Andrea Coppola

CERTIFIED TRAINER

BLENDER
The Ultimate Guide

VOLUME 2

Blender
High School

Table of contents

I

IV

V

IX

X

XI

XIII

1
INTRODUCTION

1.1. Introduction

After having learned to know Blender and to model with its powerful tools, in this second volume of **Blender – The Ultimate Guide**, we will finally face the fantastic world of colors, materials, lighting, framing and painting, thanks to which we will test the computing capability of our *computer*, generating very realistic images.

After an exhaustive dissertation in volume 1 concerning modeling, we will finally discuss about *rendering*, i.e. that computing process aimed at realistically representing the previously modeled scene.

We obviously mean for *rendering* also the computing process of the animated scenes and simulations, but these topics will be object of future volumes.

Blender basically puts at our disposal two powerful rendering engines: **Blender Render** (or **Blender Internal**), the historical engine, and the new **Cycles**, presently set as *default engine* starting from the issue 2.61, definitely more flexible, complete and powerful.

There exist, among the *Addons*, other *rendering* engines(and even more can be found on the internet, many of them *freeware* and *open source*). E.g., the *Blender Game Engine* can be used for the creation of *videogames* and for programming.

Even if *Blender Render* is being quite abandoned, and substituted by *Cycles*, a comprehensive guide must present and discuss both the main engines, in a detailed way.

Due to the organization we decided to give to this guide, since the beginning you will notice that, in many cases, we will put aside some topics and we will get them back later, or we will anticipate some.

In this way, we will maintain a logical thread.

Blender was created for the developers, and initially designed for a private use. Only after some time it was opened to the public. For this reason its interface has undergone many transformations and updating. Moreover, due to its logical planning, the functions and tools appear to be unorganized. Actually all appear in a logical order for a *developer*, but not necessarily for a *standard* user. It cannot be excluded that, in the future, the developers may change again the interface, making it more specific and simplifying the windows.

In any case, merely mentioning each function of a window, each tool, without deeply understanding some topics, would make this guide an encyclopedia (probably also not complete), a fruitless list and not a productive tool for learning such a huge *software*. For this reason, the various *tab* of the *Properties* editor, for example, will be properly discussed only when necessary, during the explanation of a special function or a certain working environment.

Each topic, each window, each function will be described in any specific and relevant setting, for each *rendering* engine, in all the aspects and for the various object types.

Moreover, as usual, you will find practical examples, suitably located in the guide, and only after having deeply learned a certain topic. We suggest to continuously practice, going beyond the exercises here proposed.

Many *tutorials, guides and books* can be found on the net, all useful beside this guide. But we believe that learning a *software* like Blender based only on *tutorials*, it is not the best way. The risk is to perform a number of operations only by memory, without the deep knowledge that only a complete guide can give.

As usual, look around. Study and copy what you find around.

Have a good reading and exercise!

2
BLENDER RENDER

2.1. Introduction to the rendering engines

In C.G. (*computer graphics*), the *rendering* engines are the tools for the computing process of a 3D scene or of an animation, according to algorithms enabling to simulate the light path and the color representation, materials and shadows, in order to obtain a proper visualization style.

In the Blender case, three *render engines are* available: the original engine *Blender Render*, the new and innovative *Cycles* and the *Blender Game Engine*, useful for the reproduction of the programming environment and of gaming, which will not be object of the present volume.

Other engines can be found among the *Addons* and many others on the internet.

The *rendering* environment, whatever it is, enables the control of a huge number of settings, parameters, criteria and factors which all affect the final outcome.

Each engine is not compatible with the others (unless special operations are performed, not possible to be here discussed) and individually manage the various aspects.

Materials, lighting, *texture*, filters and other parameters often substantially differ from engine to engine.

It is recommended to focus on a specific engine. Learning superficially the use of many *rendering* environments is counter-productive and often useless.

Blender offers two definitely performant engines, *Blender Internal* (or *Blender Render*) and *Cycles* (which we will discuss in the next section).

2.2. Blender Render

This *rendering* engine, now little abandoned since *Cycles*, extremely more performant, is being strongly adopted, is still used, especially by people using the *Blender Game Engine*, very similar in settings to this engine.

Blender has been being released starting from version 2.6x with *Cycles* set as default engine. In order to select *Blender Render* (o *Blender Render*), it is necessary to choose it on the drop-down menu *Engine to use* placed in the header of the *Info* tab.

fig. 1 selection of the *Blender Render* as *rendering engine*

2.1.1. *Render tab*

The main tab, in which all the parameters and settings of the rendering engine are located, is **Render**, represented by the icon with the camera.

In this tab some panels are located, whose settings enable a strong control of the engine.

Other fundamental settings are located in the panel *World*, while properties relevant to materials and texture can be found in the corresponding panels *Material* and *Texture* and those relevant to lighting and light sources in the panel *Lamp*.

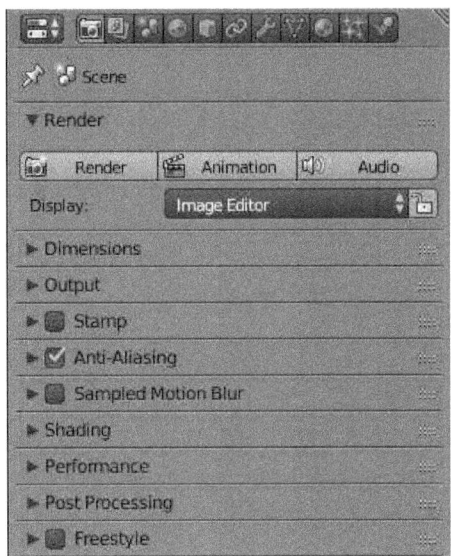

fig. 2 the *Render* tab

The **Render** panel of the Render *tab* hosts the primary engine settings. The *Display* menu let us choosing the visualization mode of the rendering process of the image or animation, choosing among:

- *Image Editor* (*default*), the editor devoted to the image visualization;

- *Full Screen*;

- *New Window*, in a new window different from the 3D view;

- *Keep UI*, for not modifying the in CPU interface unit.

Other than this menu, three switches for choosing the rendering typology are also available in the panel:

11

- *Render* (quick-select button F12) which automatically activate the *rendering* of a static image in the environment defined in menu *Display*;

- *Animation* (CTRL + F12) activating an animation rendering, whose frames are defined in the *Timeline*. Take into account that each frame amount at a single *rendering* of a static image and so *rendering process* of an animated scene may require a long computation time and many RAM and CPU resources;

- *Audio*, for mixing a sound, chosen from the *browser*, into the 3D scene.

For saving a *rendering* on disc at the end of the computation process it is necessary to digit F3.

The **Dimensions** panel manages the information relevant to the size data of the file, being either a static image or an animation.

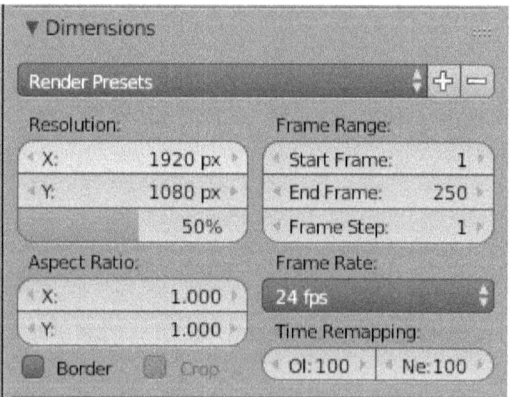

fig. 3 The *Dimensions* panel

- *Resolution* enables to insert the size of the image file of the rendered scene, in *pixel*, along directions *x* and *y*. Moreover a scale factor can be also assigned, with the button above (from 0 to 100%).

- *Aspect Ratio* defines the ratio between x and y of the rendered image (the default values are set to 1);

- The choice *Border* is very useful for rendering a portion only of the 3D scene, which can be defined with the mouse by the rectangular selection area SHIFT + B and dragging the crossed cursor;

- if the *Border* option is selected, also the option *Crop* will be activated, enabling to isolate the area defined by *Border* inside a red contour;

- *Frame Range* contains the parameters for the rendering of an animated scene, i.e. the first animation frame (*Start Frame*), and the final one (*End Frame*), visible in the *Timeline* and the frame step of the rendered frames (*Frame Step*) set to 1 by default;

- *Frame Rate* opens a drop-down menu for the choice of the frame rate (*fps*) of the animation. By *default* it is set to 24;

- *Time Remapping* defines the mappings with respect to the frames.

In the **Output** panel information relevant to the path and the extension of the rendering file can be found.

- In the text box it is possible to define the path and the directory where the frames and the rendered images will be sequentially saved at the end of the rendering process;

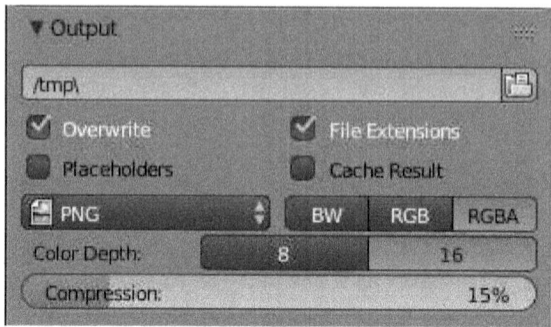

fig. 4 The *Output* panel

- The *Overwrite* option, if activated, enables to overwrite new images or files over previous versions with same name;

- *Placeholder*, is selected, creates, during the rendering process of the frames, a placeholder empty *file*;

- The *File Extensions* option enables to digit the file extension inside the box of the name of the image or animation file;

- *Cache Results* enables to save a file of extension *.exr* containing the *cache* data of the rendering process;

- The drop-down menu *Output Image* enables to choose the extension of the file containing the rendered image or animation among the most common image or video formats;

- the switches *BW, RGB, RGBA* define the color format of the rendering file, respectively *black and white, colors, colors* with transparency channel alpha, if permitted by the extension file format;

- The color depth can be set with the switches *Color Depth*, expressed in *bit*, for a better resolution and image clearness (8 and 16 *bit* available);

14

- Finally *Compression* enables to set a percentage value of file compression.

If the panel **Stamp** is activated with a flag, all the settings and characteristics defined in the panel will be given to the final rendering image.

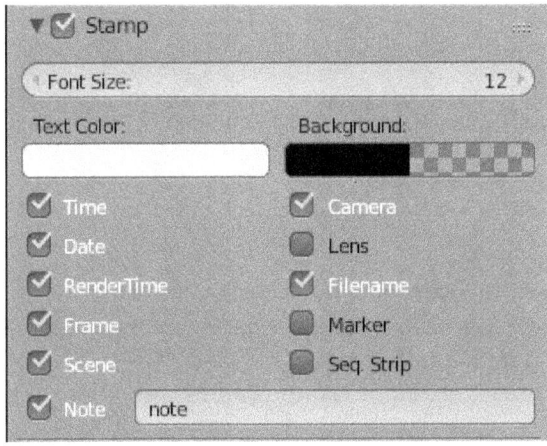

fig. 5 the panel *Stamp*

Among the information to be printed it is possible to choose: the filename (*Filename*), the date (*Date*), the time (*Time*), the rendering time duration (Render *Time*), the frame number (*Frame*), the scene name (*Scene*), the camera name (*Camera*), the lens characteristics (*Lens*), any *marker*, the name of a possible image strip in sequence (*Seq. Strip*), a note (*note*).

Moreover the font size can be set (*Fonts Size*), together with the color of the text (*Text Color*) and of the background (*Background*).

fig. 6 a *render* result with impressed information

The panel **Antialiasing**, if activated with a flag, contains the settings relevant to the detail definition of the rendered image during the vectorial transposition of the 3D models into a *raster* image.

This precision sampling parameter is defined by the *switches* 5, 8, 11 and 16, while the method and algorithm *Pixel Filter* may be defined by the drop-down menu on the right.

The flag *Full Sample* activates the *antialiasing* during rendering for a *layer*, an advanced method that will explore in the foregoing.

fig. 7 the *Antialiasing* panel

Finally *Size* defines size and thickness of the vectorial correction.

16

In the **Sampled Motion Blur** panel, if checked, it is possible to let Blender creating virtual frames between one frame and the following one which, mixed with the two original neighboring frames, determine a defocusing effect in the movement.

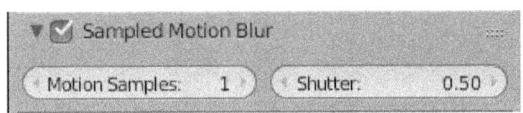

fig. 8 *Sampled Motion Blur* panel

Motion Samples sets the number of frames to be created as virtual frame in correspondence of each original frame. The higher the sample, the more uniform the defocusing effect, and obviously, the longer the *rendering* process.

Door expresses in seconds the time during which the door stays opened to burn the out of focus frame.

In the **Shading** panel it is possible to enable or disable the visualization of the *Texture* render, the shadows (*Shadows*), the *Surface Scattering* effect if existing, and the *texture* assigned to the environment if present (*Environment Map*). Moreover it is possible to choose to enable or disable the computation of the shadow projection, of the transparencies and of the reflections on objects hit by light (*Ray Tracing*) and to select what will be assigned to the transparent channel *Alpha* (if supported by file), choosing between the following options:

- *Sky*, performing the rendering of colors or chromatic scale defined in the *World* tab;

- *Premultiplied*, applying a transparent component even on the RGB colors of the image;

17

- *Straight Alpha*, assigning all information concerning transparency only to the channel *alpha*, such as to manage the resulting *file* in a photo-editing program external to Blender and a image visualizer supporting and managing the transparency channel.

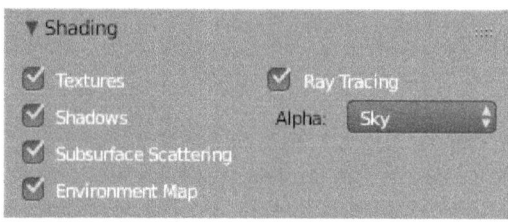

fig. 9 the *Shading* panel

The **Performance** panel manages the *rendering* settings as a function of the available hardware.

This information is very important for managing the performance of the rendering process.

The two ways *Switch Threads* enables to determine the most convenient number of computing processes, depending on the number of processors and cores of the system. These can be automatically detected (*Auto-detect*) and visualized in the counter *Threads*. If it is decided to set this option manually (*Fixed*), the counter *Threads* is enabled, letting the numerical insertion.

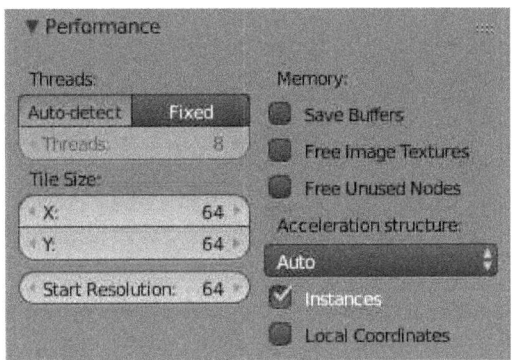

fig. 10 the *Performance* panel

Tile Size determines the size of the *tiles,* i.e. of the boxes in which the image is subdivided during the rendering, along the *X* and *Y* coordinates. We recommend to set the value 64 if the *CPU* if used for the computation, and 256 if the *GPU* is used.

Start Resolution sets the minimum value of the box at the rendering beginning, such as can gradually adapt to the previously reported values.

Then there are three options concerning the used memory: *Save Buffers, Free Image Textures* and *Free Unused Nodes* enabling to clear the allocated and not used memory in order to unload the system after the rendering process.

Acceleration Structure permits to choose from the options in the drop-down menu what kind of acceleration of the *ray tracing* must be used.

Checking the flag (or checkbox) *Instances* it is possible to reduce the file size, by considering the memory used by the instances of the scene.

The last flag, *Local Coordinates,* sets the local coordinates of the default meshes.

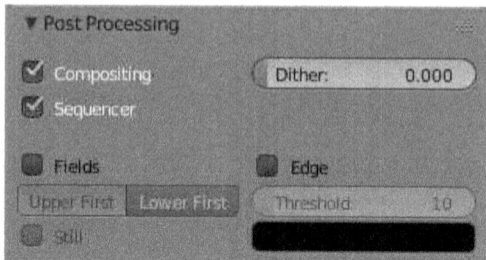

fig. 11 The *Post Processing* panel

The **Post Processing** panel conveys to specific working environments the outcome of the *rendering*, according to the chosen options.

- *Compositing* conveys the rendering to the *compositing* environment where it is possible to act in the post production of the image, by means of filters, effects and other functions;

- *Sequencer* conveys the animated *rendering* in the *Video Editor;*

- *Dither* generates a noise in the final result of the rendering in order to avoid not pleasant graphical artifacts;

- *Fields*, if checked activates a *switch* in which it is possible to define, in case of videos addressed to TV formats PAL or NSTC, which frame fields must be rendered first, among the upper (*Upper First*) or the lower (*Lower First*);

- *Still* disables time differences among the options defined by the parameters *Fields;*

- *Edge* creates a contour of the rendered geometry, cartoon style, defining the threshold in which are defined what edges

20

must be marked in the render and which color should be used (black as default).

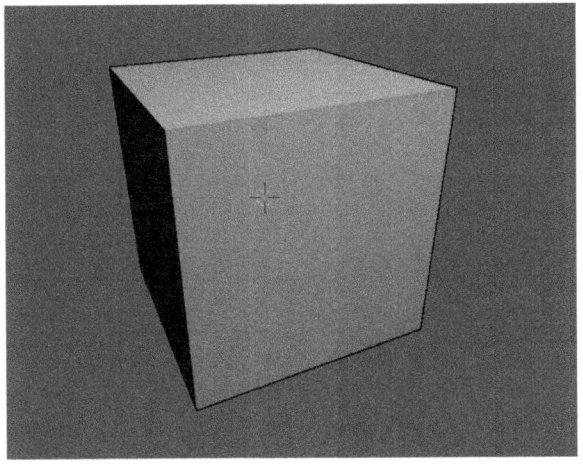

fig. 12 result of the option *Edge* checked

The **Freestyle** panel, if activated by the Addons, renders in cartoon style, marking the contours with a fixed thickness line, if the option *Absolute* is chosen in the box *Line* Thickness, or with a proportional thickness if *Relative* is used.

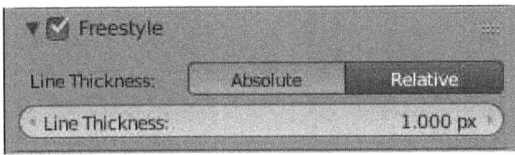

fig. 13 the *Freestyle* panel

Let us reveal in advance, since we will discuss the topic in the foregoing, the **Bake** panel, containing the information for cooking, i.e. fixing, shadows, lighting, elevations, reflections and effects on a *texture* assigned to a solid, such as to permanently fix them, unloading computation process in real time.

This function is essential for people using the texturization for creating videogames (thus unloading the computation process in real time) or virtual environment *online*, such as *Second Life*.

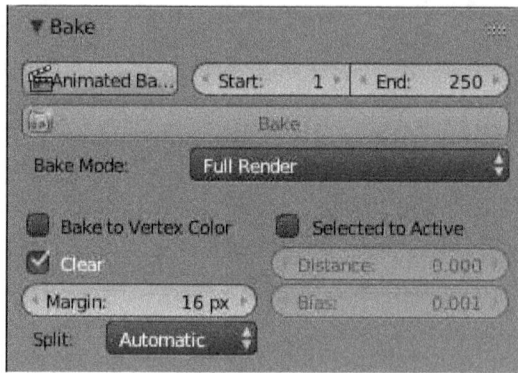

fig. 14 the *Bake* panel

2.3. Materials

After having learned how to set and configure at the best the rendering engine, we can finally start to discuss about materials.

Each object is in real composed of a material, and each material is the result of a combination of colors and physical characteristics, resulting from the incidence of the light.

The light, actually, is the key of what we are able to appreciate: colors, shininess, transparency, reflection, shadow.

Moreover, our brain is already used to select and immediately recognize the materials comprising the objects around us, based on their behavior in the various lighting conditions.

We perfectly know, and we can imagine it even without seeing it, that a metal has a shininess quite different than a plastic material, a leather or a wood object. We even recognize is a furniture finishing is a wood sheet (referred to as veneer) or a merely reproduction, even accurate, of the wood, (referred to as lamination).

We are able to notice a material because we know it in detail.

In reproducing the reality a virtual scene, comprising objects with materials applied, must reproduce the same characteristics and the same behaviors of a real configuration.

For a better understanding of the concept, it suffices to think that each material is the combination of many characteristics (referred to as shaders) behaving in a well defined manner to the light incidence.

When we will linger on the *rendering engine Cycles,* this concept will become even more complex, but definitely schematic, thanks to the use of the nodes.

Essentially, except for specific materials like glass, ice and liquids, most of the solid materials which can be found around us can be represented with a simple scheme.

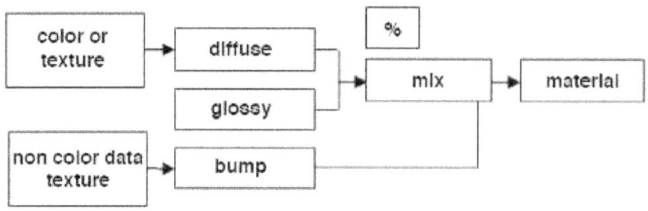

fig. 15 standard scheme for a generic material

Let us analyze the elements comprising this configuration and let's try to read them going from the right to the left. This reading will be extremely useful when we will learn to build a material with its nodes.

We can try to read and translate the scheme reproduced in a familiar language.

 A material *is given by a mix between a component of the absorbed light being diffused (diffusion) and a component which is reflected. The material will diffuse one color or a range of colors (texture). Moreover a vectorial component will determine the elevation of the material depending on a texture or on a range of monochromatic colors for which a positive elevation will be obtained with values tending toward white (upwards) and a negative elevation for values tending to black (downwards).*

Obviously many other components exist, not always present in materials, referred to as *shaders*, which will be analyzed in this section.

Looking at the scheme the difference should be clear between material and texture. The latter is only one of the (possible) components of a material. It is usually assigned to the component of diffusion (*Diffuse*).

Thus it is needed to get used to speak about material, understood as a mix of components, and not about texture, while imagining an object.

2.3.1. *Tab Material*

In order to add a material to an object (usually a mesh, but it is possible to add a material even to a curve, a surface, a text or a *metaball*) it is just needed, by selecting the object, to click on the key *New* of the *tab Material* in the *Properties Editor*.

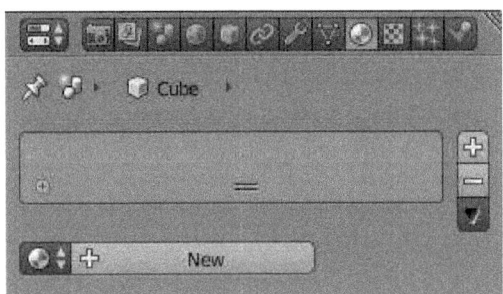

fig. 16 adding a material to an object

One or more materials may be added to a certain object. For adding one more material, it is needed to click on the key + (and on the key – to remove the material) and add it to the faces selected with the key *Assign*.

fig. 17 the *tab Material*

Once a material has been added, the *tab Material* will appear more complete and divided in several panels in which it will be possible to add components and specify characteristics and behavior of shaders, shadows and other options.

Upward it is possible to rename the material or recalling an existing one by clicking on the drop-down menu at the left hand part of the name.

In the *Outliner* the material will be associated to the attributes of the selected object.

The structure of the object *Cube* clearly appears, whose geometry is that of a *mesh*, to which the specific material is applied.

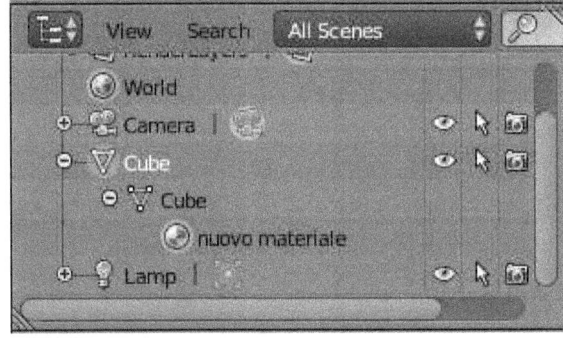

fig. 18 the *Outliner*

Going back to the *tab* Material, three small keys can be found beside the material name.

- the F key stays for fake and can be used to create a new material starting from the selected one. Once pressed, a small number 2 will appear at its left hand side, indicating that we are working on the creating of a new material, renamed as the previous one followed by a numbering in the format .00x. It is possible to create new copies which will be automatically renamed with the progressive number;

- key + adds a new empty material;

27

- key X disconnects the material from the selected object (but does not cancel the material from the project).

Next on the left hand side we find the key *Nodes* needed to use the node system for the material rendering. This system, much more complex and effective, will be explained in detail dealing with the rendering engine *Cycles*.

fig. 19 the *Node Editor*

For now it is enough to know that the node system is a graphical representation method of the component pipeline of materials, much similar to the scheme previously reported for describing the standard material.

The key *Link* adds the material to the object or to its geometrical elements depending if set as *Data* or *Object*.

Then, we find 4 switch keys.

- *Surface* makes the object to be rendered as a solid, thus visualizing the surfaces in view;

- *Wire* enables the edges rendering, by assigning them the material;

- *Volume* enables the object rendering by considering it as a volume, this option can is available only for closed objects;

- *Halo* (which can be assigned only to a *mesh*) makes the vertexes to appear as bright points in the rendering.

28

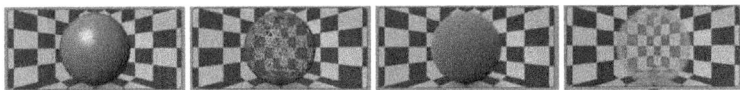

fig. 20 from left to right: representation of an object rendering in modality *Surface*, *Wire*, *Volume*, *Halo*

fig. 21 the *Preview* panel

The underlying panel is **Preview** and contains a box in which the outcome of the current material can be visualized in preview. This *preview* is real time updated in the option modification.

On the box right there are 6 icons enabling to get the material preview respectively on a flat surface, on a sphere, on a cube, on a *Monkey* (complex geometry), on a particulate system such as *hair* (which we will see in the third volume) and on a sphere illuminated by a sky in background.

Depending on the object on which the material is being applied, the most similar *preview* system can be chosen.

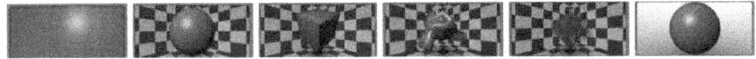

fig. 22 options of material visualization on the objects

The panel **Diffuse** contains all the information relevant to the color (or the colors) diffused by that material.

As it is well known, a light hitting an object is decomposed in three components: the absorbed part, the eventually transmitted part and a part given back to the environment (diffused and reflected).

The material will absorb a part of the colors and will give back others, the ones we actually see.

A black object, for example, will absorb all the colors without diffusing any of them, whereas a white object will not absorb any color but will diffuse all the colors (thus appearing as white).

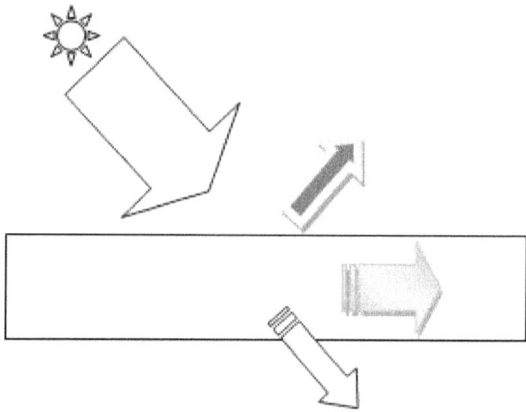

fig. 23 decomposition of a light hitting an object

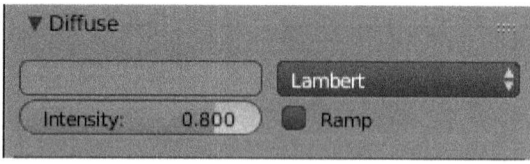

fig. 24 the *Diffuse* panel

By clicking on the first box, the palette will appear for choosing the base color of the material, according to the parameters RGB, HSV or HEX (hexadecimal), or by clicking inside the circle and directly selecting the color.

The dropper is useful for adding an external color to the palette.

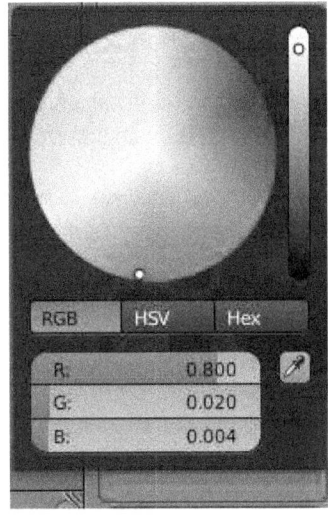

fig. 25 the palette

fig. 26 shadings algorithms

31

fig. 27 shader algorithm outcomes. From left to right: *Lambert, Oren-Nayar, Toon, Minnaert* and *Fresnel*

The drop-down menu on the left hand side enables to choose the diffuse shader method among some predefined algorithms: *Lambert, Oren-Nayar, Toon (cartoon), Minnaert* and *Fresnel*.

- The first one (*Lambert*), the *default* one, is very simple and creates a soft transition between shadowed and lighted zones;

- *Oren-Nayar* acts in a more precise way on rough surfaces, whose value is determined by the parameter *Roughness*;

- *Toon* simulate a cartoon rendering, in 2D style, with sharp shadows and light strokes;

- *Minnaert* is much similar to *Lambert*. The *Darkness* parameter has been added for the adjustment of the much lighted zones;

- *Fresnel* takes into account the index of refraction (IOR), realistically simulating the reflection behavior based in the light incidence angle and of the viewpoint. For very narrow angles with respect to the radiated surface, the reflection will be intense, whereas for wide angles the surface will reflect less.

Depending on the chosen algorithm some dedicated parameters may be added such as the size, the *roughness* or the index of refraction (*IOR*).

The *Intensity* cursor (from 0 to 1) defines the intensity used for applying the color to the object.

The *Ramp* activates a group of parameters.

Ramp enables to add colors to the shader placing them according to a sequence.

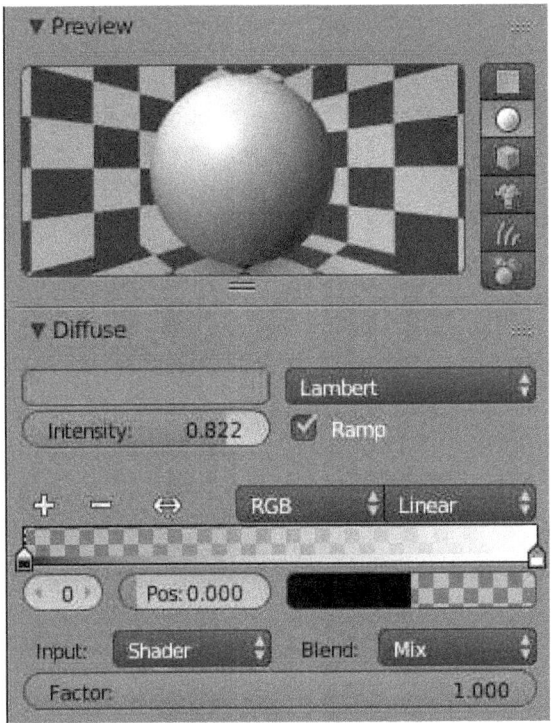

fig. 28 parameters associated to *Ramp*

The next key, represented by two opposite arrows, (*Flip*) flip the color sequence.

Next two interconnected drop-down menus can be found.

The first enables the choice of the color interpolation modality (*RGB*, *HSV* and *HSL*) affecting the options of the second menu, defining the interpolation path.

- In *RGB* modality, it is possible to choose between Ease, Cardinal, Linear, *B-Spline* and *Constant*;

- In *HSV* and *HSL* modalities, between *Near, Far, Clockwise* and *Counter-Clockwise;*

The color marker position can be manually changed (dragging the markers along the underlying color ramp), or, upon selecting the color in the counter *Index*, the color marker position can be numerically modified by inserting the value or by dragging the cursor *Pos.*

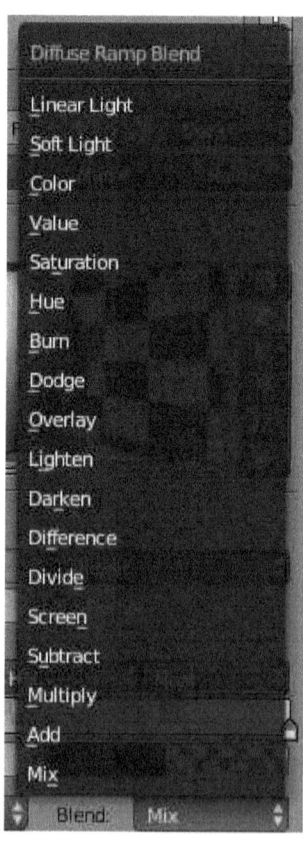

fig. 29 the *Blend* mane of the *color ramp*

34

On the right the color relevant to the selected marker of index can be defined, opening a palette.

Next, we find the two drop-down menus *Input* and *Blend*. The first one presents 4 options defining the way the color ramp acts on the object (Shader, Energy, Normal, Result); the second one defines the choices for the mixing color method on the color ramp (see image), whose factor can be set in the cursor *Blend Factor*.

Moreover a texture can be applied to the diffuse. We will see how to do it in the foregoing.

The panel **Specular** manages the parameters relevant to the specular shader.

This *shader* represents the part of light reflected by a visible object as a bright point, more or less big and more or less defined

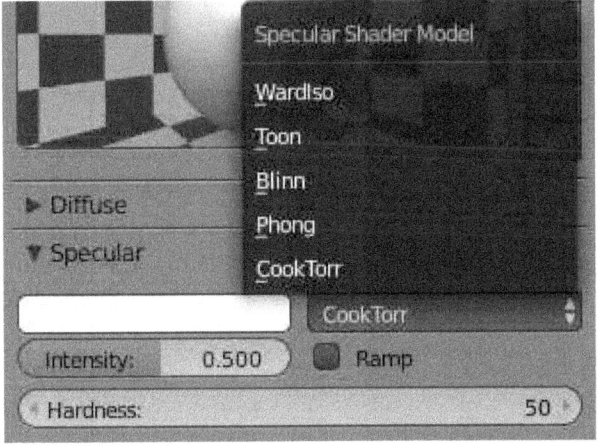

fig. 30 the panel *Specular*

35

Thus it is not, in spite of its name, a mere mirror, as in old glasses and mirrors.

The more the surface object will be smooth and uniform, the more the bright point will be defined and sharp. On the other hand it will appear blurry and vague in case of a rough surface like, for example, a frosted, anodized or sandblasted metal.

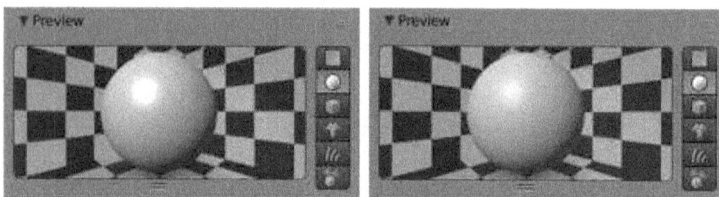

fig. 31 the *Specular* intensity reproduces effects of smooth and reflecting surfaces (on the left) with high values and rough and less reflecting with low values (on the right)

The most classic example is that of a chromed metal, whose clearness will be maximum, opposed to a anodized aluminum, in which the micro-roughness reflects light in a more soft and uniform manner.

A specific color can be set also on the *Specular Shader*, chosen with the palette, while the intensity can be defined in the cursor *Intensity* (from 0 to 1).

The counter *Hardness* determines the size of the bright point, while the flag *Ramp* activates the same previously seen commands for *Diffuse*.

The menu *Specular Shader Model*, finally, enables to determine the type of shaders, choosing between five different algorithms:

- *Cook Torr* (*Cook - Torrance*) is suitable for smooth surfaces like leather and plastic;

- *Phong*, memorable shader for the computer graphics, is suitable for smooth plastic materials or, even better, metallic ones;

- *Blinn* is similar to the previous ones but adds a control on the index of refraction (IOR) in place of the counter *Hardness*, yielding a definitely more realistic reflection;

- *Toon*, usually combined with *Diffuse Toon*, assigns a sharp and defined reflection point, typical of the 2D and cartoon graphics. The parameters *Size* and *Smooth* define respectively the dimensions and clearness of the bright point;

- *WardIso*, finally, is a very useful shader for creating very refined reflections on metallic materials. The additional parameter *Slope* enables to regulate the bright point in a more complex way and less uniform in the smoothing.

fig. 32 from left to right, the 5 models *Specular: CookTorr, Phong, Blinn, Toon* and *WardIso*

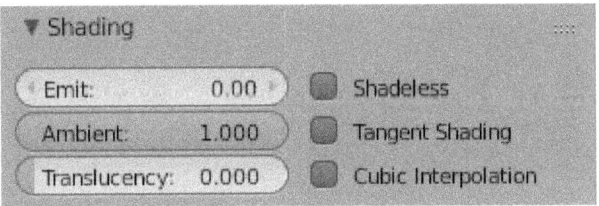

fig. 33 the panel *Shading*

The panel **Shading** adds more options, untied from *Diffuse* and *Specular*, to the general shading of the material.

- *Emit* makes the object radiating its own light depending on the value defined in the counter. It is useful for creating light

37

sources such as light bulbs or for positioning into the scene auxiliary bright panels;

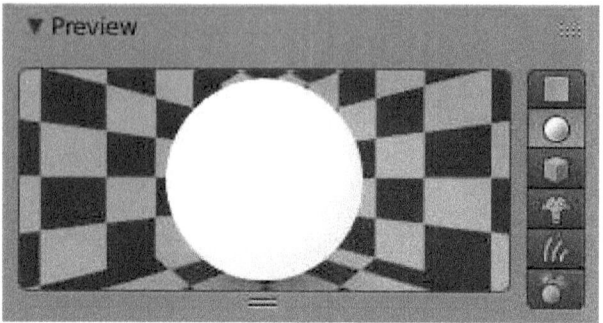

fig. 34 the effect *Emit* generates a light source

- *Ambient* defines the amount of object illumination from the environment of the scene;

fig. 35 the translucency illuminates the surface edges with respect to the current view

- *Translucency* assigns brightness to the edges of the object surface not perpendicular to the current view or to the framing;

- *Shadless*, if checked prevents lights and shadows to influence the object;

38

- *Tangent Shading*, useful for metallic materials, simulates the anisotropy effect, making the diffusion different along the surface points;

- *Cubic Interpolation* smoother the chromatic transitions between the shadowed and lighted zones.

fig. 36 *Cubic Interpolation* less sharp the transition between lighted and shadowed zones

The panel **Transparency** contains the parameters for adding a transparency to the standard *shaders*.

As already seen in the previous part, a portion of light affecting on an object is reflected, and a portion is absorbed.

Some materials, however, have a further capability, that of being partially or totally crossed by light.

This is the case of glass, ice, many fluids, semi-transparent plastic materials, some fabrics, leather etc.

Blender is able to render a transparent material in three ways, to be chosen in the upper *switch* of the *Transparency* panel.

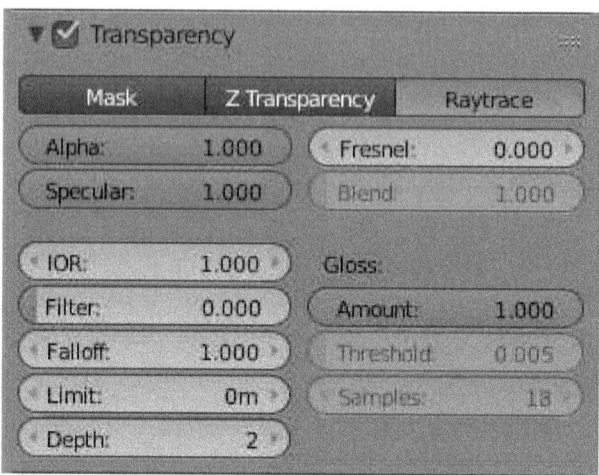

fig. 37 the panel *Transparency*

- *Mask*, acting on the parameters *Fresnel* and *Blend*, makes the object partially or totally invisible, showing the scene background;

- *Z Transparency* regulates the object transparency as a function of the current view or of the camera (remember that *Z* is the axis normal to the camera framing), using the algorithm *alpha buffer* and making the object invisible or semi-invisible, with however the possibility of adding a shader *Specular*, which will be active, instead of *Mask*, and will make the transparency more realistic, tough much simple;

- *Raytrace* simulates the realistic light path, crossing the medium, obtaining more or less background deformations according to the object curvature, transparency and reflection, depending on the index of refraction and other parameters which we will analyze in the foregoing.

fig. 38 transparency with *Mask* method

fig. 38 transparency with the *Z Transparency* method

fig. 38 transparency with the *Z* Raytrace method

The first two methods have at disposal 4 common parameters:

- *Alpha*, determining the material transparency;

- *Specular*, controlling the transparency as a function of lights;

- *Fresnel*, managing the transparency as a function of the light incidence;

- *Blend*, affecting the intensity of the *Fresnel* parameter;

Other parameters can be activated by selecting the Raytrace modality:

- *IOR* (*Index of Refraction*) simulates the light path and generates distortions depending on the angle of incidence;

- *Filter* enables to mix the transparency with the *Diffuse* such as to balance the two shaders. The parameter ranges from 0 to 1, where 0 stands for transparency only and 1 for diffusion only;

- *Limit* determines the material opacity for values greater than 0;

- *Falloff* determines the absorption amount of incidence light by the transparent material;

- *Depth* controls the refraction maximum number, i.e. the crossing number of the light rays through the material;

- *Gloss* adds a small blur such as to make the transparency not full. The *Amount* value (from 0 to 1) determines the blur amount, whereas *Threshold* and *Samples* determine, respectively, the threshold of the factors affecting the blur effect and the number of the noise samples.

NOTE: The Index of Refraction (IOR) is a value greater than 1 belonging to every (about 1 = IOR of air). Tables can be found on internet, reporting the indexes relevant to the various materials.

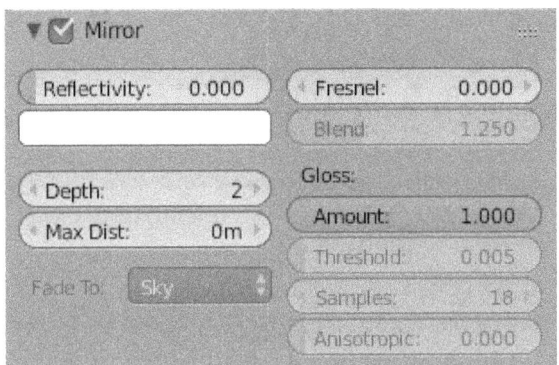

fig. 41 the *Mirror* panel

A very important shader component can be found in **Mirror** panel.

Mirror, together with *Specular*, renders a true reflection of the objects around, of the environment and of the light sources.

This mirroring will surely appear sharper and more defined on smooth surfaces and more diffused on rough or not reflecting ones.

This shader is very useful and can be found in many materials, more or less intense. It's widely used for representing mirror surfaces, chromed, lacquered, or highly reflective in general.

fig. 42 *Mirror* applied to the objects in the scene. Note how the glossy red sphere is reflected on the *Monkey* surface

Let us see which are the parameters.

- *Reflectivity* is a cursor regulating how much reflective the material is, i.e. how much the external objects will be mirrored on the reflective surface. It is possible to define the reflection color with the underlying palette.

- *Fresnel* manages the reflection as a function of the light incidence;

- *Blend* affects the intensity of the *Fresnel* parameter;

- *Depth* defines the maximum number of light bounces between reflecting surfaces;

- *Max Dist* defines the maximum range in which an object or a light ray will be reflected on glossy surface. Above that range, the reflection will become more and more blurred.

- the drop-down menu *Fade To* defines how the surface reflection will be blurred, by choosing between *Sky* (*background*) and *Material*;

The *Gloss* parameters are:

- *Amount*, determining the sharpness of the reflected image on the surface (1 = maximum sharpness and 0 no reflection);

For *Amount* values less than 1, the following parameters are activated:

- *Threshold*, beyond which certain light rays and images are excluded from the reflection computation;

- *Sample* value. The greater this value, the larger will be the reflection sharpness and the greater the computation time; and vice versa;

- *Anisotropic* effect to reflection, typical of metals. It can be set from 0 (no effect) to 1 (maximum effect). It works together with the *Tangent Shading* parameter in the *Shading panel*.

The **Subsurface Scattering** shader yields a very interesting and realistic effect, typical of some translucent materials.

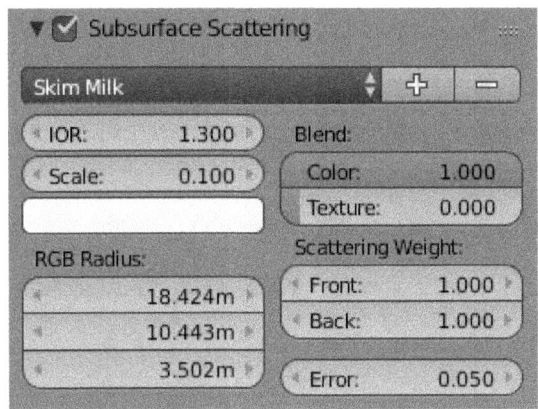

fig. 43 the *Subsurface Scattering* panel

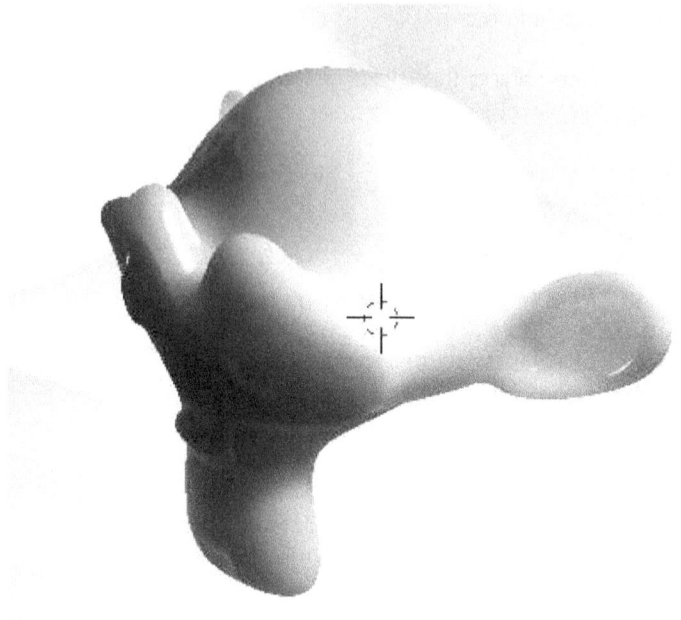

fig. 44 the light radiation crosses the surface

This effect determines, as really occurs for the *Diffuse,* a light dispersion above the surface, slightly crossing the opaque object thus obtaining a sort of radiation semi transparency.

Many examples can be found in real life: la wax, the skin, the marble, a pudding...

Try to look at your hand palm when hit by a light source.

Let us now see which are the adjusting parameters of this realistic shader.

Once clicked on the shader flag, the regulation parameters become active.

- the drop-down menu *Execute a Preset* offers 10 examples of surfaces producing this effect: *apple, chicken, cream, ketchup, marble, potato, skim milk, skin 1, skin2, whole milk.*

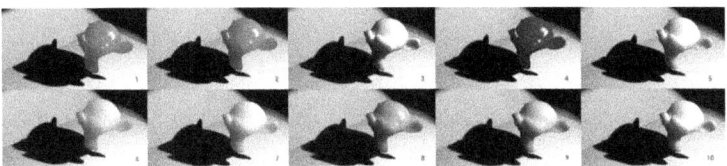

fig. 45 the 10 presets of the *Subsurface Scattering*

With the keys + and -, it is possible to add new examples and to cancel the existing ones.

- *IOR* affects the decay of the light hitting the surface, in a way proportional to the material density and inversely proportional to the decay;

- *Scale* is important for defining the scaling dimensions of the object depending on the set measure unit and the consequent effect success;

- the palette enables to define the color of the effect;

- the parameters *Blend* set the amount of the effect (*Color*) and the amount of mixing between the effect and the surface *texture* of the object (*Texture*);

- the three counters *RGB Radius* define the light amount split in the three components red, green and blue which will be emitted in the global effect;

- The two parameters *Scattering Weight* define the front light amount (*Front*) crossing the object and diffusing in the back side, and the light amount hitting the object on the non visible surface (*Back*) and crossing the object becoming visible on the front part;

47

- *Error Tolerance* controls the tolerance relevant to the algorithm precision. It is recommended not to use too high values in order to avoid artifacts.

The panel **Strand** affects the rendering of materials composed by filaments (e.g. hairs). We will quickly describe the main parameters of this panel, postponing a more accurate description in the foregoing, when we will deal with the *Particle System*.

- the parameters *Size* determine the filament size at its root and at the top;

- *Shading* defines the material and the *texture* applied to the filaments.

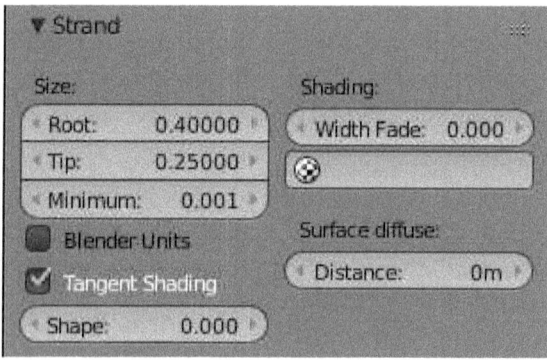

fig. 46 the *Strand* panel

The panel **Options** defined some additional parameters to the shaders assigned to the material.

fig. 47 the *Options* panel

This panel is endowed with an option series to be enabled or disabled (flags), in detail:

- *Traceable* visualize the material assigned to the object for the *raytracing* computation (set active by *default*);

- *Full Oversampling* makes the *rendering* engine to use a maximum sampling of 16 *samples*;

- *Sky* makes the material fully invisible, enabling the background visualization;

- *Use Mist* activates the mist effect, if present and defined on the tab *World* (see in the foregoing);

- *Invert Z Depth* inverts the face rendering in a way inverse with the respect to the basic methodology;

- *Light Group* assigns a group or lights lighting the material, independent from the global illumination of the scene. The flags *Exclusive* and *Local* become activated only with the assignment of a group of lights, making the selected group of lights devoted only to the object lighting;

- *Face Texture* replaces the object base color with a mapping depending on the *UV* coordinates;

- *Face texture Alpha* becomes activated only if the *Face* Texture is activated, and replaces the *alpha* channel of the object with a mapping depending on the *UV* coordinates;

- *Vertex Color Paint* replaces the base color with the colors defined in a *Vertex Color* Paint;

- *Vertex Color Light* adds colored vertices as additional illumination source;

- *Object Color* renders a pre-colored object;

- *UV Project* controls and corrects the *UV* mapping interpolation based on the framing;

- *Pass Index* assigns a number (index) to the material; this function is useful for the *Render Layer* (see in the foregoing).

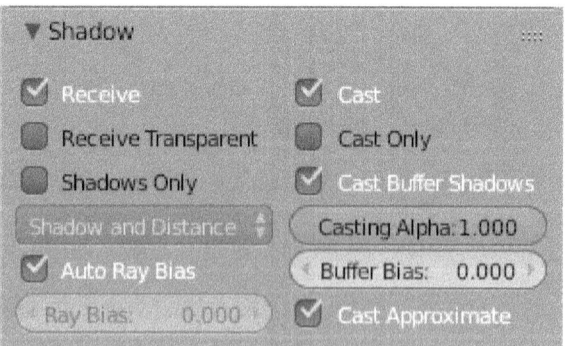

fig. 48 the *Shadow* panel

The last panel, **Shadow**, contains the settings relevant to the global managing of the shadows on the object.

- *Receive* makes the object receiving on itself the shadows generated by other objects;

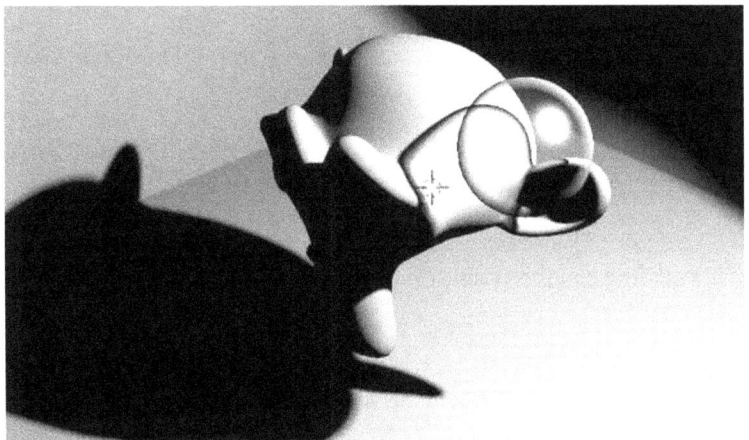

fig. 49 activating *Receive Transparent* on *Monkey*, the shadow of the transparent sphere will be projected on its surface

- *Receive Transparent*, to be used with the options of the *Transparency* panel, allows the objects to receive the projection of the shadows belonging to transparent or semi-transparent objects;

- *Shadows only* makes visible only the shadowed parts of the object, making the other shadows invisible, depending on the three options of the drop-down menu *How to Draw Shadow*;

- *Autoray Bias* corrects possible *raytracing* errors;

- *Cast* (active by *default*) allows the material and the object to cast shadows;

51

- *Cast Only* makes the object invisible and only visible its cast shadows;

- *Cast Buffer Shadows* allows the material to cast shadow if lighted by a illumination source of *Spot* type, making use of the *Buffered Shadows*;

- *Casting Alpha* controls the cast shadow amount of objects with transparent parts;

- *Buffer Bias* increases the intensity of the case shadows, depending on the option *Cast Buffer Shadow*;

- *Cast Approximate* controls the cast shadows in case of *Ambient Occlusion* use (see in the foregoing).

 EXERCISE N. 1: TESTS ON MATERIALS

In this firsts exercise, we will try to develop some materials, with the simple use of the shaders and without making use of the texture, which we will see in the next chapter.

Let us put in the *3D view* a *UV* Sphere, with the *Smooth* applied, and let us move it inside an environment with 4 faces (a floor, a ceiling and 2 walls), obtained with a cube from which we will remove one on the vertical edges.

Remember to direct in *Edit Mode* normals of the cube faces toward inside.

Let us illuminate the scene with a *Sun Lamp*, setting the intensity (*Energy*) to 1.

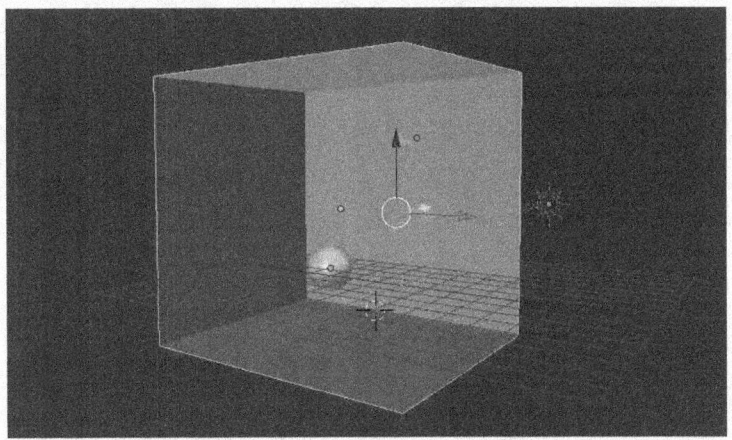

fig. 50 the scene considered in this exercise

Inside the tab *Lamp*, using the *Shadow* panel, increase the Soft *Size* parameter to 5 for smoothing the shadow.

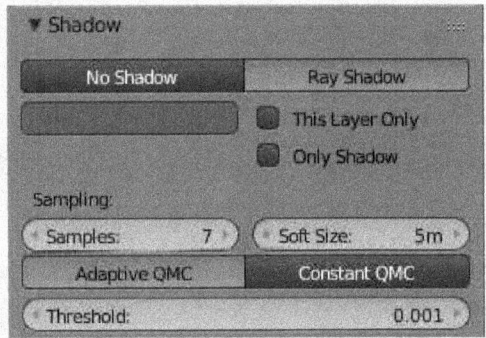

fig. 51 increasing the *Soft Size* ray in the *Shadow* panel, the shadow will appear smoother

Select the environment (the cube) and assign a new material, renamed *Environment*. Enter the panel Diffuse and select white on the palette.

Then select the sphere and set a light grey color *Diffuse*, a white lo *Specular* with *Phong* method, *Intensity* equal to 1 and *Hardness* equal to 150. Activate the flag on *Mirror* and set the *Reflectivity* equal to 0.6, *Fresnel* to 2 and *Blend* to 1.5.

Finally, place the camera in such a way as to obtain satisfying framing and launch the *rendering* pressing F12.

The outcome will be a sphere made of a glossy material, very smooth and quite reflecting, similar to porcelain.

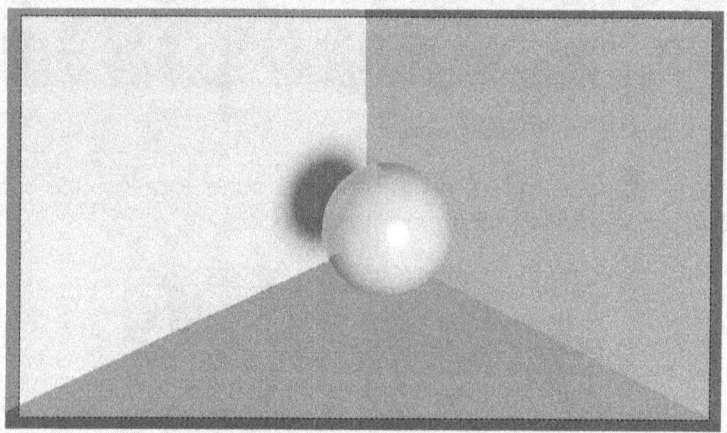

fig. 52 rendering of the porcelain sphere

Select now the sphere and set the *Intensity* and *Hardness* parameters, to 0.2 and 20, respectively. In the *Mirror* panel, set to 0.8 the *Reflectivity* and set the *Fresnel* and *Blend* to 0.3 and 0.8, respectively.

Then reduce the *Amount* value to 0.7, setting the *Threshold* to 0.5.

Finally, set the *Fade To* menu to *Material*, for avoiding the *background* to affect the reflection.

Launch the *rendering*. We will get a semi-opaque sphere, made of a material similar to anodized aluminum.

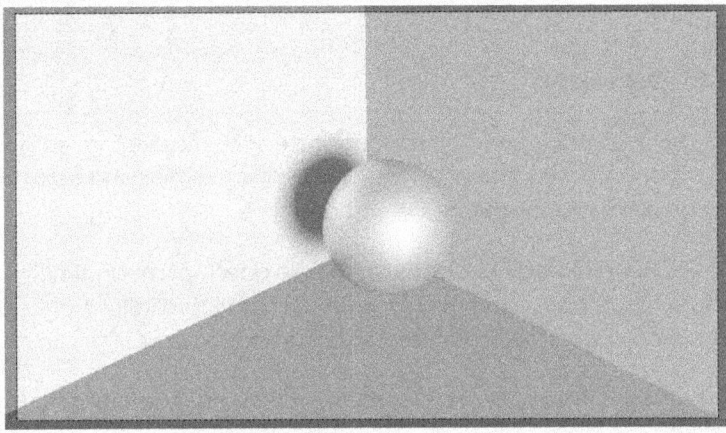

fig. 53 the rendering of the aluminum sphere

Try to play with the values, simulating other materials of common use (mirror, chrome, glass, leather...).

2.4. Texture

2.4.1. Generalities

Up to this point, we have considered a material a set of components, with the main one, the *Diffuse*, yielding the color of an object material, of monochromatic type.

As we have already understood, *Diffuse* does not mean simply a single color, but a complex type of chromatic variations (thus a single color can be considered as a particular case).

This complex number of chromatic variations is referred to as **texture**.

Imagine, for example, the wood veins, or a tiles sequence, bricks, a fabric texture, or leather.

fig. 54 *brick texture*

Thus, a *texture*, together with a *Diffuse* shader, defines the main color of the material.

Nevertheless, the *textures* can be used in many ways, e.g. as vectorial positioning factor or the vertices of a mesh (*bump* and displacement), or as mixing factor between a color and the other one. We will widely discuss on this in the next chapters, especially dealing with *Cycles*.

Generally, the *textures* used as *bump,* or as a vectorial element, are in monochromatic scale (grey scale) or bi-chromatic (per the *displacement*), in which an effect is applied to certain values associated to a color, instead of another one.

Other than being applied to an object surfaces for defining the various material components and depend on the lighting, the *textures* can be applied to backgrounds.

Blender offers the possibility of choosing between two main texture families: the image textures, being uploaded by a graphic file; and the procedural textures, generated by the code, by means of a complex computation system.

Finally, the *textures* can be associated to one or more materials.

Before further continuing the topic, discussing in detail the various texture typologies, we can include in the project and we can associate to materials and objects, it is necessary to anticipate two fundamental topics: the **Unwrapping** and the functions of the **UV/Image Editor**.

2.4.2. Unwrapping

First of all we will explain the meaning of unwrapping and why this function is necessary when an image texture must be applied to a mesh.

57

In order to tell to Blender (or to any other software of 3D modeling) how a *texture* must be applied to a surface of a solid, it is necessary to open in some way the solid making it temporally bi-dimensional to be able of being superimposed and compared to the *texture*.

To execute this operation, especially in case of complex solids, the geometry become bi-dimensional will appear often deformed. Don't worry about this: as a matter of fact the *mesh* has not been modified. Actually the conceptually inverse process occurred, i.e. the enveloping of the *mesh* with a picture which will adapt to the texture in any place.

The unwrapping method is a trick to make simpler an operation that would be quite difficult on the screen. Thus it is necessary to open the *mesh* and to place it on a flat surface, than to apply on it the *texture*, and finally to wrap it again.

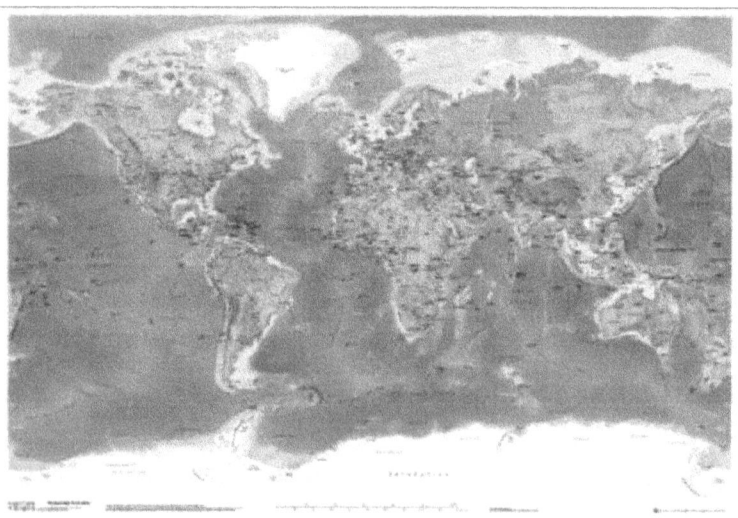

fig. 55 the planisphere

Think about, for example, to the planisphere which is actually obtained by unwrapping the globe.

Similarly, we can think about unwrapping some edges of a cube made of cardboard thus obtaining an unwrapped cube with a T or crossed shape.

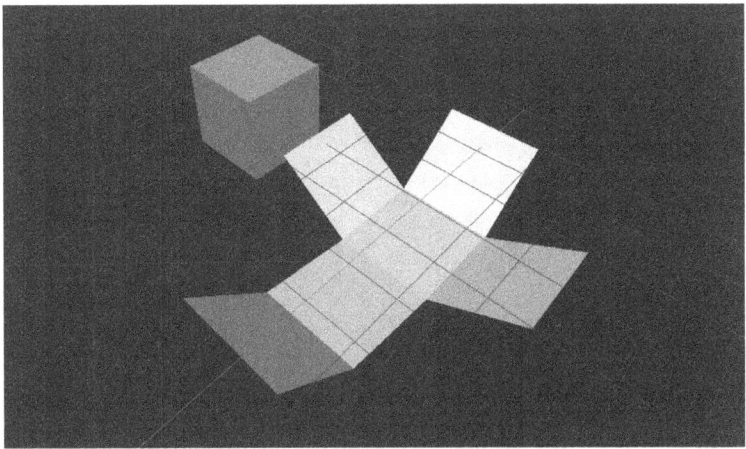

fig. 56 an unwrapped cube

Blender provides several methods for unwrapping a mesh.

First of all select the mesh to be unwrapped, enter in *Edit Mode* with the TAB key, select with A all the vertices (or, in specific cases, select the vertices relevant to the faces to be unwrapped only) and, with the mouse arrow on 3D view, digit U, standing for *Unwrap*.

A drop-down menu will appear, from which it is possible to choose the most suitable method for the mesh unwrapping.

Let us here describe the 9 methods for unwrapping a mesh or a part of it.

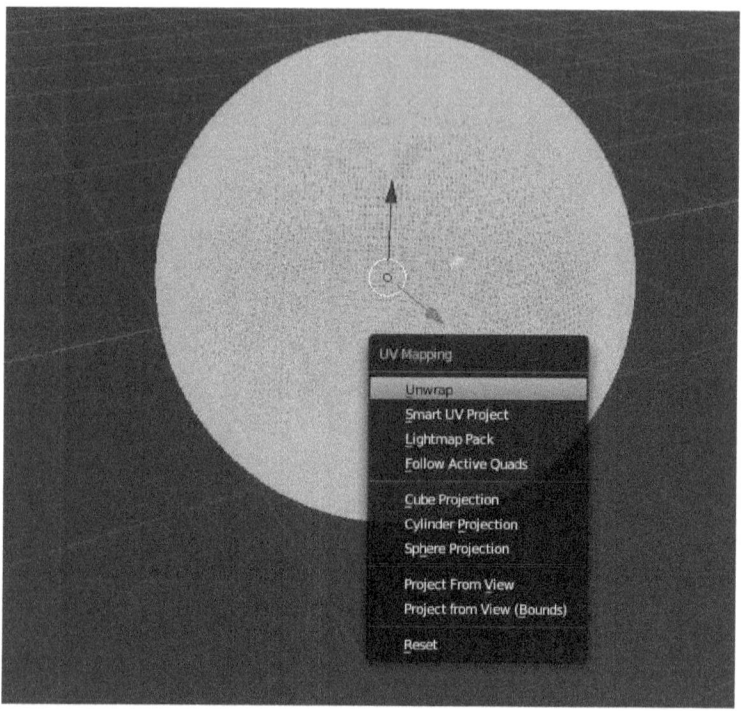

fig. 57 *Unwrap* menu (*UV Mapping*)

- **Unwrap** is usually employed as manual method, associated to the marking out of certain unwrapping lines. These lines, as already anticipated, can be applied to the selected edges by means of the CTRL + E command (or by opening the *Edge* menu of the 3D view header in *Edit Mode*) and by choosing the option **Mark Seam**. The marked out edge will become red. Obviously it is possible to cancel the edge marking out, by selecting the edge and pressing CTRL + E, thus choosing the **Clear Seam** option. Marking out an unwrapping is actually not a simple matter. It is needed to behave as a tailor that, using the chalk, mark on the fabric the guiding lines for cutting. In order to unwrap complex meshes more cutting lines are necessary, chosen with knowledge among decades of solutions. Only a bit of exercise will make simpler the operation. Once marked the cutting lines, in *Edit Mode*, it is needed to select with A all the *mesh* vertices, by pressing U, and then choose the *Unwrap* option. In order to visualize the mesh faces unwrapped along the marking out lines, it is needed to open the **UV/Image Editor**, choosing among the various possibilities. In this editor it is possible to visualize images and superimposed unwrapped meshes, to select faces, to move their vertices, to visualize rendered images and other functions related to the images. We will analyze in detail this editor in the next section.

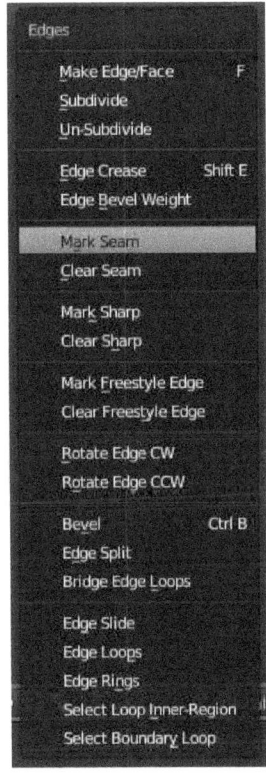

fig. 58 the menu *Edges* where the marking out options of the edges *Mark Seam* and *Clear Seam* can be found

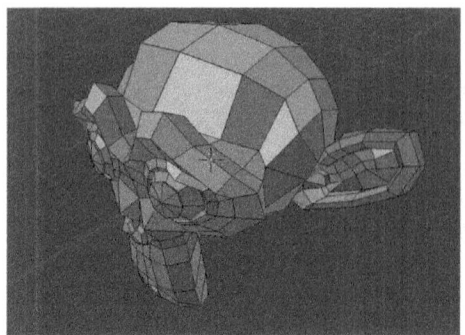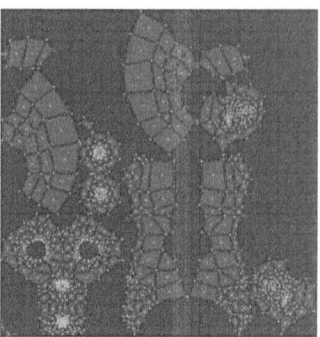

fig. 59 example of unwrapping of the *mesh Monkey* (on the left) with the *Mark Seam* and visualization of the unwrapped mesh parts in the *UV/Image Editor* (on the right)

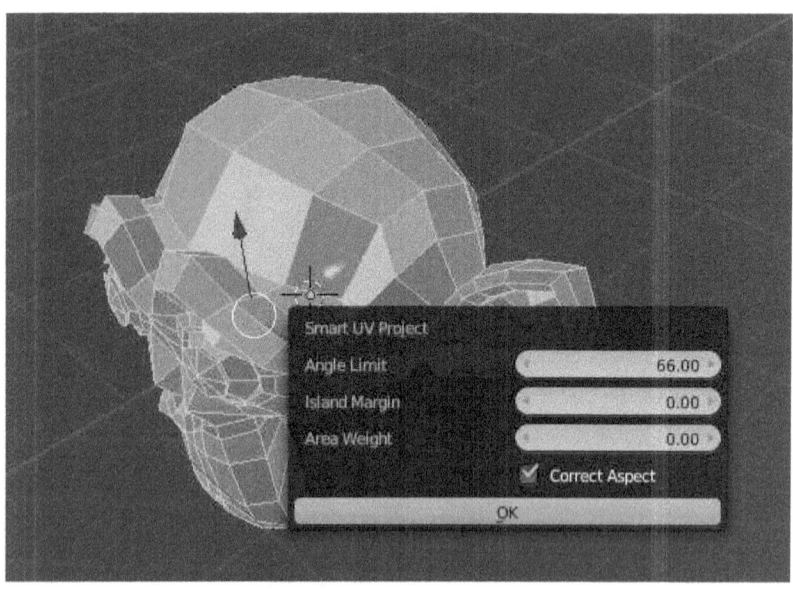

fig. 60 confirmation of the unwrapping options in *Smart UV Project*

- **Smart UV Project** is an automatic method of mesh unwrapping. With this method, Blender tries to mark the mesh after having analyzed it and after some options have been set by the user in the *Smart UV Project* popup, appearing after the choice of the method and the confirmation. We don't recommend this method in case of much complex solids and for particularly defined meshes.

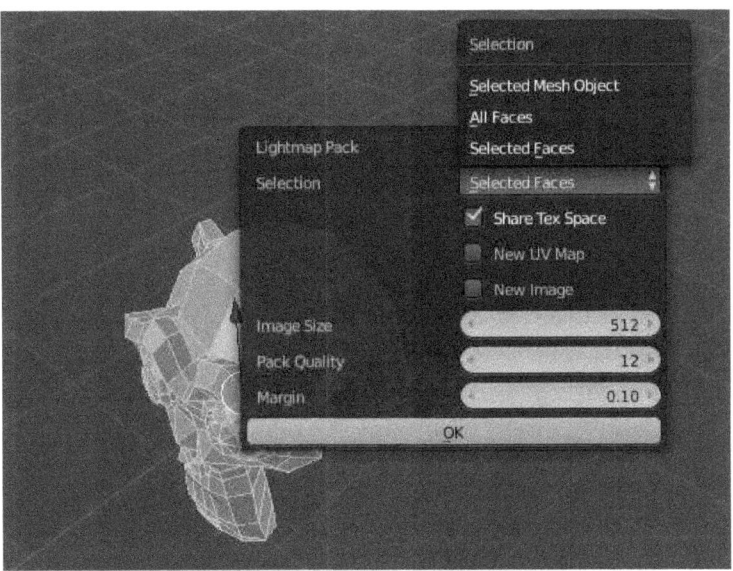

fig. 61 confirmation of the unwrapping options in *Lightmap pack*

- **Lightmap Pack** groups together and organize all the selected faces in the texture range, depending on the dimensions defined by the user in the window appearing once the option is chosen. Generally this method is recommended for very simple and regular objects like cubes or parallelepipeds. In the window it is possible to choose the faces to be selected (*Selected mesh Object, All Faces, Selected Faces*), mapping the whole object into a single *UV Map* (*Share Tex Space*), mapping the object into a new empty *UV Map* (*New UV Map*)

63

or in a new image (*New Image*). Moreover it is possible to define the image dimensions in *pixel* (*Image Size*), the unwrapping definition (*Pack Quality*) and the margins (*Margin*).

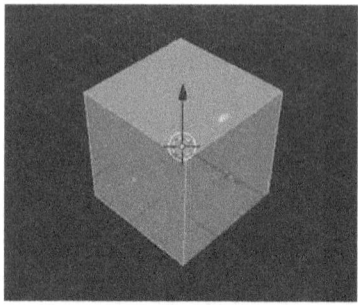 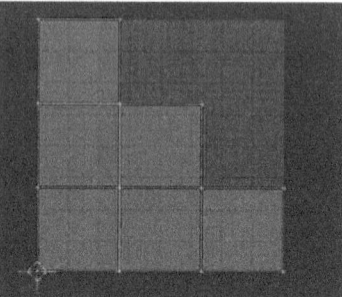

fig. 62 *Lightmap Pack* applied to a cube (on the left) and the outcome in the *UV/Image Editor* (on the right)

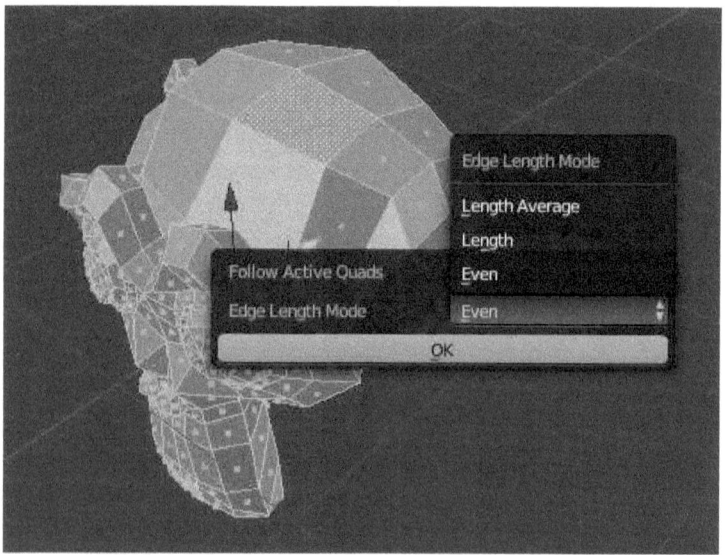

fig. 63 *Follow Active Quads*

- **Follow Active Quads** enables to unwrap the *mesh* following a loop starting from or following one or more active selected faces. In the confirmation window it is possible to choose 3 options from the menu *Edge Length Mode*: Even places uniformly all the faces in the *UV/Image Editor*; *Length* places the faces depending on the edge length of the active face; *Length Average* depending on the average length of the loop edges.

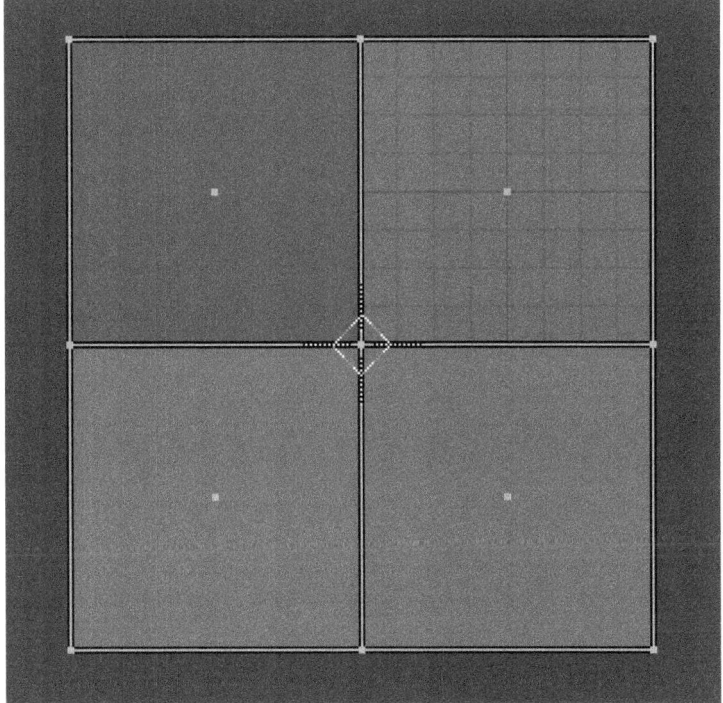

fig. 64 the cube unwrapping outcome using *Cube Projection*

- Suitable for solids like cubes or parallelepipeds, **Cube Projection** unwrap the mesh by projecting all the UV vertices of the mesh on the 6 faces of a cube and yielding in the *UV/Image Editor* a regular and orderly face decomposition. This option is particularly suitable for cubic shapes.

- Similarly, **Cylinder Projection** unwraps a cylindrical object. In order to use this function, the unwrapping procedure must be developed by vertically positioning the cylinder in the 3D view. All the faces of the cylindrical surface will be placed equally-spaced in the *UV/Image Editor*. It is recommended to unwrap the cylinder step by step (first the rectangular faces with the *Cylinder Projection* method, and then the circular bases, seen by the top, with the method *Project from View* which we will discuss in the foregoing.

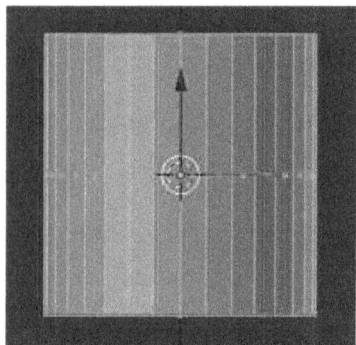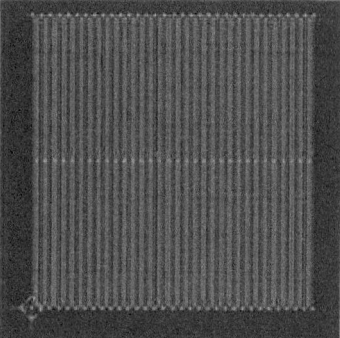

fig. 65 the cylinder unwrap outcome with *Cylinder Projection*

- **Sphere Projection** applies to a sphere the same methodology used for the cylinder. A good method to unwrap a sphere (*UV Sphere*) is to deselect the two poles (the top and bottom vertices), place the *mesh* with frontal view (with the two poles placed on the top and the bottom, respectively) and press U - *Sphere Projection*. All the faces of the sphere will be projected on the plane of the *UV/Image Editor* such as to be visualized equally spaced and uniform, easily to be mapped.

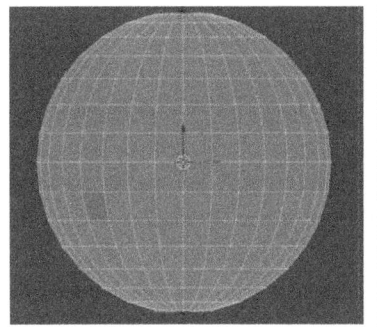 

fig. 66 the unwrapping sphere outcome with *Sphere Projection*

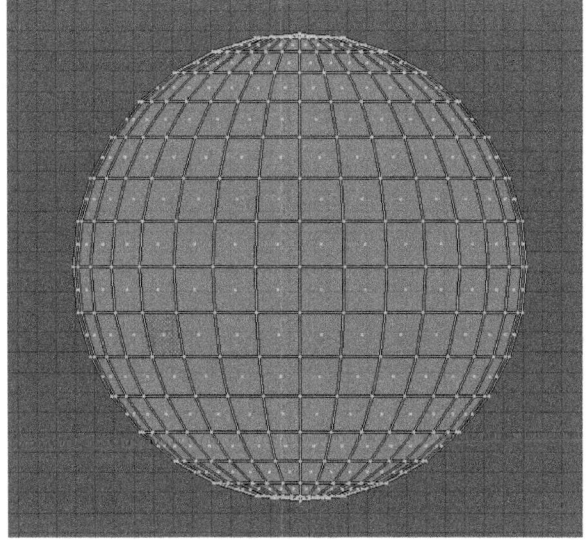

fig. 67 the unwrapping outcome of the same sphere in frontal view with *project From View*

- **Project From View** is a very useful method when the user wants to leave unchanged and proportions the shape of the selected faces of a mesh. For example, it is used for mapping a floor, unwrapped with this method with view from upside, or, in general, any object according to the current view. *Project*

67

Front View, actually projects the current view on the *UV/Image map*.

- **Project From View (Bounds)**, finally, projects according to the current view the vertices, the edges and the faces of the mesh on the *UV/Image Map* and maximize them, at the same time, with respect to the margins of the reference texture.

2.4.3. The *UV/Image Editor*

This editor, as previously said, is very useful for managing image files, textures, backgrounds e unwrapped meshes.

The editor, like all the other ones, has a header (placed by default downside) and a working area.

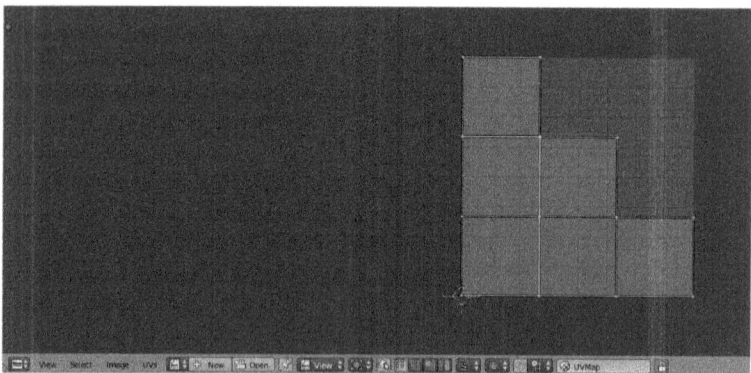

fig. 68 the *UV/Image Editor*

Inside the working area it is possible to visualize the images and, eventually, the previously unwrapped meshes superimposed to the images. For making visible the meshes unwrapped and deformed according to the unwrapping method it is necessary that the mesh be in *Edit Mode* modality in the 3D view and be selected. In fact in the working area of the *UV/Image Editor*, only

68

the vertices, edges and faces selected in the 3D view will be visualized.

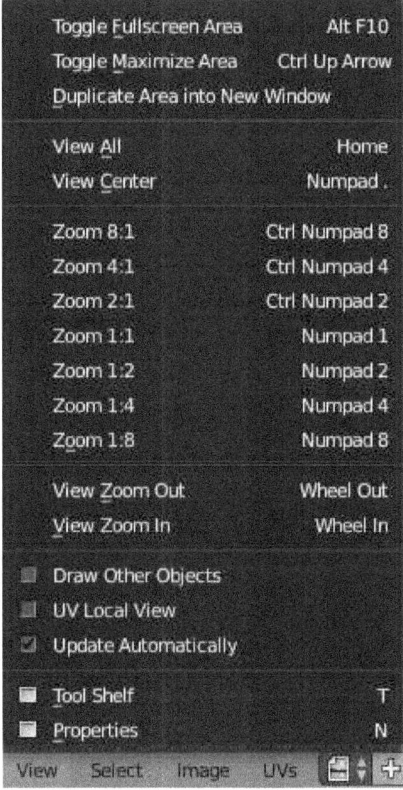

fig. 69 the *View* menu

The **View** menu in the header contains all the tools related to the image or the *VU Mapping* visualization in the working area, analogously to the menu in the 3D view.

- T and N open or close the lateral tabs **Tools Shelf** and **Properties** relevant to the *UV/Image Editor*, which we will analyze at the chapter end.

- **Update Authomatically** updates authomatically the window content after the changes.

- **UvLocal View** visualizes only the *UV Mapping* faces with the image actually assigned;

- **Draw Other Objects** shows other selected objects sharing the same image and the *UV Mapping*;

- **View Zoom In** (WM forward) and **View Zoom Out** (WM backward) carry out the image zoom;

- **Zoom 1:8, 1:4, 1:2, 1:1** (8-1 NUM), **2:1, 4:1, 8:1** (CTRL + 1-8 NUM) carry out the predefined zooms of the image and the *UV Mapping*;

- **View center** (. NUM) centers and maximizes the image and/or the *UV Mapping* in the working area;

- **View All** (Home) visualizes and rescales the image and/or the *UV Mapping* in the working area;

- **Duplicate Area Into New Window** duplicates the working area in a new window;

- **Toggle Maximize Area** (CTRL + upward arrow) (see 3D view);

- **Toggle Fullscreen Area** (F10) (see 3D view).

The **Select** menu collects the operations relevant to the selection, already analyzed in detail in the section relevant to the header of the 3D view. The function *Select Split* (key Y) is added, enabling to exclusively select the faces separated from the others.

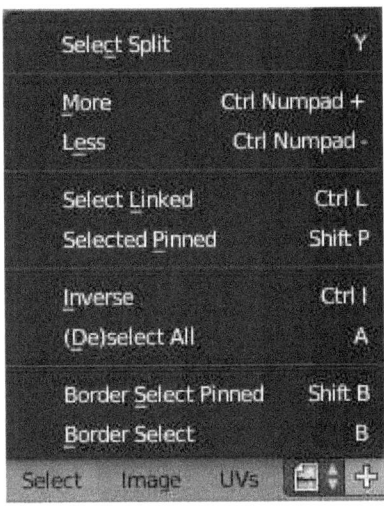

fig. 70 the *Select* menu

The **Image** menu contains:

- **New Image** (CTRL + N) creating a new empty image in the working area in which dimensions and sampling can be inserted;

- **Open Image** (CTRL + O) opening an image from the browser;

- **Read Render Layers** (CTRL + R) reading and representing the current rendered scene, if present;

- **Save All Images** saving all the images located in the working area;

- **Replace Image** replacing with a new current image the previous one;

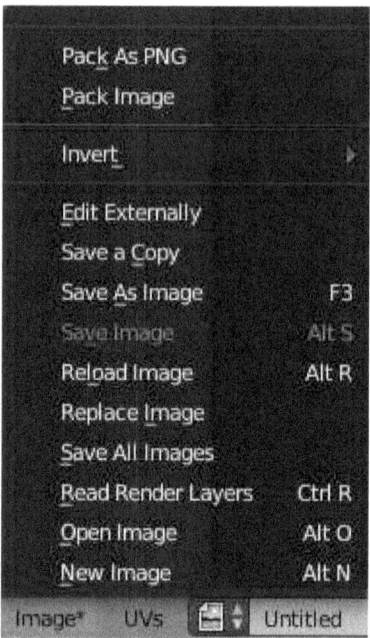

fig. 71 the *Image* menu

- **Reload Image** (ALT + R) reloading and updating the current image;

- **Save Image** (F3) saving the current image or the render just made;

- **Save a Copy** saving a copy of the current image;

- **Edit Externally** enabling to modify the image loaded in a photo editing application external to Blender;

- **Invert** opening a drop-down menu in which it is possible to fully invert all the image colors (*Invert Image Colors*) or separately only the channels of the primary colors red, green and blue or the transparency (*Alpha*);

72

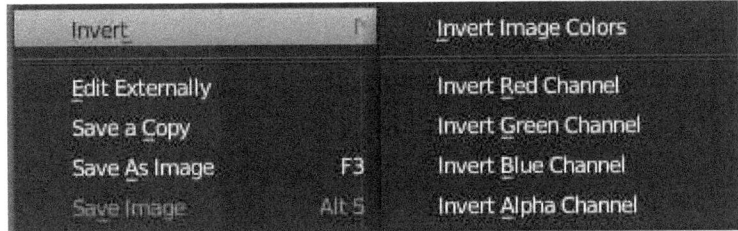

fig. 72 the *Invert* submenu

- **Pack Image** packs the image as integral datum of the *file* **.blend;*

- **Pack As PNG** packs the image as integral datum of the *file* **.blend* with related extension **.png.*

The **UVs** menu contains all the information related to *mapping.*

- **Snap to Pixels** attach the selection to the nearest *pixel* during the *UV* editing;

- **Constrain to Image Bounds** constrains the *editing* inside the image edges;

- **UV Sculpt** (Q) enables in the *Tools Shelf* a panel with the sculpture brushes dedicated to the editing of the *UV* mapping;

- **Live Unwrap** unwraps, in real time, the region selected during the transformation of the fixed vertices (*pinning*);

- **Unwrap** (E) executes the edited object unwrapping;

- **Pin**(P) and **Unpin** (ALT + P) sets or cancels the selected vertices setting as linked in different unwrapping multiple operations, i.e. when certain vertices belong to different unwrapping operations, see, for example, the cylinder unwrapping;

73

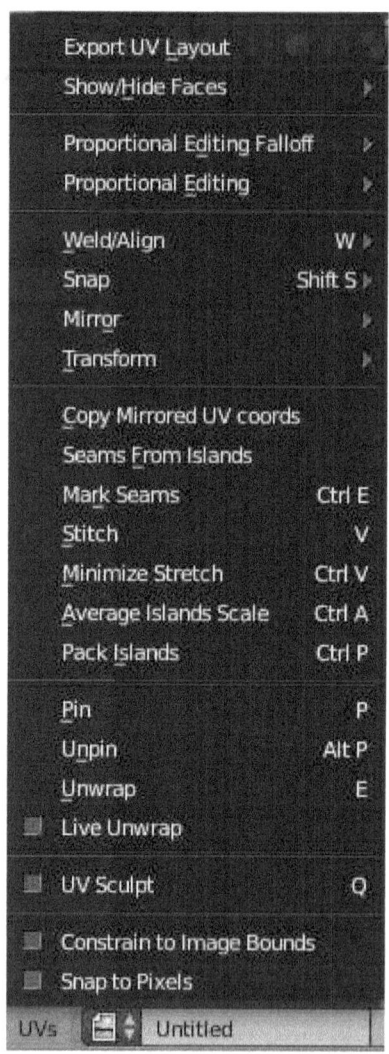

fig. 73 the *Uvs* menu

- **Pack Islands** (CTRL + P) automatically modifies all the regions such as fill as much as possible the available image space;

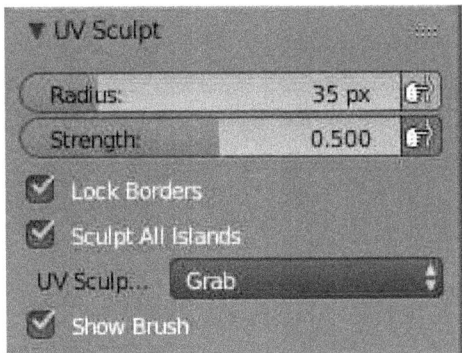

fig. 74 the *UV Sculpt* panel

- **Average Island Scale** (CTRL + A), regulates and makes an average of the areas dimensions (islands) resulting from the *UV Mapping*, based on the true face dimensions.

- **Minimize Stretch** (CTRL + V) reduces, as a consequence of the *unwrapping*, the island stretching and prevents the formation of too sharp angles;

- **Stitch** (V) stitches two selected vertices depending on their proximity;

- **Mark Seams** (E), see above;

- **Seams From Islands** sets the mesh unwrapping depending on the disposition of the *UV Mapping*;

- **Copy Mirrored UV coords** copies the mirrored coordinates along the x axis based on a in turn mirrored *mesh*;

- the **Transform** and **Mirror** menus contain the same transformation tools available for the objects and elements of the 3D view;

- **Snap** (SHIFT + S) activates a menu much relative to the snap between cursor and pixel of the *UV Mapping*;

75

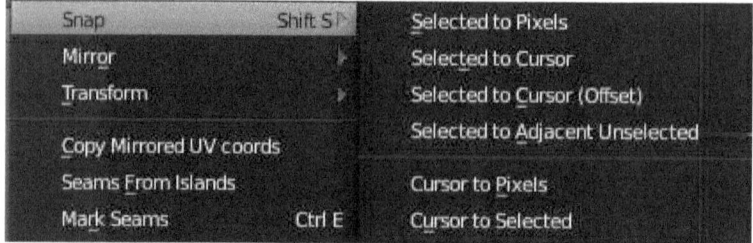

fig. 75 the *Snap* submenu

- **Weld/Align** (W) activates a submenu in which are defined the alignment modalities of the *UV Mapping* pixels and the possible copy removal;

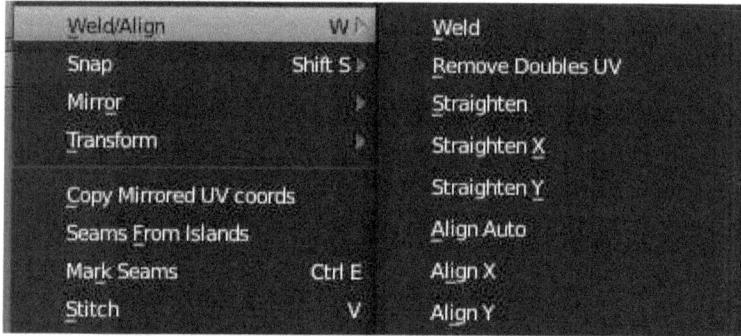

fig. 76 the *Weld/Align* submenu

- **Proportional Editing**, **Proportional Editing Falloff** and **Show/Hide Faces** offer the same functions already analyzed in the case of the proportional editing proportional and object visualization;

fig. 77 the commands relevant to the file import

76

- **Export UV Layout**, finally, exports on an external file the current *UV Mapping* layout.

Next, on the right of the *UVs* menu, we can find a sequence of commands relevant to the file import in the working area of the *UV/Image Editor.*

The first icon opens a menu from which it is possible to recall all the image files present or already downloaded of the scene, being either texture or render.

The text box enables to visualize and modify the image file name.

F, + and X have the same functions previously described (copy of the current file, add a new file, delete a file).

The icon between + and X enables to unpack the *file* from the project, such as to reduce the size of the saved *file* *.blend.*

fig. 78 other commands of the *header*

The icon with the pin shows the image without any regard for the selected file.

Then, the drop-down menu with the picture enables to upload one of the three different image types:

- *View*, visualization of an image file;

- *Paint* activates in the *Tools Shelf* the commands for the *Paint* applied to the *UV Mapping*. The *Painting Mode* will be explained in the foregoing;

77

- *Mask* activates the settings for the *mask Editing*.

Next we find the icon opening a menu relevant to the transformation methodology (rotation, scaling and positioning) with respect to the *2D Cursor* of the *UV Mapping*.

The next group of icons activates the tools relevant to the selection type and transformation methodology.

fig. 79 tools for the selection and transformation methodology

In detail:

- The first icon depicting an arrow and two vertices, if selected, enables the selection, at the same time, of both the vertices relevant to the *UV Mapping* and the *geometrical* vertices of the mesh to which they refer;

- The next group of 4 icons enables the selection, respectively, of the vertices, the edges, the faces and the full islands of the *UV Mapping* in order to perform the transformations (displacement, rotation and rescaling) for adapting the *UV Mapping* to the underlying *texture*;

- The menu icon *Sticky Selection Mode* enables to choose the selection modality of the elements in some way related to each other. For example, *Shared Vertex* selects all the vertices related in the geometry to the one selected in the *UV Mapping*, whereas *Share Location* selects all the vertices having, in the geometry, the same position and the same position/dimension.

The next commands, similarly to the corresponding ones in the header of the 3D view, activates the functions of proportional editing and snap.

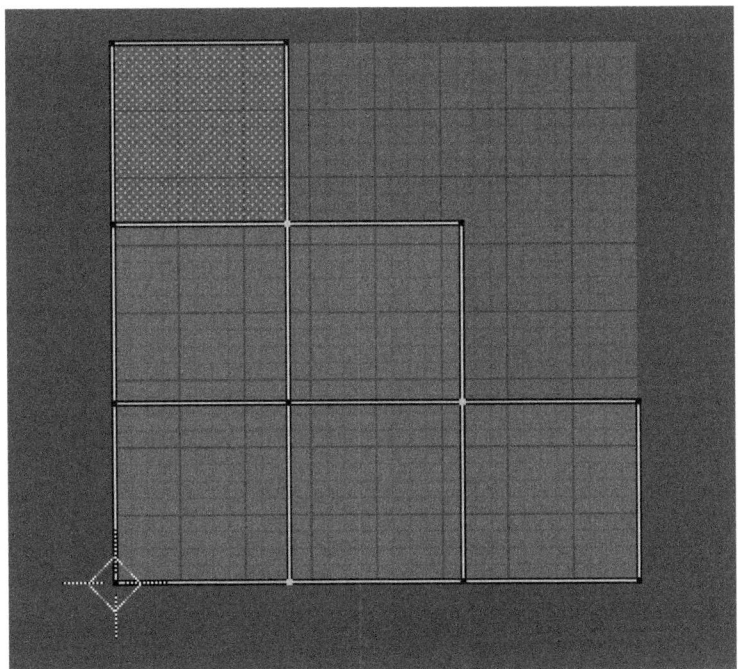

fig. 80 *Share Vertex*

Finally we find the command *Active UVMap* activating the *UVMap* in the editor and the lock, automatically updating all the other spaces of the relevant window, highlighting the changes due to the interactive operations such as the transformations.

fig. 81 the icons *UVMap* and lock

After having analyzed the functions and the options of the *UV/Image Editor* and having explained how to unwrap a *mesh* with the *unwrapping*, we can discuss the textures, both of image, video and procedural type.

Tab texture: the Image texture and the procedural texture

Let us discuss now how to upload a texture and associate it to a material.

Select an object to which a material has been applied and enter the *tab Texture* placed inside the *Properties Editor*.

As for the case of materials, it is possible to add to a texture an ongoing project, uploading the texture from the browser or creating it.

By clicking on *New* a new empty texture will be created.

The icon at the left hand side of the command *new* opens a menu in which it is possible to upload textures, if present.

fig. 82 the *tab Texture*

As for the case of a material, it is possible to change the texture name by typing the new name it the relevant box, to duplicate an existing texture to be modified by clicking the key F, to create or cancel a new texture by clicking on + or X, respectively.

80

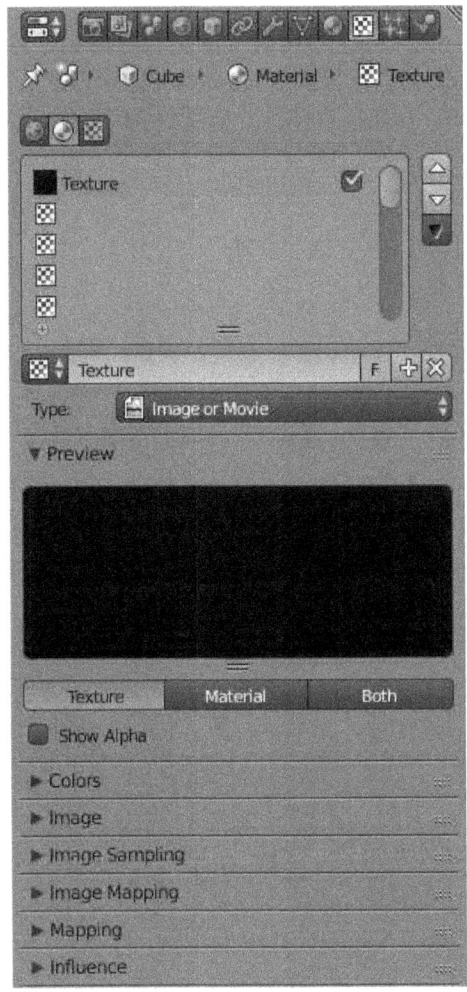

fig. 83 the *tab Texture* with a new open *texture*

NOTE: By adding several *textures* to a material *shader*, these can be mixed together or be used to affect several material parameter (color, *displacement...*).

The drop-down menu **Type** enables to choose the texture type to be uploaded.

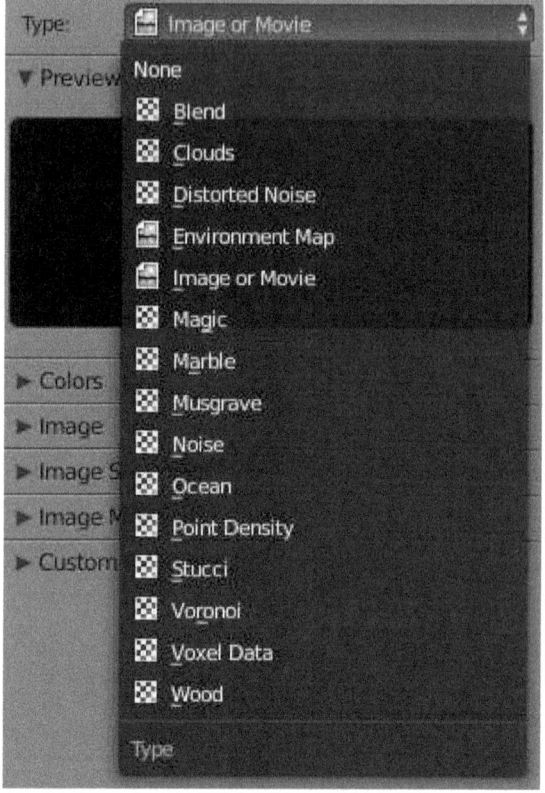

fig. 84 the menu *Type*

It is possible to choose whether to upload from an existing file an image texture, a movie, or one of the procedural texture which will be described in the foregoing.

Every texture has a **preview** in the preview panel, in which three commands can be find enabling to visualize the *texture*, the

82

material or both of them at the same time. The flag *Alpha* enables the preview of the transparency channel.

Blend creates a texture by the mix of two or more colors.

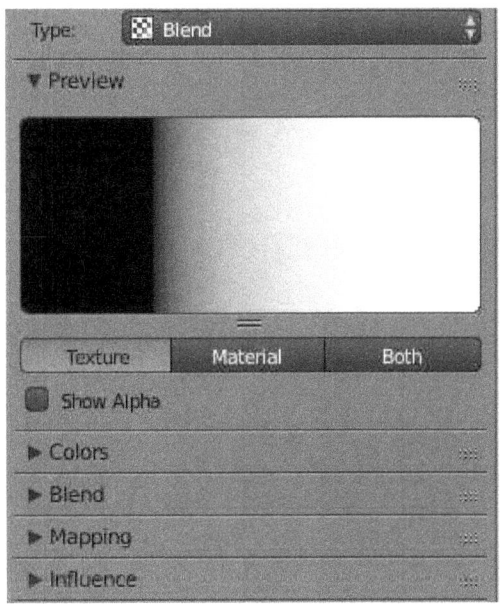

fig. 85 the procedural texture *Blend*

It is possible to add, to delete or to mirror in the panel **Colors**, by activating *Ramps*, a *Color Ramps* of two or more colors. The panel and the contained parameters are analogous to those present in the menu *Diffuse*. Moreover it is possible to modify the brightness, the contrast and the saturation, without affecting the quality and detail of the procedural texture.

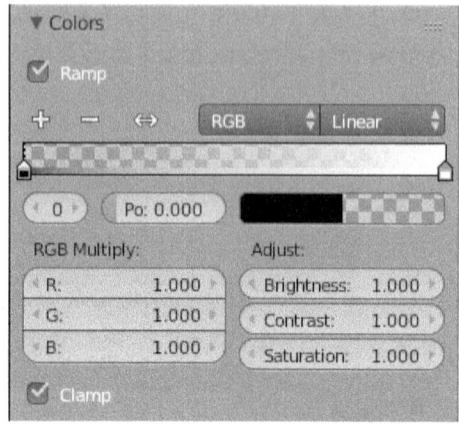

fig. 86 the *Colors* panel

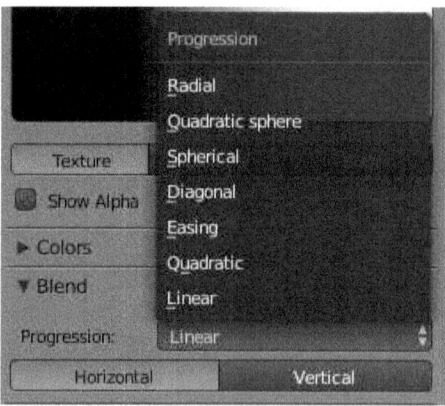

fig. 87 the *Blend* panel

In the **Blend** panel the disposition of the color ramp (*Horizontal* or *Vertical*) and the progressive model (*progression*) are defined), in the drop-down menu offering 7 choices.

The **Mapping** panel contains all data relevant to the texture mapping on the object faces to which is associated by means of

84

the material. Mapping amounts at placing, scaling, and rotating a texture such as it correctly and proportionally fits.

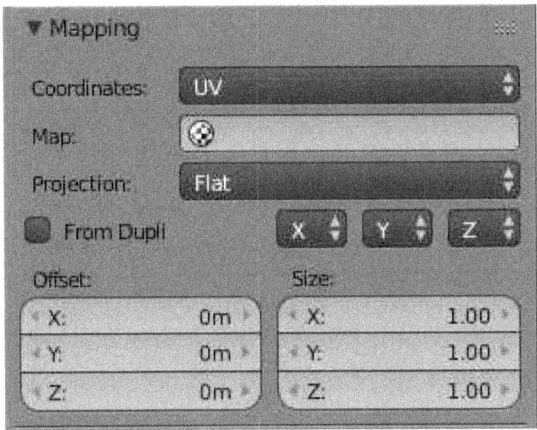

fig. 88 the *Mapping* panel

- *Coordinates* opens a drop and down menu in which several coordinate systems can be find for the application of the texture to the faces.

- *Tangent* sets the vectors tangent to the mesh as texture coordinates;

- *Stress* computes the coordinates to result optimized for meshes undergoing massive modifications with the use of the modifiers;

- *Reflection* employs the reflection vectors as coordinate system;

- *Normal* sets the texture coordinates along the vectors normal to the mesh faces;

- *Window* sets the coordinates such as they are always parallel to the current view;

- *Sticky* generates a *texture* coordinate system such as the *texture* has the same shape of the *mesh* projected on a plane from the current view;

- *Strand/Particle* applies the texture to a particulate system, if present;

- *UV* employs the texture standard coordinate system;

- *Generated* (default option) assumes as coordinate system the native coordinates of the object on which the texture is applied, without deformations;

- *Object* employs as coordinate system the system of another object specified in the relevant text box.

- *Projection* defines the projection method chosen among *Sphere*, *Cube*, *Flat* and *Tube*.

- *Offset* defines the texture position on the object with respect to the *x*, *y* and *z* axes.

- *Size* defines the scaling, thus the texture resize with respect to the object, according to the *x*, *y* and *z* directions.

The last panel **Influence**, on the other hand, contains all the options for the influence of the texture on the material.

The flags, divided by sectors (*Diffuse*, *Shading*, *Specular* and *Geometry*) activate or deactivate the *texture* influence on the relevant parameters of the material shaders and of the mesh geometry.

The drop-down menu *Blend* offers several solutions concerning the texture action on the various parameters.

Negative inverts the *texture* colors and *Stencil* enables to use the *texture* as a mask.

Finally *Bump Mapping*, defines how the *texture* will behave as displacement factor on the material, if at least one of the *Geometry* flags is activated. More specifically, the texture will be a vectorial scale factor for the displacement effect, i.e. the elevation, similarly as it can act on the other shader parameters.

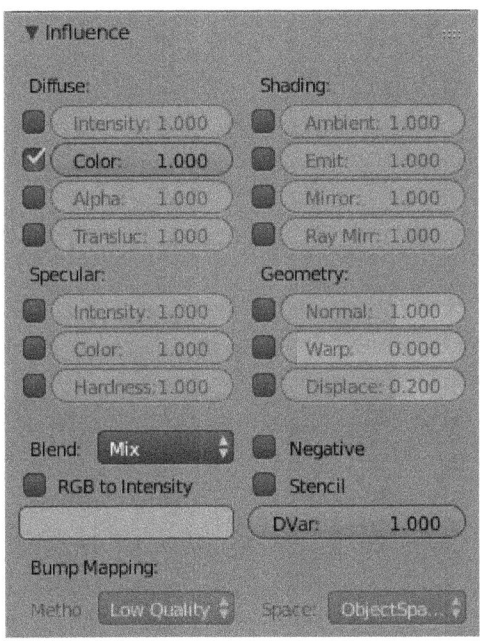

fig. 89 the panel *Influence*

NOTE: All the panels, except the one having the same name of the procedural texture, are shared by all the textures. The panel named as the texture is the one managing its characteristics in detail.

87

fig. 90 the *texture Blend* applied to a sphere

CLOUDS

fig. 91 procedural texture *Clouds*

Clouds is a procedural *texture* much used, generating a cloudy effect or a noise depending on the chosen settings.

Since, as specified in the note, all the panels are shared by the *textures*, we will analyze only the specific one named *Cloud*.

Choosing between *Grayscale* and *Color*, the cloudy texture will have a coloring in gray scale or colors.

Soft and *Noise* define the noise incidence (*Noise*).

Basis defines the kind of noise applied to the *texture* chosen among 10 solutions, as in figure, depending on the desired effect.

Size determines the scale, i.e. the dimensions, of the mapping on the object.

Nabla is a multiplicative factor for the displacement functions.

Depth defines the detail level of the effect.

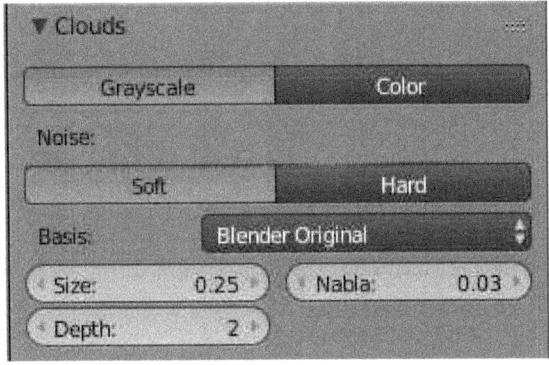

fig. 92 the *Cloud* panel

fig. 93 noise typologies (from left to right): *Blender Original, Blender Perlin, Improved Perlin, Voronoi F1, Voronoi F2, Voronoi F3, Voronoi F4, Voronoi F2 . F1, Voronoi Crackle, Cell Noise*

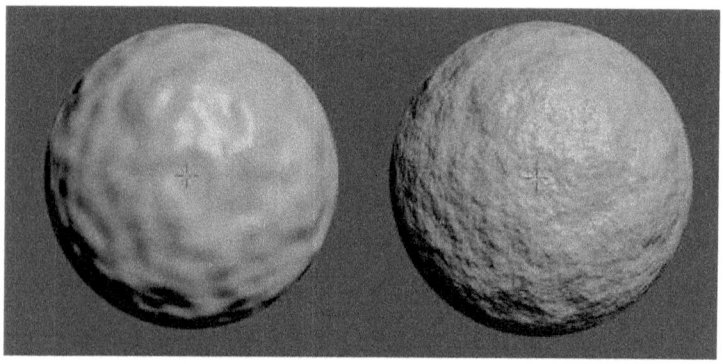

fig. 94 a texture *Clouds* applied as color and as displacement to a sphere with *Depth* set to 1 (on the left) and to 5 (on the right)

Distorted Noise generates a disturbance like *Clouds* (the parameters are much similar).

In particular it enables to operate with a distortion of the cloudy effect, much similarly to *Clouds* and with the same option choices in the two menus *Noise Distortion* and *Basis*.

90

In fact in the panel **Distorted Noise**, the *Distortion* parameter is present in place of *Depth*.

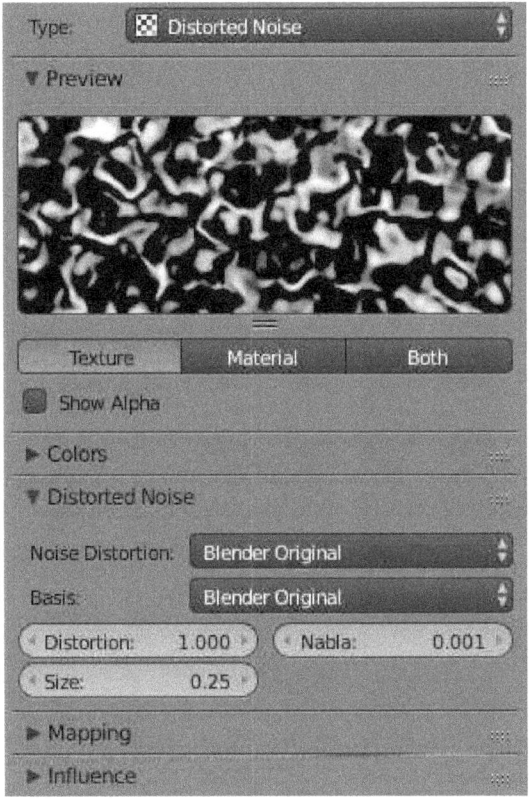

fig. 95 procedural texture and panel *Distorted Noise*

Set also as *displacement*, this *texture* generates a very interesting effect.

Try to practice, by creating complex geometries and applying the texture *Distorted Noise*.

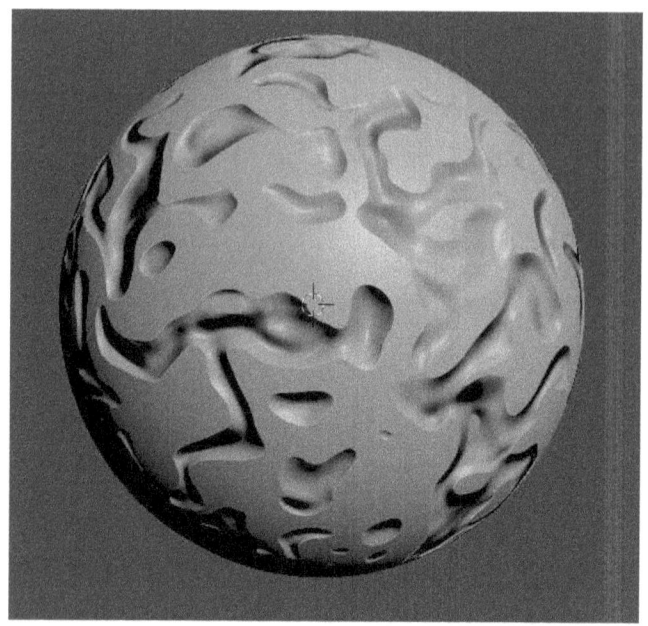

fig. 96 a *Distorted Noise* texture applied as color and displacement to a sphere

IMAGE OR MOVIE

The **Image or Movie** option enables to set as texture an external file as a image, a sequence of images or a video.

Thus it is not a procedural *texture*, but the placement of an image or a video on a surface object.

 Different from the procedural textures, Blender must unwrap the mesh according to a suitable method in order to apply the image or video to a mesh surface. This operation is referred to as unwrapping.

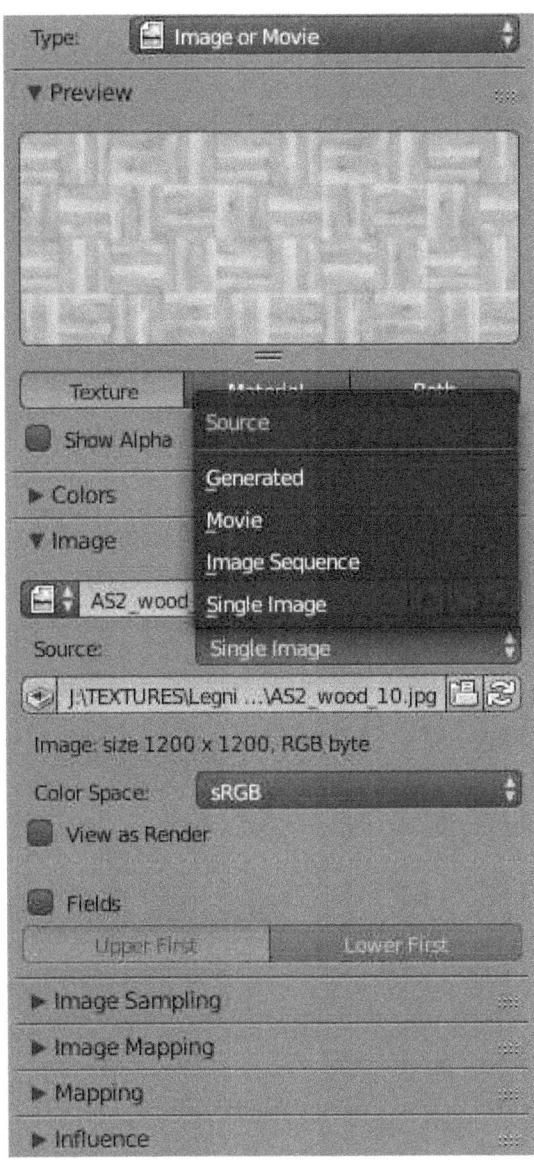

fig. 97 *Image or Movie*

93

EXERCISE N. 2: TEST ON MATERIALS

Suppose to create a base element of a modern kitchen and to assign to the front parts (doors, drawers...) a material whose color is defined by an image texture.

First, as usual, it is necessary to clearly know what one wants to get, using an external reference.

The piece of kitchen is composed of three main parts: the cabinet, with shelf or extractable guides; the front (doors or drawers); the regulation feet, on which is attached the baseboard.

The cabinet is composed of:

- 2 vertical elements, the sides, 72 cm height, usually 56 deep and 1.8 cm thick;

- 1 top and 1 base shelf, with variable width depending on the kitchen composition (in our case, for a base with width 60 cm, the width of the horizontal shelves will be given by the difference between 60 cm and 1,8 times 2, thus equal to 56.4 cm), the deepness will be 56 and the thickness 1.8;

- 1 central shelf with width 56.4 cm, deepness 46 cm and thickness 1.8, placed at the center of the room;

- 1 back panel, wide 56.4 cm, with height 68.4 cm (72 – two times 1.8) and thickness 0,8 cm.

Let us start defining one of the two side panel. Insert a cube and resize the dimensions:

$$x = 0.018; \ y = 0.56; \ z = 0.72.$$

Remember to apply the scale with CTRL + A.

Add a modifier *Bevel* with the parameter *Width* equal to 1 mm and switch off the effect by clicking on the icon with a eye.

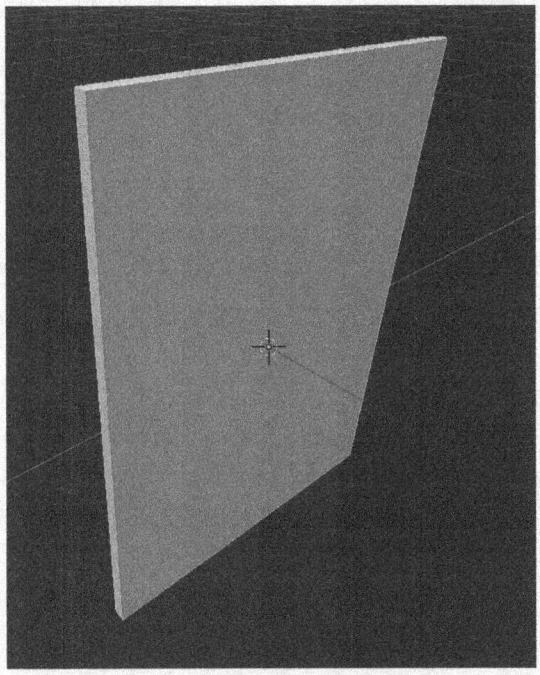

fig. 98 side panel of the kitchen basal element

Create a linked duplicate (ALT + D) of this side and translate along the x direction by 58.2 cm.

Select now the two elements and digit SHIFT + S for positioning the *3D Cursor* at the center between the two panels (*Cursor To Selected*).

The next elements to be generated will be placed in correspondence of the *3D Cursor*, i.e. between the side panels.

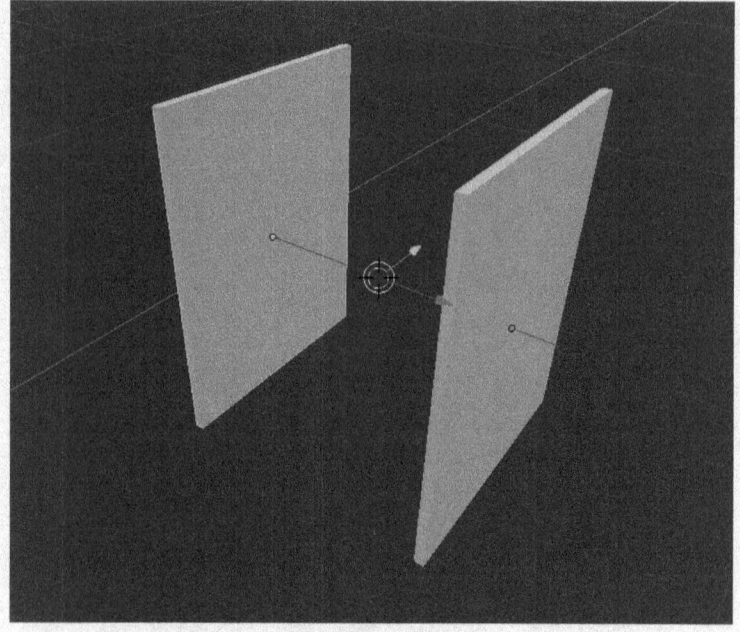

fig. 99 placing of the *3D* Cursor between the two sides

Create a new cube and resize it such that:

$$x = 0.564; \ y = 0.56; \ z = 0.018.$$

Apply the scale and translate the object with G + Z by 35.1 cm (i.e. half of 72 cm – half of 1.8 cm).

The object will be moved at the top.

Create a linked duplicate and move it downside by 70.2 cm (72 - 1.8).

The base panel will appear correctly positioned at the center.

Select the 4 elements and take care that the *3D Cursor* be aligned with their centers.

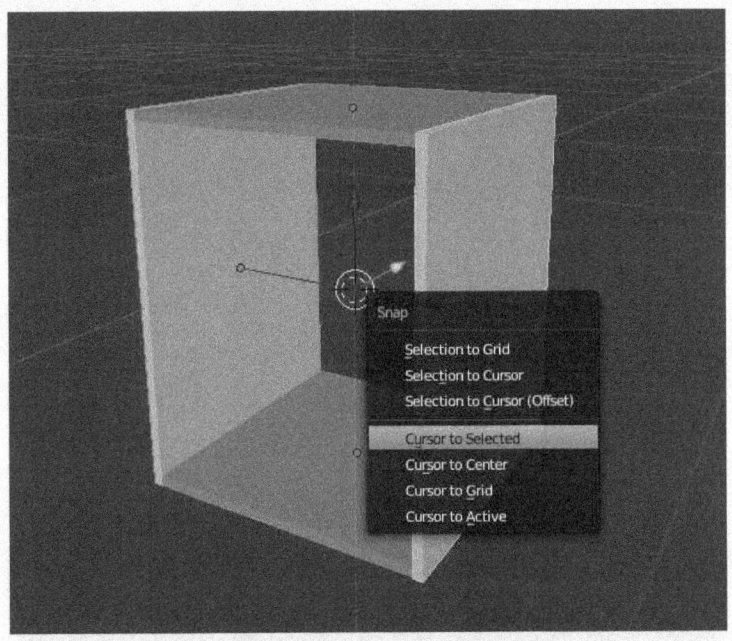

fig. 100 placing of the *3D* Cursor between the 4 elements of the cabinet

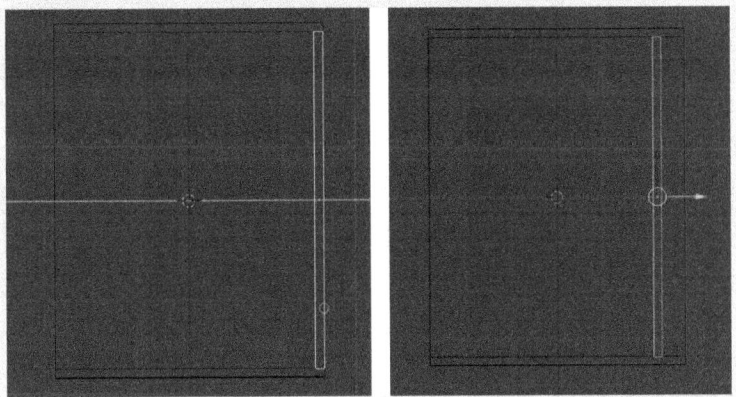

fig. 101 placement of the back panel

Insert a new cube (the back) and resize it:

$x = 0.564; y = 0.008; z = 0.684.$

fig. 102 cylinder placement

In lateral view (1 NUM), drag toward the y direction the back panel with the magnet activated (key CTRL during the drag operation) till it clasps to the side external edge, then move it again toward the inner side by 5 cm (G, Y, .05 -).

Select now the 4 elements and, with CTRL + J, group them together in a single mesh which we will name cabinet.

In *Top* view (7 NUM), create a cylinder of radius 3.5 cm and height 2 cm.

Apply the scale.

Place the cylinder at about 8 cm from the left edge and the same from the front edge.

Go in frontal view (1 NUM) and place the cylinder base coinciding with that of the element, then move by 15 cm downside.

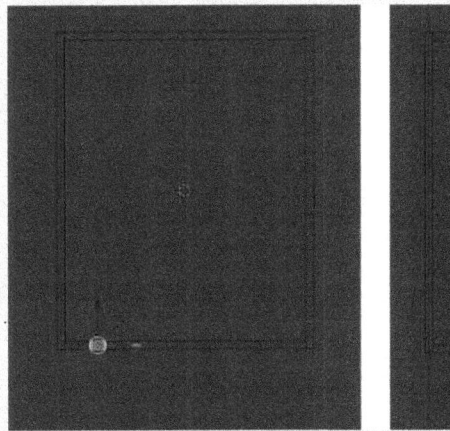

fig. 103 cylinder displacement

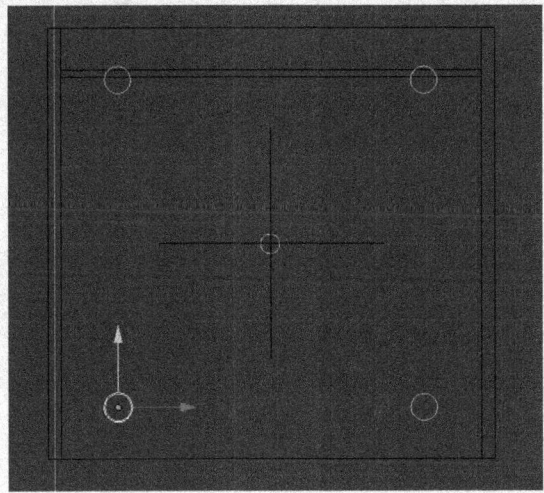

fig. 104 *Mirror* on the cylinder

Then add an *Empty* on the *3D Cursor* and with the cylinder selected assign a modifier *Mirror*, which will mirror with respect to the *Empty* both with respect to *x* and *y*.

Enter in *Edit Mode* and execute a sequence of *Inset*, *Extrude*, *Scale* and *Grab* on the top cylinder base such as to shape the cabinet foot. With *Mirror* activated, the modification will occur on all the four feet.

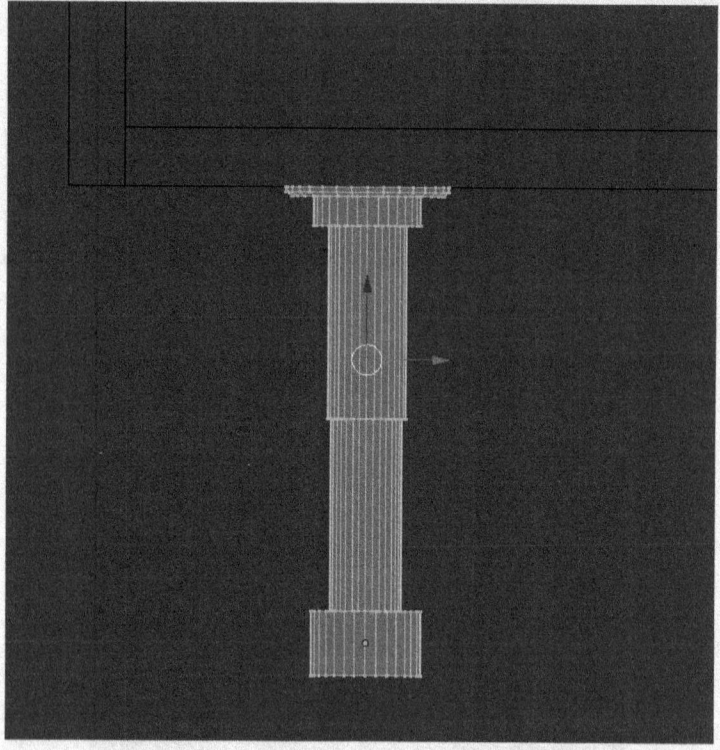

fig. 105 the cabinet foot

Add *loops* very close to the foot element borders.

fig. 106 *loop*

Pressing H, remove for now the cylinder top portion from the view and in wireframe, select the vertex as in figure 107.

Then, scale with S inwards to obtain 8 slots.

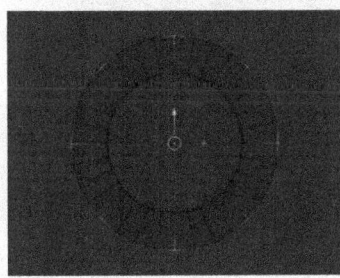 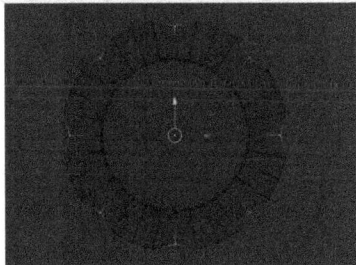

fig. 107 slots of the foot

Press ALT + H to unhide the other vertices of the foot and add a modifier *Subdivision Surface* with 2 divisions and then a *Smooth*.

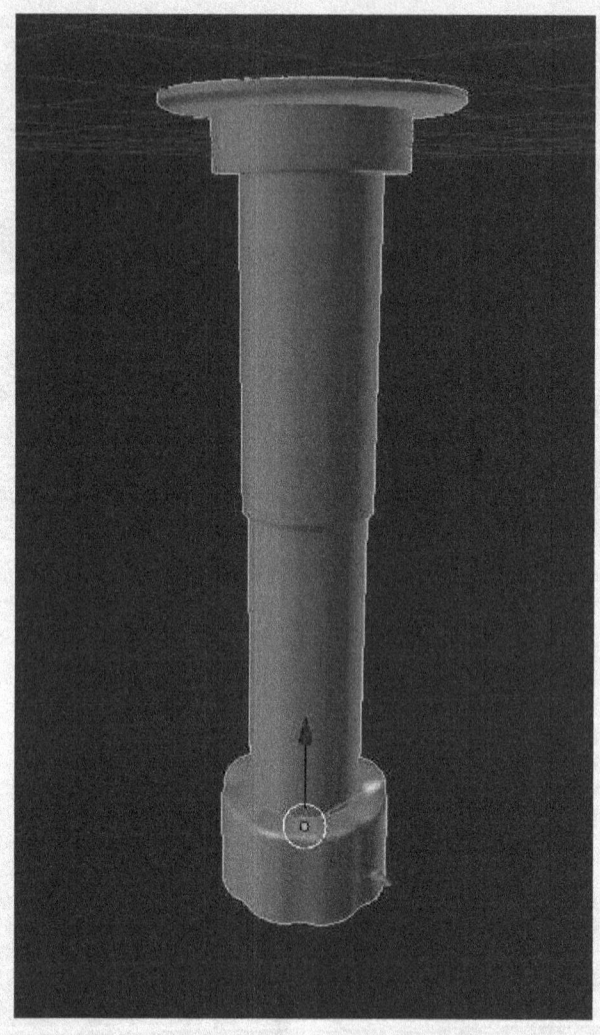

fig. 108 completed foot

Rename the object *feet* and apply the *Mirror*.

Then remove the visualization flag of the *Bevel* on the cabinet.

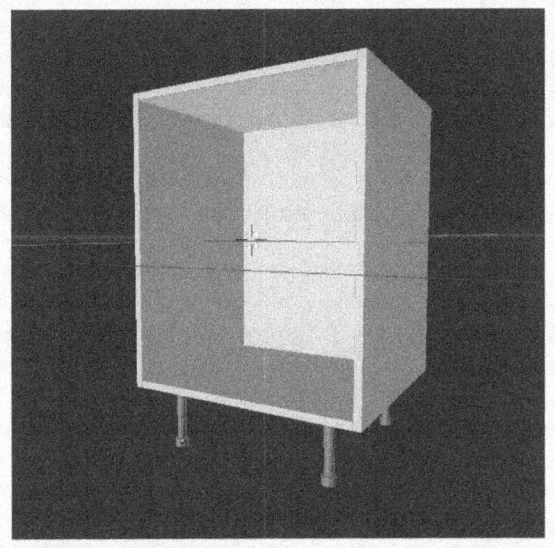

fig. 109 cabinet and feet

fig. 110 placing of the *3D Cursor*

We can now create the door.

Since the door will remain closed, the internal shelf is not visible and so we will not model it.

Select the 4 frontal vertices of the cabinet and digit SHIFT + S to place the *3D Cursor*.

In *Object Mode*, add a new cube and rescale it:

$$x = 0.597; \; y = 0.018; \; z = 0.717.$$

This way the door will be 3 mm smaller that the cabinet, just to prevent friction between neighboring doors.

Place the door such as the distance from the cabinet be 3 mm. This will create realistic shadows between the elements.

Apply the scale and rename the element door.

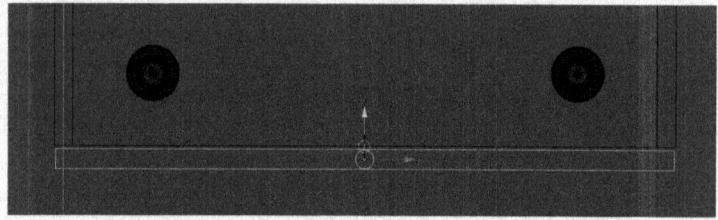

fig. 111 the door

Add *Bevel* to the door, and set the ray 2 mm and 4 segments.

Add also the *Smooth* and, obviously, the modifier *Edge Split* to have a correct shading on the flat faces.

Select now the *Lamp and set it as* Sun.

Place it to correctly light the door.

fig. 112 *Bevel*

Select the door and add a material we will rename *wood*, then, on the *tab Texture*, add a new image texture, loading the file *wood.jpg*.

Enter in *Edit Mode* and select all the door vertices, then digit CTRL + E and choose *Mark Seam* from the menu, such as to fully unwrap all the elements comprising the door.

Open the *UV/Image Editor* e observe the outcome.

The 6 faces of the door have been unwrapped and horizontally placed on the *UV* plane with the underlying *texture*.

First, on the *UV Image/Editor*, rotate the faces appearing with the grain not aligned to the remaining.

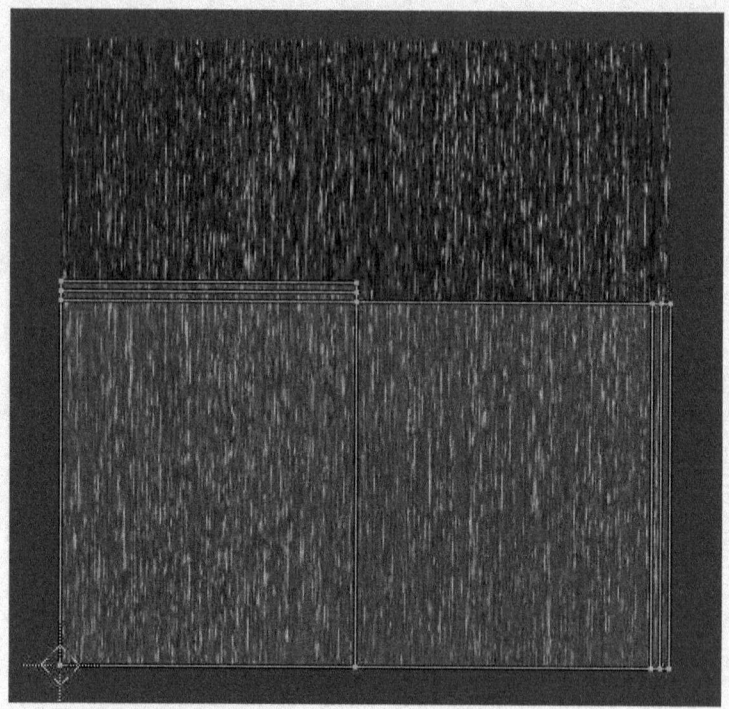

fig. 113 *unwrap* of the door *mesh*

Keep in mind that the grain must be parallel to the long edges of the door lateral faces.

Clicking on the icon *UV Selection: Island*, select all the lateral faces (they can be superimposed and horizontally displaced) and rotate them by 90°.

Then repeat the same procedure for the other faces.

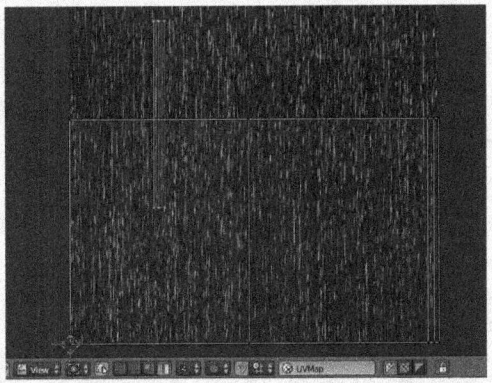

fig. 114 rotation by 90° of the lateral faces on the *UV Image/Texture Editor*

fig. 115 rotation by 90° of the other faces on the *UV Image/Texture Editor*

Go in *Rendered* visualization mode in the 3D view (SHIFT + Z) observe the outcome.

We can rescale and place the unwrapped selected faces in the *UV Image/Texture Editor* such as to adjust the grain.

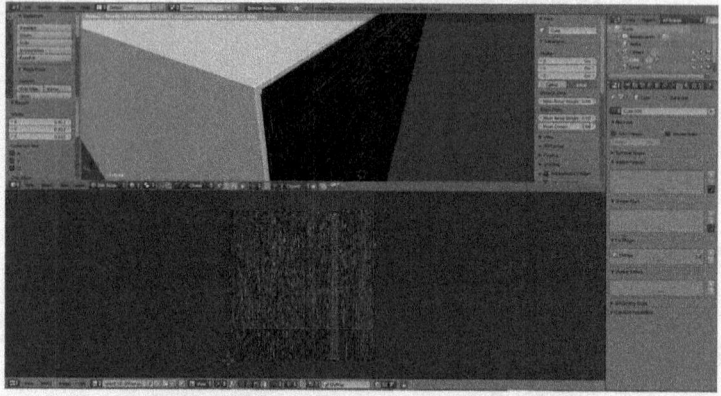

fig. 116 pre rendering mapping effect

Add a *bump* effect, which will be discussed in detail in the foregoing, with a value higher than 0 in the *Geometry* section on the *Influence* panel (*tab Texture*), checking *Normal*.

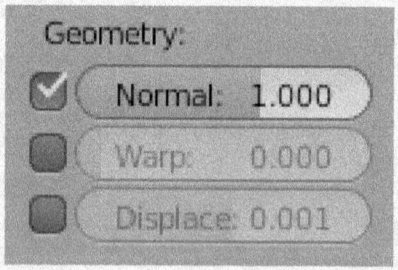

fig. 117 *Normal*

We can further apply a bit of reflection to the material in the *Mirror* panel, setting the value 1.450 in the *Fresnel* box, thus regulation the index of refraction (IOR). Define now the laminate color of the cabinet.

Create a new material, naming it *grey*, and change the color on the palette in *diffuse*.

Finally assign a semi gloss black color to the feet. The outcome should be similar to the one shown in figure 119.

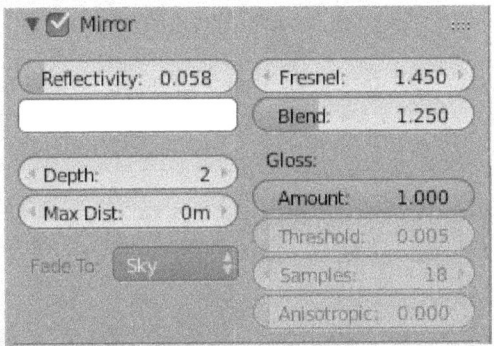

fig. 118 the reflection with *Mirror*

fig. 119 *render* of the kitchen cabinet

Environment Map generates reflections coming from a *background texture*.

Thank to the *raytracing*, they result much quick to be computed, especially if the blur is set, requiring a lesser number of samples.

Reflecting the light along all the 6 possible space directions (*x* and - *x*; *y* and - *y*; *z* and - *z*), yields a diffuse and realistic reflections.

In order to obtain correct outcomes for an *Environment Mapping*, the *Coordinates* menu must be set on *Reflection* in the *Mapping* panel.

fig. 120 the panel *Environment Map* panel. On the left the available options in *Static* and *Animation* modality; on the right in *Image File* modality

There are three modalities defined in the first panel **Environment Map**:

- *Static*, computing the texture only one time during an animation rendering, thus reflecting always the same image;

- *Animated*, computing continuously the rendering for each animation frame, thus reflecting the actual image;

- *Image* File, enabling to upload a *background* image from the *browser*. This option makes the rendering quicker and gives also the possibility to modify or use the *Environment* Map in an external application.

Moreover it is possible to set the *mapping* of the *Environment Map*, in planar mode (*Plane*) or cubic (*Cube*), to ignore the objects belonging to selected layers and to define limiting values for the reflection (*Clipping*), for values beyond the limits set in *Start* and *End* the reflection will not happen.

Resolution determines the quality of the reflection resolution during the rendering, whereas *Depth* defines the number of rebounds between reflecting objects. This parameter should be carefully employed based on the desired effect, since any further reflection will yield longer computing time during the rendering.

By setting the modality *Image File*, it is possible to upload an image to be reflected.

A fixed image (*Single Image*), an image sequence (*Image Sequence*), or a movie (*Movie*) can be uploaded from the browser, or the image can be mathematically generated (*Generate*).

Once the image file has been uploaded or generated, the color space method can be used, choosing from the options in *Color Space* and the image in the *render* can be visualized, by selecting the option *View as Render*.

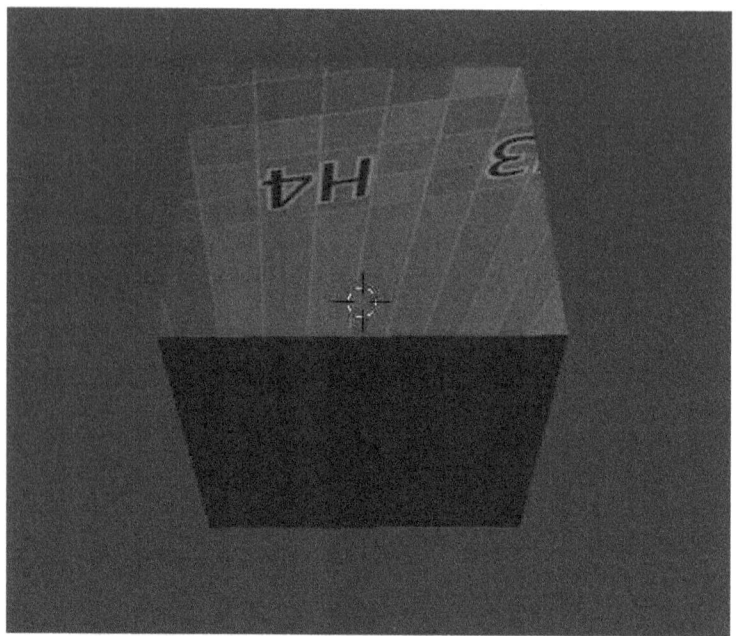

fig. 121 *reflection render of Generate Color type Image*

Using *Generate* for creating the image, on the other hand, the dimensions in *pixels* can be defined and inserted in the counters *X* and *Y* and the type of image can be set: *Blank*, *Color Gria*, or *UV Grid*.

In the underlying panel **Environment Map Sampling**, the menu *Filter* define the filter type to be used for the image sampling, chosen between:

- *Box*, cubic type filter;

- *EWA* (*Elliptical Weighted Average*), which generates an elliptic path for the sample weights, and then divide the outcome by the sum of the weights;

- *FELINE* (*Fast Elliptical Line*), uses several isotropic probes in different points, for producing an anisotropic filter and reducing the *aliasing* artifacts without sensibly increasing the *rendering* time;

- *Probes*, affecting the maximum sample number (a high number yields less blur to the angles far and oblique, with unavoidable increase of the computing time).

The counters Eccentricity and *Filter* Size define the maximum sample number for eccentricity and blur effects (higher values generate reduced blur to the angles far and oblique, but also yield increases computing time).

The flag on *Minimum Filter Size* uses *Filter Size* as minimum value expressed in pixels.

MAGIC

The procedural texture **Magic** generates a color image computed with trigonometric algorithms.

In the **Magic** panel only two parameters are available:

- *Depth*, determining the depth of the generated noise;

- *Turbulence* determining the turbulence effect of the texture.

Magic is useful for obtaining mapping on the meshes with a definitely fuzzy outcome.

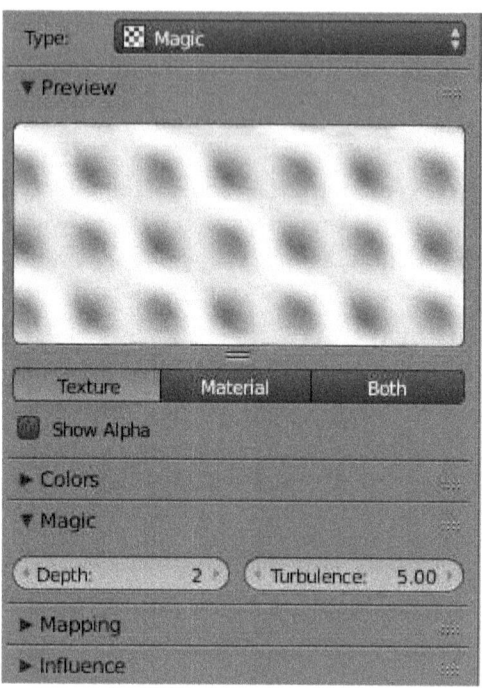

fig. 122 the procedural texture and panel *Magic*

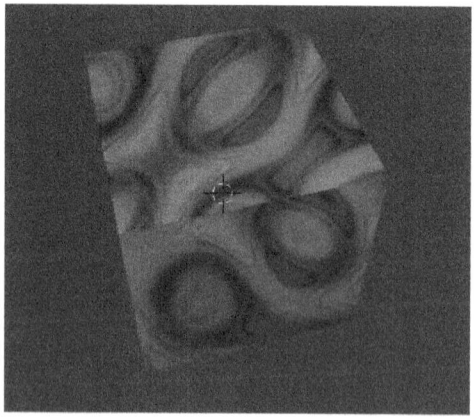

fig. 123 the procedural texture Magic applied to a cube

114

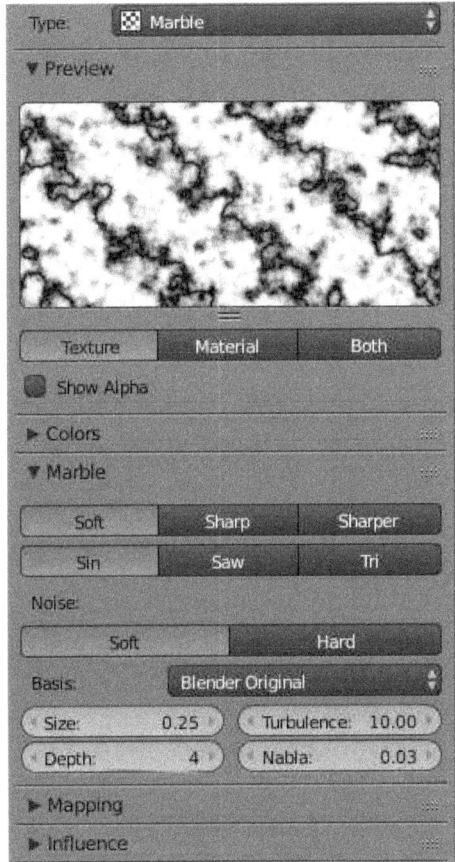

fig. 124 the procedural texture and panel *Marble*

Marble generates a procedural *texture* simulating the natural veining pattern typical of the marble and granite.

The three switches on the top of the panel **Marble**, Soft, *Sharp* and *Sharper*, enable to choose the veining definition.

115

The underlying three switches *Sin* (sinusoid),*Saw* (saw tooth shape), *Tri* (triangular wave), set the mathematical model used for generating the veins.

The noise influence can be managed by one of the two switches *Soft* and *Hard*.

The menu *Basis* builds the mathematical model generating the veins, choosing it by one of the available procedural textures.

Size determines the veining size; *Turbulence* the deformation; *Depth* regulates the effect depth and definition; *Nabla*, like for *Clouds*, is a multiplicative factor for the displacement functions.

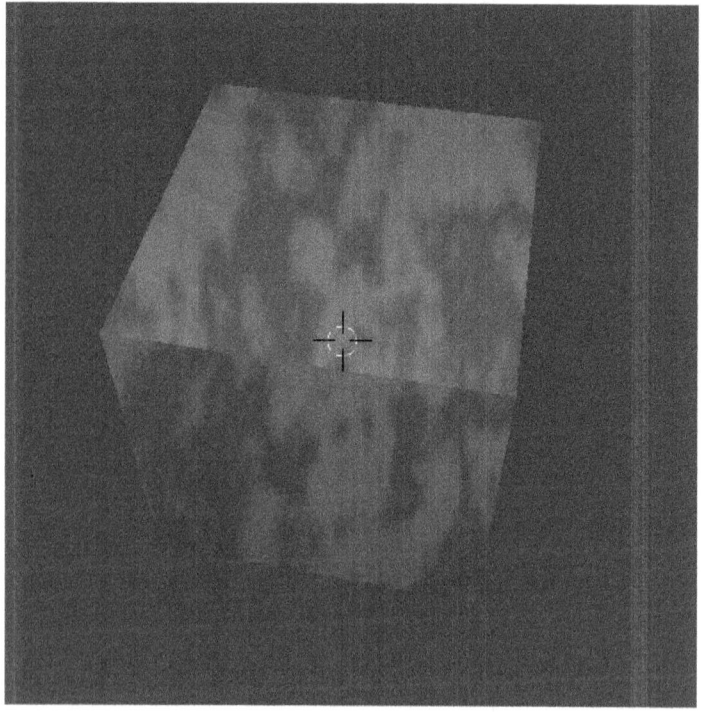

fig. 125 the *marble* texture applied to a cube

Musgrave generates a procedural texture according to a fractal structure.

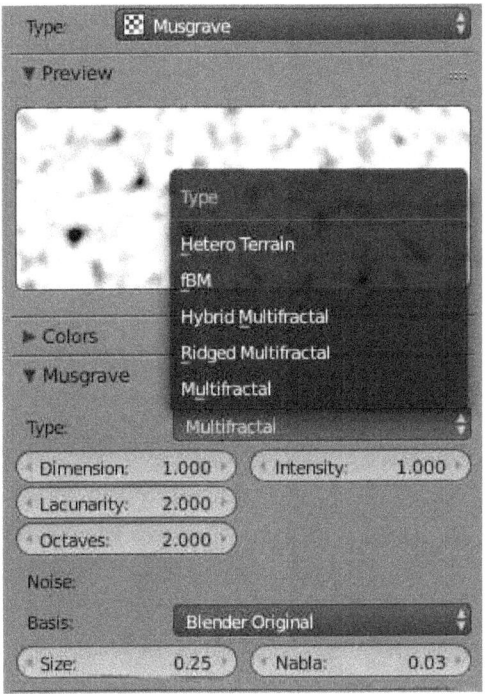

fig. 126 the procedural texture and panel *Musgrave*

This kind of texture is devoted for simulating on a mesh, for example, a spotted cloak or a hilly ground.

In the panel **Musgrave**, once chosen the disturbance typology from the menu *Type* (*Multifractal, Ridged Multifractal, Hybrid Multifractal, fBM* or *Hetero Terrain*), the dimensions of the weave (*Dimension*), the intensity (*Intensity*), the split between the next fractals (*Lacunarity*) and the number of frequencies used in the fractal subdivision (*Octaves*) can be set.

117

In order to determine the base structure of the noise it is possible to choose a reference procedural texture between the ones available in the menu *Noise*, defining the specific sizes (*Size*) and the multiplicative factor for the elevation (*Nabla*).

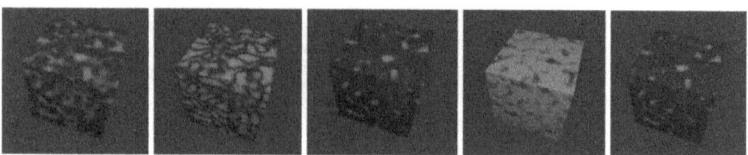

fig. 127 *Musgrave* applied to a cube. From left to right, *Type* set to *Multifractal, Ridged Multifractal, Hybrid Multifractal, fBM, Hetero Terrain*

NOISE

fig. 128 procedural texture *Noise*

Noise is one of the procedural texture most used and simple.

It has not a dedicated panel, since its point weave can be simply rescaled, translated and rotated in the panel *Mapping* to be applied to the material.

Usually the *texture* is made correspond to the *bump* or to the *displacement*, setting a value greater than 0, for obtaining a displacement effect similar to the textured finishing of a wall or a gall glazing, keeping into account that the elevated vertices will correspond to the clearer areas of the *texture*, whereas the depressed ones to the darker areas.

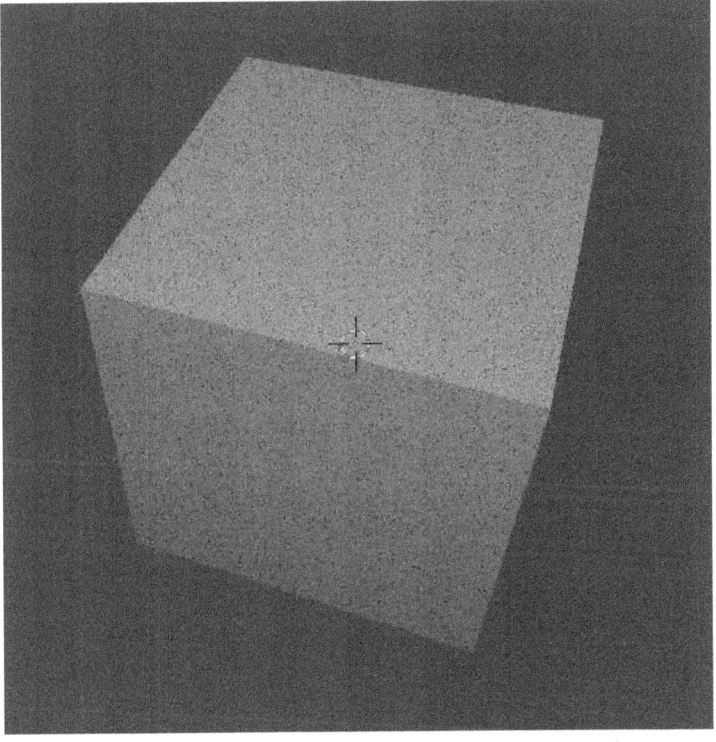

fig. 129 *Noise* applied to a *mesh*

OCEAN

This procedural *texture* is needed to be associated to the modifier *Ocean* for simulating sea waved surfaces.

The modifier *Ocean*, not yet discussed, belongs to the group *Simulate*, of which we will discuss in the foregoing.

Thus, for now, this *texture* will not be analyzed.

fig. 130 panel of the procedural *texture Ocean*

POINT DENSITY

Point Density renders a point set (mesh vertices or particle system) like it were part of a 3D volume, using a user defined radius.

The rendered points are represented spherical by default, with various smoothing options *Falloff* and turbulence options for modifying the outcome, with the addition of small details.

The first two options we find in the panel **Point Density** enable to choose the source of the point cloud. These can be generated by a particle system (*Particle System*) or by object vertices (*Object Vertices*).

In the box *Object* it is thus possible to select which object (particulate or mesh) the *texture* will be referred, whereas *Radius* determines the effect action radius.

120

120

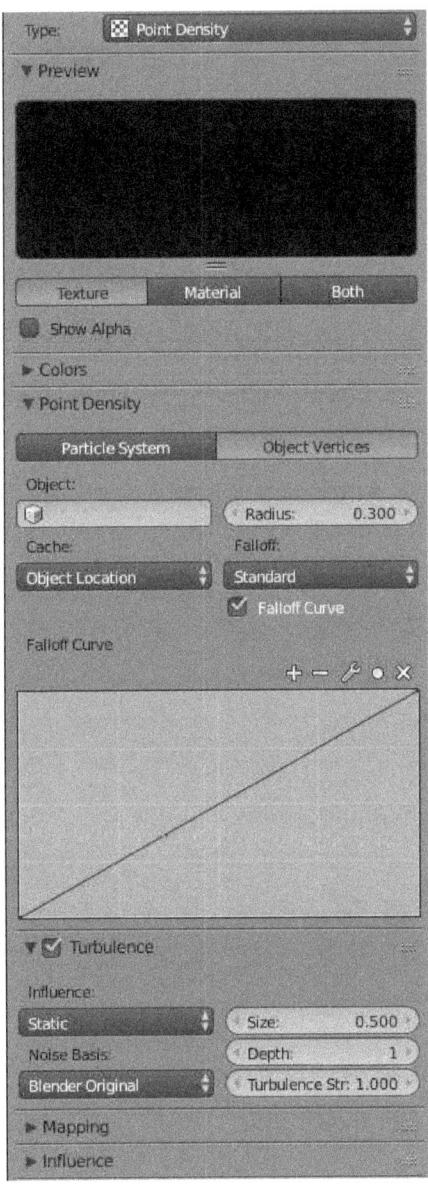

fig. 131 procedural *texture* and *Point Density* panel

Particle System activates a drop-down menu named *Color Source* to be used for defining the color data, i.e.:

- *Constant*, constant color;

- *Particle Age*, color intensity depending from the age of the generated particles;

- *Particle Speed*, color intensity depending to the particle speed;

- *Scale*, depending on a value scaling the particle velocity;

- *Particle Velocity*, defines the RGB color components as a function of the XYZ particle velocity components;

Menu commons to the two options *Particle System* and *Object Vertices* are *Cache*, influencing how the visualized particles are hidden and *Falloff*, determining the particle attenuation method based to the items contained in the drop-down menu. The flag *Falloff Curve* activates a manual area where it is possible to draw the damping curve.

The **Turbulence** panel contains some options regulating a noise addition (a turbulence) to the rendered particles.

The *Influence* menu regulates the way the turbulence must be added, i.e.:

- *Static*, in which the added noise remain unchanged, static, method more suitable for the static images;

- *Particle Velocity* generates a turbulence based on the particle velocity;

- *Particle Age* generates a turbulence based on the particle age;

- *Global Time* generates a turbulence based on the current frame (for the animations).

The *Noise Basis* menu uses the behavior of a procedural *texture*, chosen from the list, for determining the turbulence behavior.

Size determines the turbulence scale; *Depth* the detail level; *Turbulence Strength* the strength of the added turbulence.

STUCCI

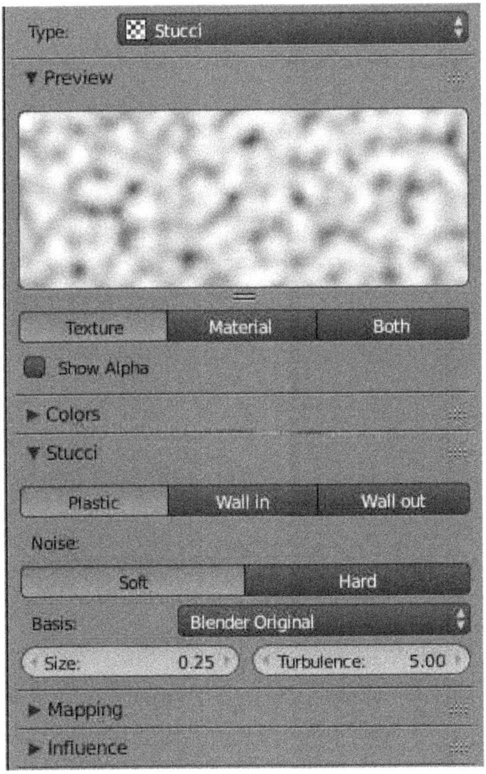

fig. 132 procedural *texture* and *Stucci* panel

123

Stucci is a fractal type texture and it is usually used for simulating an uneven surface similar to a wall plaster.

Like for *Noise, Clouds* and other similar procedural *texture*, by applying it on the *bump* or on the *displacement* generates an elevation without necessarily modifying the color.

Three main options are available in the *switch* of the **Stucci** panel. The options set the *texture* parameters for simulating, respectively, the behavior of a plastic material (*Plastic*), or of inner rough wall (*Wall In*) and of an external rough wall (*Wall Out*).

The underlying *switch Noise* enables to choose the influence strength of the *texture* between *Soft* and *Hard*, whereas the menu *Basis* uses an auxiliary procedural *texture* for determining the fractal behavior.

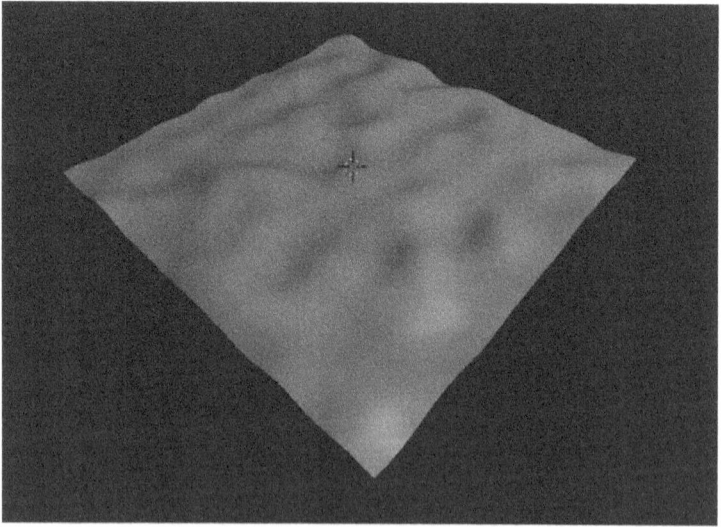

fig. 133 *Stucci* applied to a surface

Size sets the dimensions of the fractal (or of the grain), whereas *Turbulence* add a further noise effect (turbulence) to the *texture*.

VORONOI

Voronoi creates a cell pattern, more or less regular.

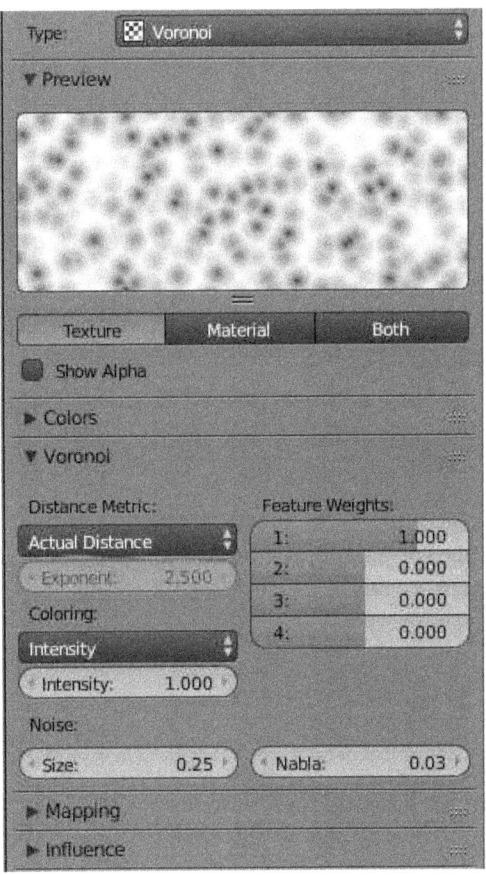

fig. 134 procedural *texture* and *Voronoi* panel

The first choice in the **Voronoi** panel (*Distance Metric*) opens a drop-down menu defining the algorithm generating the *texture*.

There are 7 algorithms: *Actual Distance, Distance Squared, Manhattan, Chebychev, Minkovsky 1/2, Minkovsky 4, Minkovsky.*

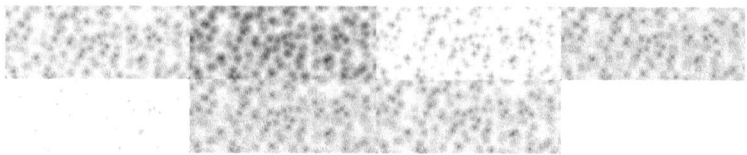

fig. 135 from left to right and from top to bottom, the 7 algorithms *Distance Metric*

The four cursors *feature Weights* represent the values of the four constants *Worley*, which are used for calculating the distances between each cell of the *texture* based on the metric distance.

The *Coloring* menu presents 4 settings: *Intensity; Position, Position and Outline; Position, Outline and Intensity*, using as much base noises in different methods for computing the color and the intensity in generating the *texture*.

The flag *Intensity* scales the noise general global intensity of the *texture*.

Size and *Nabla* are the same parameters already described in other procedural *texture*.

VOXEL DATA

Voxel Data is the second texture useful for generating simulations of volumetric effects (like for *Point* Density).

The default setting, *Smoke*, is usually used for the *rendering* of smoke simulations inside the environment of rendering *Render Blender*.

126

As a matter of fact this *texture* renders a source typology named *voxel*, working in a way much similar to an image *texture*, but in 3D.

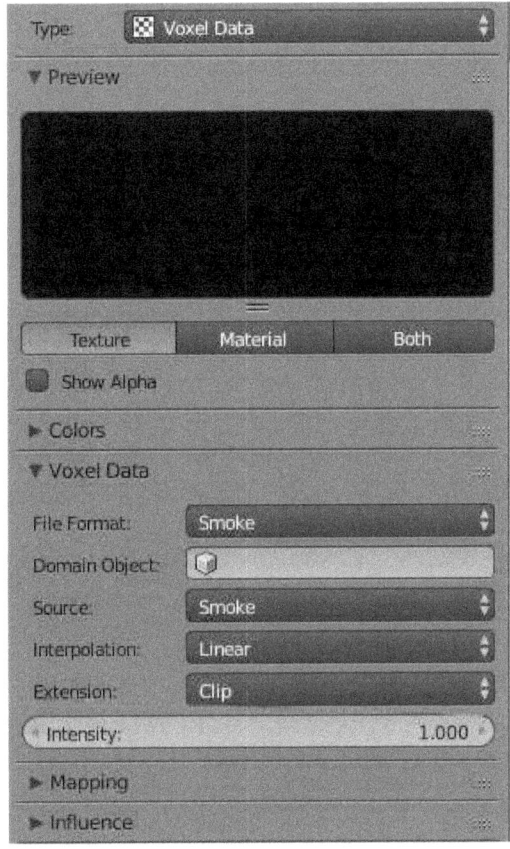

fig. 136 procedural *texture* and *Voxel Data* panel

In the panel **Voxel Data**, several data typologies are available for generating the texture (*File Format*), like *Smoke*, *Hair*, *Image Sequence*, *8 bit* Raw, *Blender* Voxel; four different sources (*Smoke*, *Heat*, *Flame* and *Velocity*), and various interpolation methods (*Nearest* Neighbor, Linear, *Quadratic*, *Cubic Catmul-Rom*, *Cubic B-Spline*).

Extension determines in which way the texture must be extrapolated, while *Intensity* determines the application intensity of the texture.

WOOD

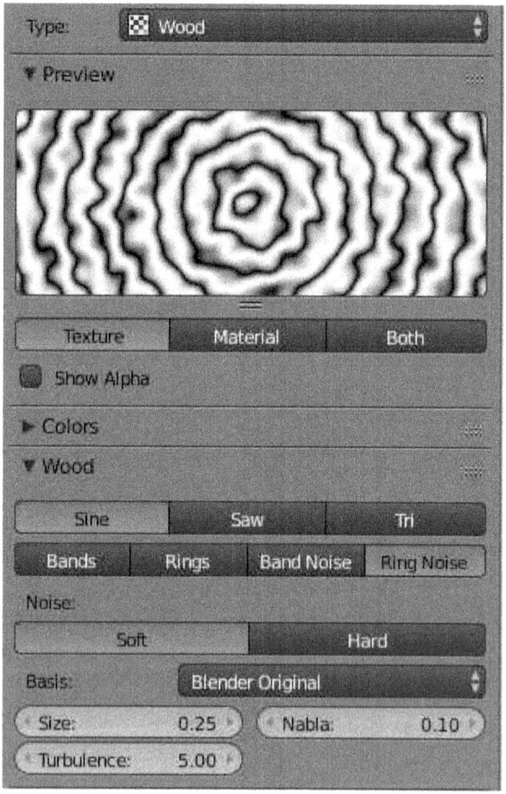

fig. 137 procedural texture and *Wood* panel

128

The last (but not least) procedural *texture* we will describe is Wood.

This *texture* generates veins similar to those of the wood. It is very used for simulating barks or trunk sections, but also parallel or annular waves.

In the **Wood** panel it is first of all possible to choose from the *switch* the wave type that will be generated, between sinusoidal (*Sine*), soft and smooth; *Saw* (saw tooth shape) and *Tri* (triangular), both of them hard and sharp.

The second *switch* is a group of 4 buttons regulating the vein shape.

- *Bands* generates parallel waved veins;

- *Rings* generates concentric rings;

- *Band Noise* generated parallel bands with a noise;

- *Ring Noise* generates concentric rings with noise.

Soft and *Hard* force the *texture* to act softly or hardly.

Basis enables to upload a procedural *texture* acting as noise method (*Noise*).

Size, Nabla and *Turbulence* are the same parameters already previously described for other textures.

Rather than for determining the color of the material associated to this *texture* (even if obviously it is possible to color using the options inside the panel *Colors* and possibly a *Color Ramp*), *Wood* is more suitable for generating elevation on a surface (*bump* or *displacement*).For visualizing the *texture Wood* it is necessary that the *mesh* have been previously unwrapped (*unwrap*).

129

2.5. Illumination

The illumination is one of the main factors for a optimal result.

Like in photography, light and framing play a fundamental role.

To light a scene means amounts at point a finger and put in evidence what we want to underline and describe. A wrong illumination not only will yield bad images, but may not focus the attention on the desired detail.

This is way often, other than the base illumination, it may be necessary to use auxiliary light sources, precisely as in a studio.

When a new scene is created, it is necessary to have clear in mind if one wants to accurately reproduce the reality, thus simulating the real illumination, or to use one or more light sources to adapt the light to the scene. The choice depends on what one wants really show.

Blender put at disposal 5 types of direct light sources, other than global light sources taken from the environment and indirect illuminations, such as light bounces between neighboring objects and relevant mutual surface coloration (*Indirect Lighting*).

The first are obtained inserting a Lamp with SHIFT + A in the scene and, in the *tab Lamp* of the *Properties* window it is possible to determine the nature between *Point, Sun, Spot, Hemi* and *Area*, already described in volume 1 of this guide, in the *Lamp* panel.

Let us recall in more detail the typologies and characteristics of the 5 direct illumination sources (*tab* **Lamp**):

2.5.1. Tab Lamp

Point is a point wise illumination source radiating in all the directions.

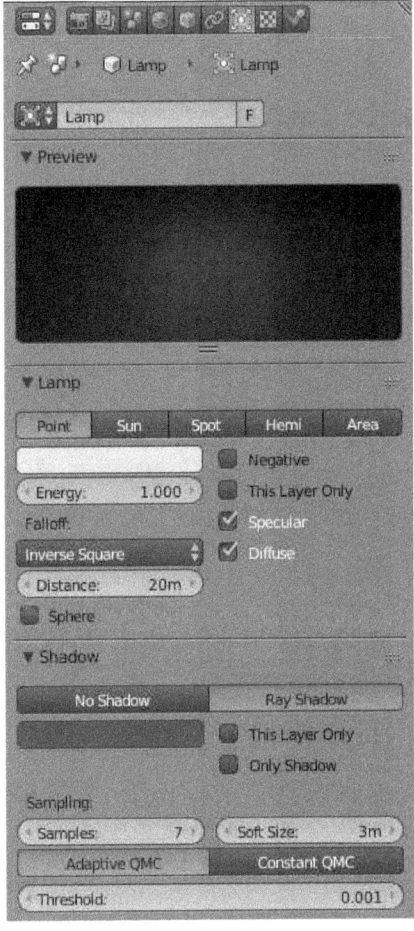

fig. 138 panels and parameters for managing the illumination source *Point*

131

In the **Lamp** panel the color and light can be determined, by clicking in the suitable box opening a palette, and the radiation power, setting the value in the counter *Energy*.

Checking *Negative* the illumination effect will be inverted, thus projecting a negative illumination.

By checking *This Layer Only* the light source will radiate only on the objects grouped on the same *layer*.

By checking *Specular* and *Diffuse* (active by *default*) a specular reflection and a diffuse illumination will be created, respectively, on the objects hit by the light rays.

The *Falloff* menu enables to define the way the light will decay with the distance, by choosing the method among 6 options: *Constant*, *Inverse Linear*, *Inverse Square*, *Custom Curve* and *Lin/Quad Weighted*.

Distance defines, instead, the maximum decaying distance of the light, i.e. the number of meters (if the space unit is set on meters, obviously), the light source will act on the scene, before switching off.

The flag *Sphere* sets the intensity to zero beyond the distance set by the lamp, enforcing an sharper and less pale illumination.

In the **Shadow** panel all the parameters relevant to the managing of the shadows produced by the light source can be found.

The *switch No shadow / Ray Shadow*, respectively, disables or visualizes the shadow projection of the objects hit by the light rays on other objects.

The underlying palette enables to determine the shadow base color.

fig. 139 the effect of a illumination source of *Point* type

This Layer Only works such that only the objects grouped together in the same layer will produce a shadow.

The check on *Only Shadow* will show only the shadows and not the radiated surfaces.

The *Sampling* section contains the options affecting the quality and definition of the projected shadow.

In the counter *Samples* it is possible to insert the sample number, whereas *Soft Size* determines the softness of the projected shadow. Low values will produce sharp shadows, high values, soft and smooth shadows.

The underlying *switch* can be used to determine the method for the shadow generation: *Adaptive QMC* generates less defined but quicker shadows, depending on the *Threshold*, whereas *Constant QMC* generates more defined shadows, but according to a slower computing process.

Sun simulates the illumination due to the sun. It is a very powerful illumination source, with parallel rays and sharp shadows, all along the same direction. The *Lamp Sun* can be placed in an point of the scene. Being a directional light source, only the direction is important, which can be defined b rotating the dashed base vector connected to the lamp itself.

The panels **Lamp** and **Shadow** are the same as in the previous case.

Another dedicated panel **Sky & Atmosphere** is present, in which the parameters for the sky simulation and the neatness of the atmosphere are contained.

Both of them can be activated b checking *Sky* and *Atmosphere*.

Sky generates a sun visible in the sky, if framed, more or less neat depending on the settings.

On the right a panel can be opened on which it is possible to upload *presets*, which can be created and saved with the key +, or canceled with the key –. Three presets are available by default simulating a generic sky (*Classic*) with a strong and blurry sun; a sun in a desert scene (*Desert*), where the sun generates a red light; and a mountain sun (*Mountain*) with neat air and sharp sun.

Turbidity simulates the effect of the sky neatness. Any low values the sun will appear sharp and defined; at high values a blurry and cloudy effect will be achieved.

fig. 140 panels and parameters for the management of the illumination source *Sun*

If in the *tab World* of the *Properties* editor a sky in *background* is activated (which we will analyze in the foregoing), the menu *Bending* determined and defines the mixing method between the sky in the *tab World* and the one set in *Sun Sky & Atmosphere*. The cursor *Factor* (from 0 to 2) manages the balancing between the two systems.

fig. 141 the effect of a illumination source of type *Sun*

The section *Horizon, Brightness* determines the horizon luminosity, whereas *Spread* its diffusion and neatness.

Color Space defines the color range according to what has been set in the underlying *switch: SMPTE, REC70* or *CIE. Exposure* regulates the illumination exposition and strength of the generated sky.

On the other hand, the section *Sun* contains the settings of the generated sun.

Brightness regulates the brightness, *Size* the dimensions (at larger size a larger solar sphere will appear and vice-versa), whereas *Back Light* (cursor from -1 to 1) the arc type around the solar sphere.

Atmosphere generates an effect on the sun light simulating an atmosphere more or less rarefied.

The section *Intensity* has two parameters: *Sun* regulating the sun influence with respect to the atmosphere; *Distance* representing a multiplicative parameter as a function of the unit measure set in Blender.

The section *Scattering* defines the scattering effect of the radiation through the parameters *Inscattering* (light scattering factor) and *Extinction* (damping factor of visibility).

SPOT

Spot simulates the illumination generated by a halogen lamp.

This light source generates a unidirectional light, defined b a light cone more or less visible.

The dedicated panel **Spot Shape** contains the settings relevant to the generated light cone.

This cone can be visualized in the scene by checking the option *Show Cone* and may have the shape of a square base pyramid instead of circular base, by checking the option *Square*.

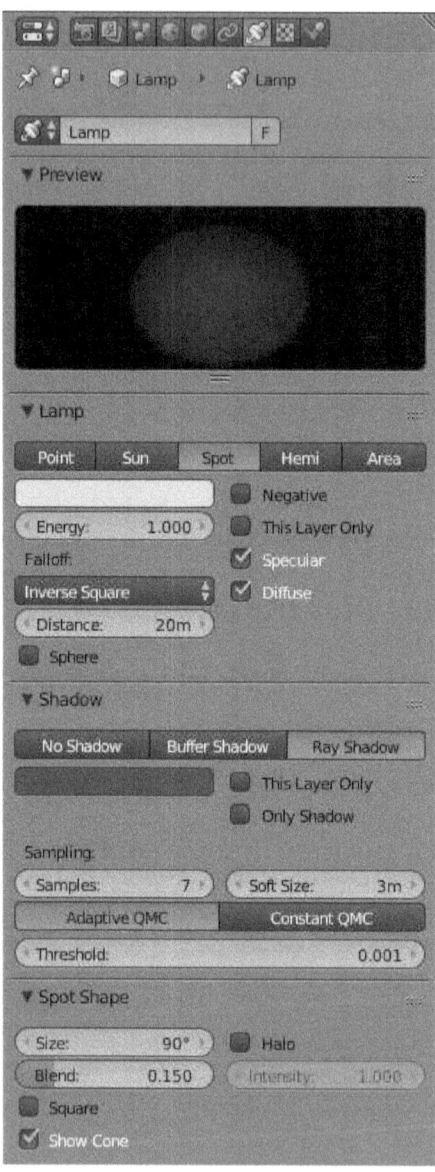

fig. 142 panels and parameters for the management of the illumination source *Spot*

138

Size indicates the light cone opening in degrees, whereas *Blend* defines the neatness of the projection cone on the other surfaces.

Halo shows indeed the light cone into the scene (and not only the projection), whereas *Intensity* determines the intensity, and thus the one visibility in the space.

fig. 143 the outcome of an illumination source of *Spot* type with *Halo* activated

 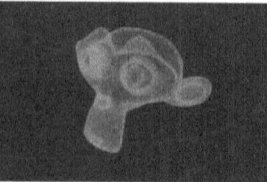 

fig. 144 *Suzanne* illuminated by a light source at its right hand side (image on the left); application of a *Halo* on its left hand side (image at center); effect on the umbrella on *Suzanne* (image on the right)

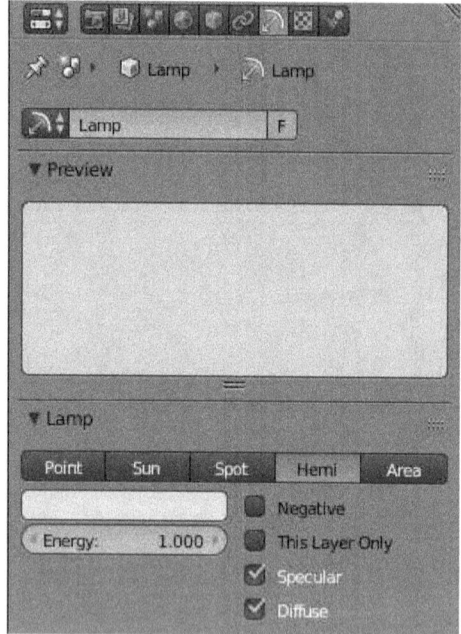

fig. 145 panels and parameters for the management of the illumination source *Hemi*

Hemi simulates the illumination effect obtained with the typical umbrella employed in photographic studios. This umbrella is constituted by a concave panel, supported by a tripod or any other support, uniformly reflecting an opposite light source, illuminating zones in shadow of a subject whose primary illumination source be opposite.

The zones in shadow will be lighted and better defined, without generating further shadows.

Hemi has not dedicated parameters. It has only those parameters defined in the panel **Lamp**, common to all the light sources.

It does not exist a panel *Shadow*, because *Halo* does not project any shadow.

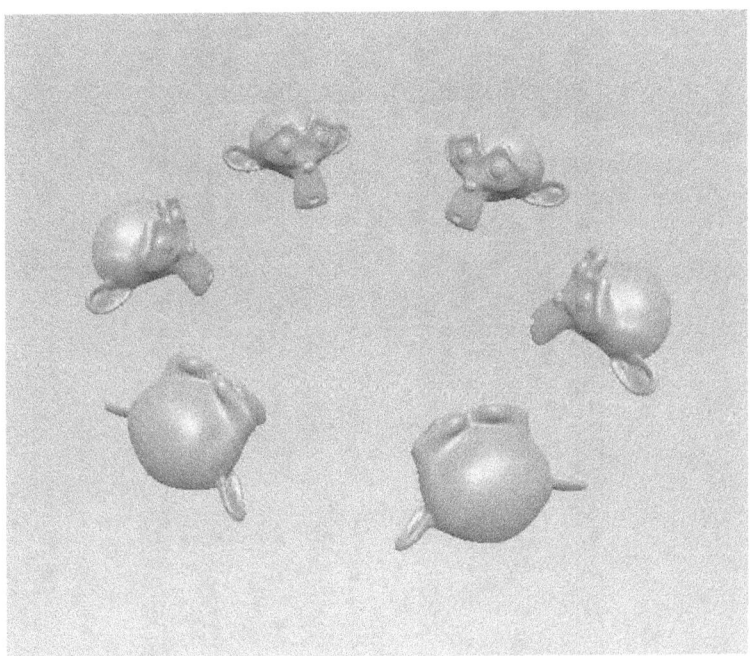

fig. 146 effect of an illumination source of *Hemi* type

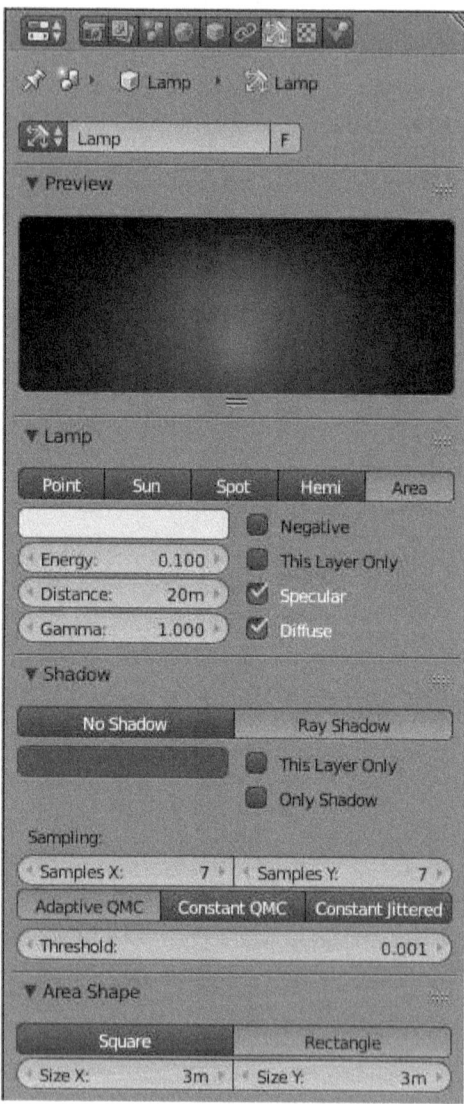

fig. 147 panels and parameters for the management of the light source *Area*

Area produces a scattered light, similarly to that generated by *Halo*, but with shadow projection.

It is indeed an emitting panel, much useful for illuminating scene details or to be reflected on smooth objects.

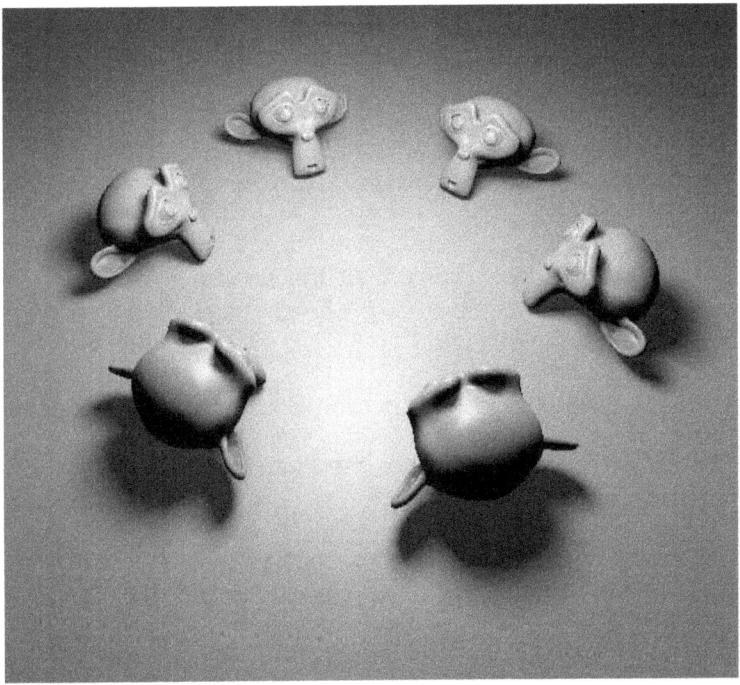

fig. 148 the outcome of an illumination source of type *Area*

In the **Lamp** panel the counter *Gamma* has been added, regulating the intensity of the main channel of light coloration, in such way that, for high values, the resulting color tends to white with a regular scale.

In the panel **Shadow**, the samples relevant to the shadow definition are split along the X and Y axes, whereas a third sample elaboration method is added, *Constant Jitterea*, accentuating the definition depending on three further options appearing with it: *Humbra* (accentuating the fully shadowed zones); *Dither* (adding a noise to the shadow at 2 x 2 *pixel*); *Jitted* (adding a point noise to the shadow contour).

In the panel **Area Shape** it is possible to choose the shape of the emitting panel between *Rectangle* or *Square* and, as a consequence, the dimensions *Size X* and *Size Y*.

2.5.2. Tab World: Global illumination sources

The tab **World**, represented by the icon with the earth globe in the *Properties* editor, contains all the settings relevant to the background of the ongoing project and to its general illumination.

In *Render Blender* modality, the *tab World* is divided in 6 panels.

The first panel **World** regulates the global illumination and the scene base colors.

It is possible to define what kind of background will be rendered, by checking one or more of the three available options:

- *Paper Sky* will render a flat background, without shades;

- *Blend Sky* will render the scene background with a natural progression of two colors: the one of the horizon and the one of the zenith;

- *Real Sky* will render the scene background with a horizon placed as a function of the current view.

Moreover it is possible to regulate in the suitable three color palettes the base colors of the horizon (*Horizon Color*), of the zenith (*Zenith Color*) and of the surrounding ambient (*Ambient*

Color) affecting the scene global illumination. B setting this latter color n black, the ambient will not affect at all the scene illumination, which will depend only on the *Lamps* inserted in the 3D environment.

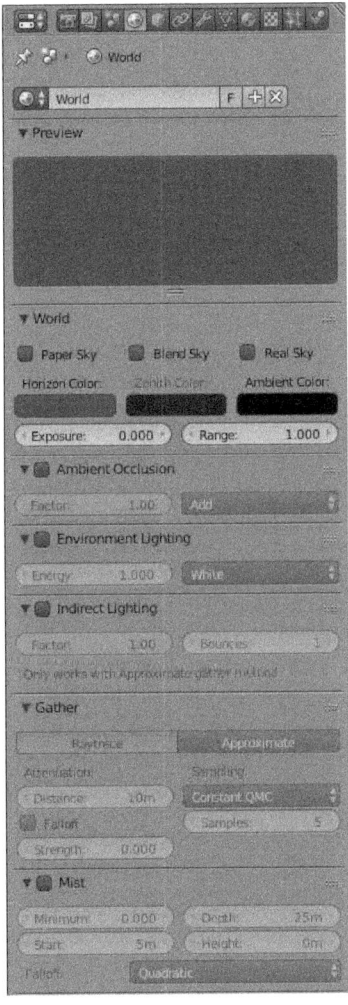

fig. 149 the tab *World*

fig. 150 the rendered scene with the horizon color set to gray and the sky (Zenith Color) to pale blue, checking the two options *Blend Sky* and *Real Sky*

B setting the value of the *Exposure* counter it is possible to increase the exposition, by acting on it, whereas the cursor *Range* determines the coloring influence with a parameter ranging from 0.2 to 5.

The **Ambient Occlusion** panel, if activated with a check, enables to light the scene in such a way as to mutually overshadow the objects based on the distance.

As a matter of fact the ambient occlusion can be observed in correspondence of the edges between walls or between wall and ceiling, or near the shadow zones between a furniture at the floor, where the light can only partially arrive. In those zones a much attenuated and soft shadow can be observed.

Thus the ambient occlusion illuminates and shades the scene even in the absence of direct or indirect lights.

fig. 151 the ambient occlusion generates a soft shadow

Factor (from 0 to 1) determines the amount of the ambient occlusion effect.

The menu on the right of the cursor *Factor* defines the way the ambient occlusion and the external illumination (direct or indirect) will mutually act. *Add* simply adds the illumination sources and the relevant shadows, whereas *Multiply* multiplies the illumination sources, yielding a darker outcome.

The **Environment Lighting** panel, if activated, favors the scene to the lighted from the environment. The cursor *factor* sets the intensity the background will illuminate the objects on the scene, whereas the menu on the left defines the illumination color, chosen among white, the sky color set in the *World* panel (*Sky Color*) or a background color inserted as a *texture* (*Sky Texture*).

147

fig. 152 the sky (*Sky Color*) lights the scene

fig. 153 the red sphere slightly influences the coloring of the cube surface

The panel **Indirect Lighting** makes the objects in a scene to act in the illumination contributing to color the surfaces, as a consequence of the light bounces. The bounces can be set in the cursor *Bounces*, whereas the intensity in the cursor *factor*.

This indirect lighting is effective only when the underlying panel **Gather** is activated and set in *Approximate* modality.

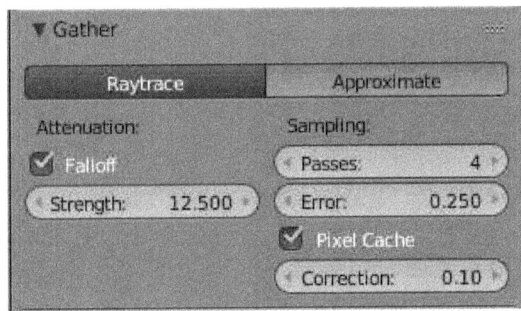

fig. 154 the *Gather* panel set to *Approximate*

This modality activates a set of regulation parameters.

- the check on *Falloff* manages the minimum attenuation distance of the action;

- *Strength* the influenco strength influence of the bouncing light on the mutual coloration of neighboring objects;

- *Passes* defines the number of computing processes;

- *Error* defines the effect quality. For low values the computation will be slower;

- *Pixel Cache*, if checked, regulates at the best the interpolation between neighboring pixels;

- *Correction* regulates the color correction.

149

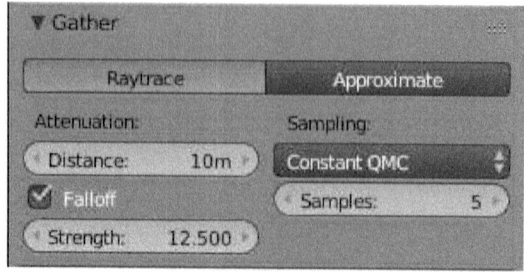

fig. 155 the *Gather* panel set to *raytrace*

fig. 156 the *Mist* effect

The *Raytrace* modality computes the effect in a more precise way, though slower.

The attenuation is regulated by an accurate distance (*Distance*).

Falloff and *Strength* have the same functions of the previous modality.

The *Sampling* menu enables to choose the method for the shadow and bounce generation, whereas *Samples* defines the sample number for the definition in the rendering process.

The last panel is **Mist** and enables, if activated, to add to the environment a fog or mist effect.

Minimum defines the minimum intensity of the mist general effect in the scene.

Depth is the distance beyond which the mist effect will be gradually visible (*Fade in*) in the scene.

Start is the distance from the camera of the starting mist effect.

Height regulates the mist intensity with respect to the height ($z = 0$).

Falloff opens a drop-down menu defining the mist shading method, between *Quadratic*, *Linear* and *Inverse Quadratic*.

3

CYCLES

3.1. Introduction to Cycles and to the use of nodes

This *rendering* engine, being set in Blender as default engine from version 2.61, has become a fundamental reference for most of the 3D *artist* using this powerful 3D modeling engine.

Provided with an almost immense versatility, *Cycles* has by now substituted *Blender Render* (or *Blender Internal*).

The *Cycles* methodology definitely differs from that of its celebrated predecessor. *Cycles* is aligned to the most professional *rendering* engines, giving to the user a global view of the object materials, the scene lighting, and the *compositing*.

In order to set *Cycles rendering* engine (if a different engine were set as default one), it is necessary to choose the option in the *header* of the *Info* panel.

fig. 157 choice of the *Cycles* engine

For understanding the logic and conceptual operating mode of *Cycles* a bit of exercise and much initiative is necessary.

Cycles uses a connection system of events and information, referred to as **nodes** which can be interconnected for creating a logic line of reasoning, not necessarily consequential of additive as it was the case in *Blender Render*.

To make it clearer with an example, we know that a material is given by the sum of several *shader*. But it is not necessary that these *shader* must obey to the logic of the cascade, i.e. be one

155

next to the other. It is likely that, as a matter of fact, either the *shader* and the other elements (nodes) may interfere in a non linear way.

Examples will follow, clarifying this concept that for now may appear hard and contorted, but will be a very useful and fundamental resource for obtaining very photorealistic results.

3.1.1. *Tab Render*

First, before discussing the practical use of this *rendering* engine, as already done for *Render Blender*, we must analyze the *software* and *hardware* settings of this engine, contained in the *tab Render* of the *Properties* editor.

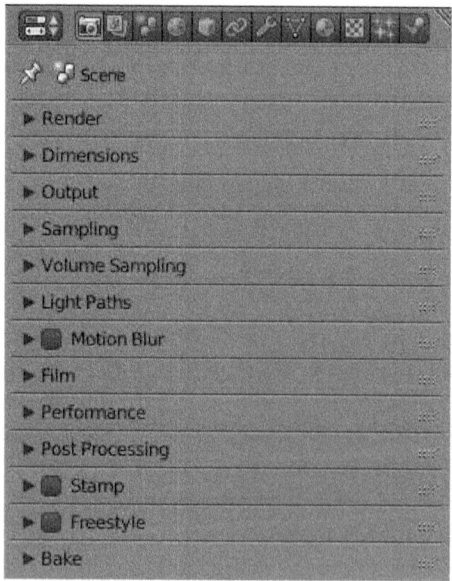

fig. 158 *tab Render* of the *Properties* editor

The panels contained in this *tab* slightly differ from those relevant to *Render Blender*. In fact some settings are adapted to the case of *Cycles*, which is definitely not compatible with *Blender Render* and vice-versa.

Thus it is necessary to highlight that, once some materials have been created with *Blender Render* or *Cycles*, switching from a *rendering* engine to another one will make useless the previously done work.

Some panels, as previously said, are the same and the relevant settings will not be here repeated, referring to the previous section. The panels common to both the rendering engines are: *Dimensions, Output, Stamp* and *Freestyle*.

The following panels are not present in *Cycles*, substituted by other dedicated panels: *Antialiasing, Sampled Motion Blur, Shading*.

Some differences can be found, on the other hand, in: *Render, Performance* and *Post Processing*.

Finally, the following ones are panels exclusively dedicated to *Cycles*: *Sampling, Volume Sampling, Light Paths, Motion Blur* and *Film*.

The panel *Bake* will be finally described at the end of this section.

The **Render** panel gives the possibility of using the *GPU* as *hardware* for the rendering, is this option is set in the preferences (*Cuda*).

fig. 159 The *Render* panel set on *GPU Compute*

In this panel it is possible to start the *rendering* processes of a image (*Render* button), of an animation (*Video* button) or of a sound sequence (*Audio* button).

The menu *Display* defines in which editor their rendering is visualized. *Image Editor* visualizes the result of that editor; *Full Screen* mode; *New Window*; *Keep UI* such as the user interface (*UI*) will be not modified.

Feature Set enables Blender to accept *features* from external developers.

Device allows you to choose the computation will be performed by the *CPU* or by the *GPU*.

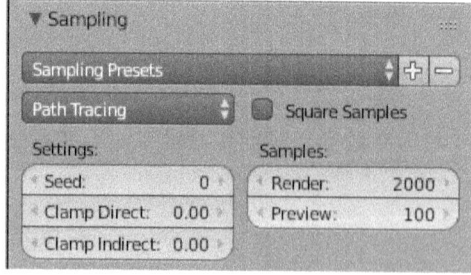

fig. 160 The *Sampling* panel

158

The **Sampling** panel acts in the algorithms of the rendering sampling.

The first drop-down menu allows you to act in the *Preview* phase or in the *rendering* (*Final*).

The second menu is referred to as *Integrator* and allows you to set the *rendering* algorithm for the lighting computation.

By setting the parameter on *Path Tracing* the algorithm makes *Cycles* to compute the largest part of lighting configurations, by using the light bounces, especially those related to direct light. It may not be suitable for special lighting cases as the *caustics*.

By setting instead the parameter on *Branched Path Tracing* each light bounce will be spread such as to get many more samples. This process will obviously require more computing time.

The section on the right (*Samples*) defines the sample number which must be computed in the *rendering*.

These must be set by the user depending on the power of his computing system and on the final result, which should be obtained. The larger the sample number, the better the *render* definition. It is possible to set the sample number for the final rendering (*Render*) and for the preview (*Preview*).

The section on the left contains the settings (*Settings*) of the sampling process.

Seed is a random generator of samples, yielding a different sample configuration in correspondence of each value.

The two following parameters are useful, though of difficult and delicate use, for managing the noise and disturbances of the *rendering* caused by several reasons. Before explaining their use, let us analyze the main disturbance sources.

Noise can be present in a rendered scene due to many reasons, first of all a too poor lighting (e.g. it is much complicate to obtain acceptable *renders* in semi-dark conditions). Other noise sources are the sharp contrasts between lighted and shadowed zones (due to strong light sources burning the image); a not sufficient number of bounces, especially between shiny or transparent surfaces; the presence of *caustics* (The reflections and shadows usually generated by liquids on solid surfaces, i.e. in swimming pools); lighting panels in not enough lighted surfaces...

All these factors may generate noise like grains or, even worse, *fireflies*, i.e. white *pixel* in the scene.

A first attempt for solving the problem is to go straight and correct the lighting. It will be necessary to randomly redistribute the light rays inside the scene, such as not to get too specific luminous points. In order to achieve this many more sample are necessarily needed.

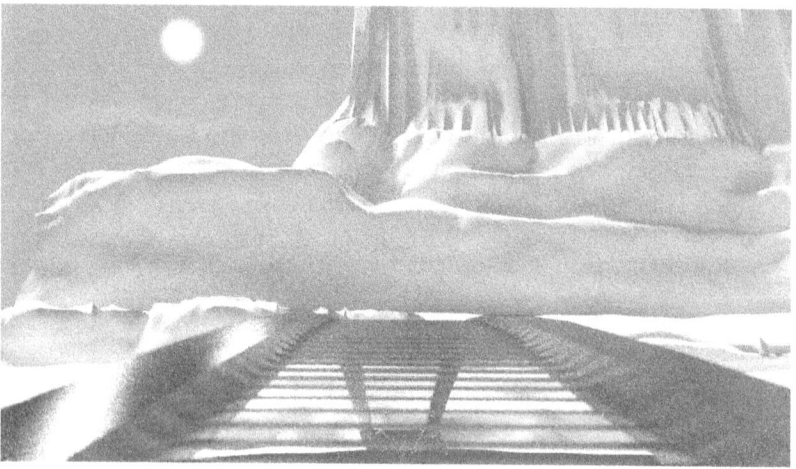

fig. 161 this rendered image produced much noise and *fireflies* (especially on the ice bridge)

160

We can also reduce the noise with some other tricks, blurring the luminous points, making them bigger and less intense. The focusing settings will be of the outmost importance to achieve this result.

A third method consists of not producing the caustics, by eliminating them from the computing process (see in the foregoing).

In case of specular surfaces (glasses, mirrors and highly reflecting metals) or transparent surfaces, it will be necessary to compute the maximum bounce or transmission number and set it in the *Light Paths* panel, as we will see in the foregoing.

Other than these methods, we can try to act on the *Clamp* parameters (*Direct* and *Indirect*).

These options switch off all the *pixels* having an intensity beyond a certain threshold and reduce the noise reducing also the precision. With a value set to 0, this option is disabled.

fig. 162 the same scene in which, on the left, a noise is present, caused by the strong illumination; on the right the noise turns out to be reduced

The problem relevant to these parameters is that they affect too much the luminosity of the whole scene. Though they attenuate the zones too lighted and eliminate the fireflies, they reduce the brilliance and the realism of the previously defined colors.

It is thus necessary a trade off between the noise reduction and the achieved final result.

Volume Sampling sets the volume and volumetric effect sampling.

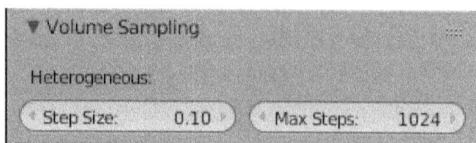

fig. 163 the *Volume Sampling* panel

Step Size defines the distance between samples during the volume rendering process, such that, for lower values, the outcome turns out to be improved but the computing time increases.

Max Steps sets the maximum step number inside the volume, before the sampling process be stopped, in order to avoid waiting times too long, especially for very large objects.

The **Light Paths** panel, already discussed at the beginning of the first volume, is very important for defining in Blender the light behavior depending on the scene and the project under construction.

In this panel the bounces between surfaces and the crossing number of transparent surfaces are defined.

162

It should be taken into account that increasing the values beyond the limits enforced by the scene, if not strictly necessary, may turn out to be counter-productive implying needless too long computing times.

For example, imagine a scene with only two reflecting bodies, moreover largely far apart to each other. Depending on the point of view, setting a too large bounce number on glossy surfaces may force Blender to further compute not necessary light bounces.

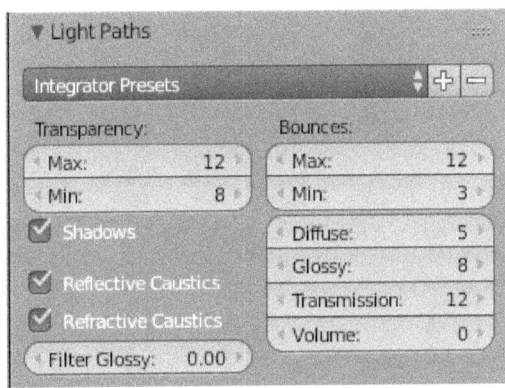

fig. 164 the *Light Paths* panel

Obviously predefined and preset values do not exist, since dependent only on the ongoing project.

The first item in the panel is a menu in which to define the desired type of illumination: (*Direct Light*), (*Full Global Illumination*) or *Integrator Preset* yielding a preset setting. Other personalized settings may possibly be added or eliminated.

In the left part we find the *Transparency* section, where to set the minimum and maximum number of passages of the luminous rays through the transparent surfaces.

163

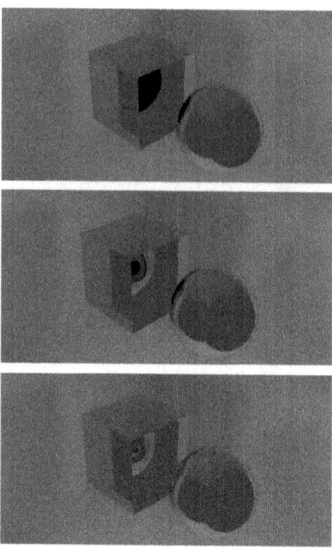

fig. 165 the same scene representing two completely glossy solids reflecting to each other with the *Glossy* parameter respectively set to 1, 2 and 8 bounces. Note how the largest bounce number cancels the black zones, indicating an interruption of reflections and light bounces

Shadow allows the light to project shadows on the transparent objects.

On the right, in the *Bounces* section, the generic (minimum and maximum) bounces can be set and, more specifically, the light bounces on the color (*Diffuse*), with the reflections (*Glossy*), with the transmissions (*Transmission*) and through the volumes (*Volume*).

The flags on *Reflective Caustics* and *Refractive Caustics* activate or deactivate the effects produced by the caustics, adding an improved realism, with detriment of the quality and the computing time, whereas *Filter Glossy* reduces the noise produced by too many bounces.

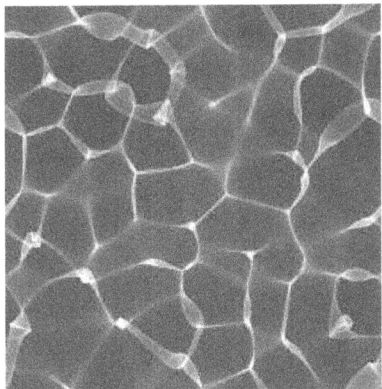

fig. 166 the caustics produce on the water the typical spider-web luminous effect

The **Motion Blur** panel, if the flag is activated, enables you to obtain the typical motion blur relevant to any moving object.

The *Shutter* panel sets the shutter opening and closing time between a frame and the following one, determining the blurring effect between the consecutive images.

fig. 167 the *Motion Blur* panel

Cycles simulates the real light behavior and, with it, the virtual camera behavior.

For this reason, the virtual film characteristics can be further defined in the **Film** panel, on which the picture is being taken or the video is being recorded.

165

fig. 168 the *Film* panel

Exposure regulates the exposure.

Transparent, if the flag is activated, renders and impresses on the virtual film a transparent background, if no background has been set.

A filter acting on the pixels can be defined in the drop-down menu on the right, choosing between *Gaussian* and *Box*, further regulating the definition in the *Width* counter.

Performance slightly differs from the same-name panel in *Render Blender* environment.

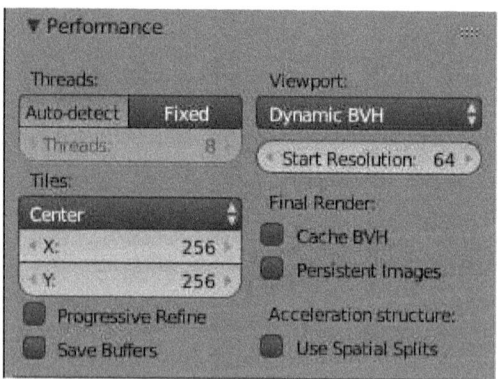

fig. 169 the *Performance* panel

The parameters *Thread*, *Tiles* and *Start Resolution* are the same as those previously analyzed, with the addition of the drop-down menu *Tile Order* forcing Blender to follow a certain image composition method during the rendering process, starting for example from the center, from left to right, from the top etc.

It is recommended, after specific technical testing, to set the values of *X* and *Y* (*Tiles* dimensions, or *rendering* boxes) to 256 if the *GPU* is used and to 64 if the *CPU* is used.

The *Viewport* menu allows you to choose if getting a faster *rendering* or a more accurate image refresh during the computing phase. This can be defined by choosing one of the two options at disposal:

- *Dynamic BVH*, yielding a longer rendering and a more accurate refresh;

- *Static BVH*, using the opposite method.

By checking *Cache BVH*, the rendered image will be kept in memory in the disc, if the geometry will not be modified.

Persistent Images keeps in memory the rendered image in case of a new rendering of it, with the goal of speeding up the computation process.

By checking the last option *Use Spatial Splits* Blender tries to speed up the computation process.

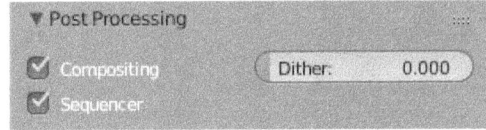

fig. 170 the *Post Processing* panel

The **Post Processing** panel is similar to that relevant to the *Blender Render* engine.

It allows you to activate or deactivate the *compositing* functions (if activated, see in the foregoing) and the *sequencer* functions, in order to operate in post processing on the images and on the final result supplied by the rendering computation.

Moreover, it allows you to set a noise limit (*Dither*) in the *rendering* for a better post processing.

Once Cycles has been optimally set based on the hardware at disposal, we can start to discuss about materials.

3.2. Materials

As already discussed, a material is composed by a series of parameters and shaders mutually interacting.

This rendering engine develops the material composition just with the interaction between parameters (defined as nodes in *Cycles*).

3.2.1. Tab Material

In order to assign a material in *Cycles*, the same procedure valid for *Blender Render* is followed.

In the *Material* tab, it is necessary to click on *New* for creating a material starting from 0, or, by clicking on the icon on the left representing a colored sphere, to upload an existing one, if present.

fig. 171 creating a new material in *Cycles*

By choosing *New* all the panels relevant to the materials of Cycles will be activated, which we start to examine one by one.

fig. 172 the *Material* tab in *Cycles*

170

The upper part of the panel has not differences with *render Blender*.

It is present, in fact, the list of materials assigned to the object, the name of the selected current material and the **Preview** window.

It is recommended to read again what has been previously discussed in the chapter relevant to *Blender Render*, if some functions were not yet be clear.

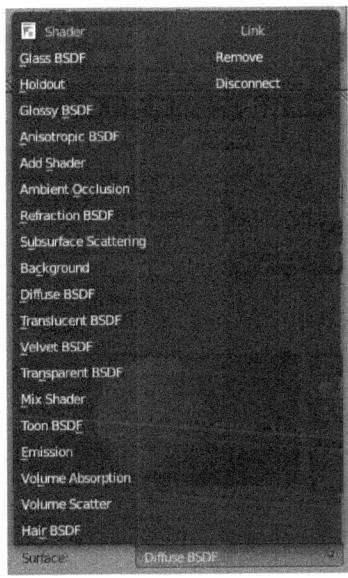

fig. 173 the menu associated to the *shader*

The most important panel, on which the whole material composition is based, is **Surface**.

In this panel all the shaders, the textures and the mathematical and vectorial functions are reported, defining the behavior of each element, according the logic graphically defined in the nodes.

By creating a new material, only two nodes will be automatically activated: a color (*Color*), a roughness parameter (*Roughness*) and possibly a relief effect (*Normal*) is obviously associated to the Diffuse.

On the right hand side of each item a small point is reported, indicating that, by clicking on the button, a menu will appear devoted to the type of selected node (or element).

For example by clicking on *Diffuse* a list will appear enabling to change the shader type among the ones available in the list.

A material can be created using this panel, however we don't recommend to work on this panel, unless in the case of simple and brief operations, instead advising to use the **Node Editor**, which we will explain in a short.

While information (nodes) are being added to the complex system determining a material, this will update in real time either in the *Node Editor* and in specific panels in the *Material* tab.

Moreover, next to each *shader* a small button at the left hand side will appear, with a small + or a – indicating the possibility of expanding or contracting, revealing the additional information. An example will be made in the foregoing.

The **Volume** panel works in an analogous way ad refers to volumetric effect, which will be discussed more specifically in the foregoing.

The **Displacement** panel will be deeply described in the foregoing and so, at this time, will not be discussed.

Finally, the last panel, **Settings**, contains all the settings relevant to the material applied to the object.

The first two flag options refer to the surfaces.

By checking *Multiple Importance, Cycles* will adopt an increased sampling for the indicated material. The option deactivation may reduce the overall noise for large dimension objects emitting few light with respect to other light sources.

Transparent Shadows, if checked, will permit an increased sampling for the transparent materials (to which a *Transparent shader* is associated). The deactivation implies reduced rendering times but less defined shading.

On the other hand the second two options, on the right hand side, refer to the volume.

The *Volume Sampling* menu will determine the computing method of the color sampling on the volume. *Distance* is indicated for dense volumes with far lights; *Equiangular* for low dense volumetric effects and close illumination; *Multiple importance* combines the previous two options.

The second menu, *Volume Interpolation*, computes the interpolation method of the shading according to one of the two options at disposal: *Linear* for the less defined volumes (faster computation); *Cubic* for highly defined volumes (slower computation).

The flag on *Homogeneous* yields shorter rendering times making uniform the volume density.

The palettes *Viewport Color* and *Specular Color* enable to assign a color to the selected object with that determined material, respectively for the *Diffuse* and the reflection, such as to be able to recognize in the 3D view the material nature even in *Solid* modality.

The cursors *Alpha* enable a visualization in the 3D view of the transparent channel, if existing.

Pass Index, finally assigns an indexed number to that material, such as to be assigned to external functions, like for example the *Render Layers*, of which it will be discussed in the foregoing.

Now, the summary description of the *Material* tab panels can be certainly interrupted, because we must finally introduce the concept of nodes, the true heart of Cycles, which will be deeply explained.

3.2.2. The *Node Editor*

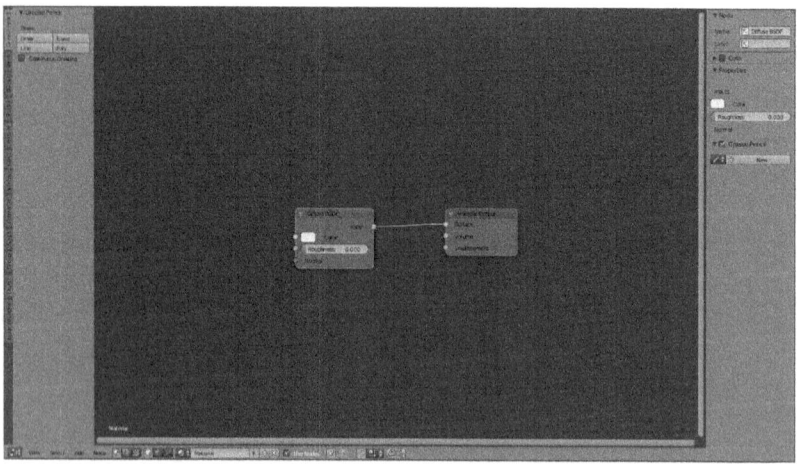

fig. 174 the *Node Editor*

174

It is recommended to work with more windows alongside, such as to be able to visualize in the 3D view in real time the outcome of a material modification done in the *Node Editor*.

Substitute, for example, the *Timeline* editor with the *Node Editor* (the corresponding icon depicts two small interconnected rectangles) and widen it.

Like all the editors, also the *Node Editor* has a *header* and, in detail, also the lateral bars *Tools Shelf* and *Properties* devoted to the nodes.

In the central working area, once the new material has been created, the two interconnected nodes *Diffuse* and *Material Output* will be reported. This is the graphical representation of what specified in the previous *Surface* panel.

This configuration means that the material (*Material Output*) is defined by a diffuse white color (*Diffuse*).

In order to make easier the node reading, it is recommended to read from the right to the left.

Inside the *Node Editor* it is possible to navigate like in the 3D view, making a displacement holding pressed the mouse wheel and making a zoom by rotating it. It is not possible to orbit since the window is two-dimensional.

The same nodes can be selected with the same selection methods of the 3D view objects; scaled, clicking and dragging the borders; duplicated, with SHIFT + D; canceled, with X or CANC.

But what do we exactly mean with?

 Graphically represented by smoothed triangles, the nodes are a set of sources of data, filters, mathematical functions or destinations, joint together by mean or specific connections

named *socket* **(colored point at the box ends), along a flux (a curve).**

Several kinds of nodes exist, suitably grouped by Blender depending on the primary function. Some node groups at this time will not be visualized since belonging to the compositing environment, which we will see in the foregoing.

Blender has nodes available for the material creation, divided in ten groups.

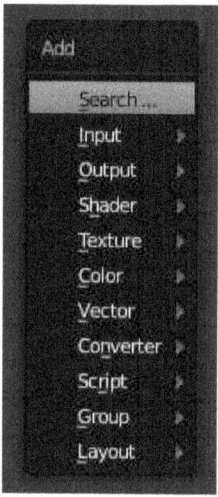

fig. 175 node insertion divided by groups

- *Input* group comprising all those source node to be assigned to other specific node groups;

- *Output* group, comprising the destination nodes, i.e. of *output* of the interaction system of nodes;

- *Shader* group, one of the most important and used, including all the shaders, characterizing each material;

176

- *Texture* group, including all the nodes having any relation with the textures;

- *Color* group, in which are contained the nodes regulating the color;

- *Vector* group, including the nodes acting on the parameters related to the relief and the mapping;

- *Converter* group, including the nodes useful for executing computations and mathematical functions between the other nodes parameters;

- *Script* group, related to the programming, which will not be discussed here;

- *Group* group, enabling to group together the nodes;

- *Layout* group, enabling to visualize the nodes inside boxes, for a simpler reading and understanding of the connections;

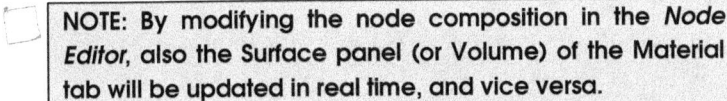

NOTE: By modifying the node composition in the *Node Editor*, also the Surface panel (or Volume) of the Material tab will be updated in real time, and vice versa.

The just created material, as said, is simply represented by a diffuse color. If we launch the *rendering* we get a flat image, simple. This because, as previously explained, each object reacts to the light in a different way and depending on the material characteristics is composed of, containing several interconnected shaders. Obviously a material composed of a single simple color (Diffuse) is not realistic. Almost all materials, though simple, for example have a reflection component and often any relief.

fig. 175 the rendered cube on which a simple Diffuse material has been applied produces a shadow if illuminated, but does not reflect other objects or light spots

For creating a complex material it is then needed to add new nodes and interconnect them depending on a precise logic.

For adding a node in the *Node Editor* three methods can be found:

1) analogously to the 3D view, nodes can be added with the key combination SHIFT + A;

2) selecting the relevant keys inside the *tabs* of the *Tools Shelf* of the *Node Editor*, already suitably divided based on the previously described grouping;

3) by selecting the node from the corresponding group clicking on the menu *Add* placed in the *header* of the *Node Editor*.

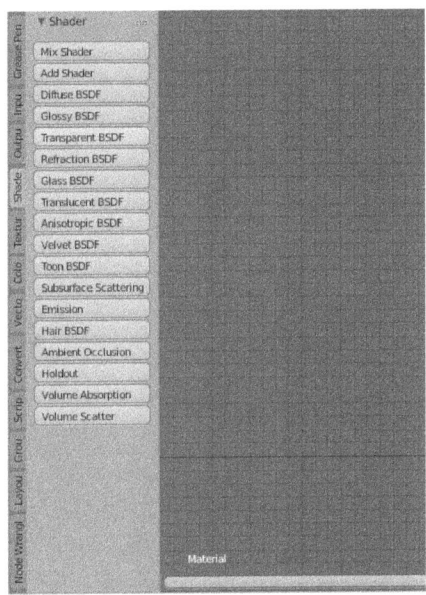

fig. 177 inserting a node from the *Tools Shelf* of the *Node Editor*

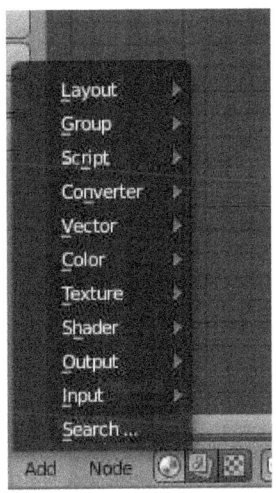

fig. 178 inserting a node from the *Add* menu

179

The scheme previously analyzed concerning the base composition of a generic material, with *Cycles* assumes an even more clear meaning.

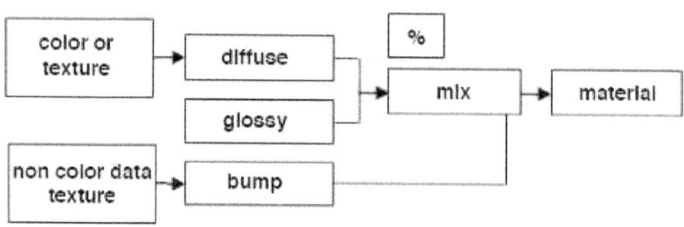

fig. 179 basic scheme of a material composition

This scheme, as a matter of fact, already represents a node configuration, which can be faithfully reproduced.

Get used, at least at the beginning, to schematically think a configuration, even drawing the scheme on a paper, can be a very good working method.

But how to interconnect the nodes?

Thanks to special "cables", named *fluxes*, represented by a curve.

These fluxes join, as said, two or more *sockets*. In order to connect two nodes by means of the *sockets* it is needed to drag, holding pressed the LMB, a *socket* till the second one and the flux (the curve) will appear, automatically linking near a socket. By releasing the LMB the choice will be confirmed.

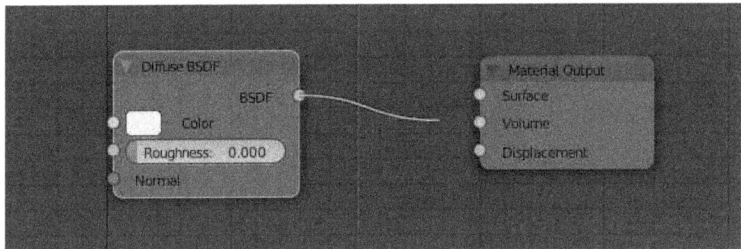

fig. 180 connection between two nodes

It will be certainly clear that the various nodes are endowed with several *sockets* in input (left side) and in output (right side) and that these *sockets* are of different colors.

 First it is good to clarify that only sockets in input with sockets in output can be connected (even more than one at the same time).

The *socket* colors represent specific functions, in detail:

- **the** green **sockets transmit or receive data relevant to the shaders (*shader*);**

- **the** yellow **socket transmit or receive data and information relevant to the colors;**

- **the** gray **sockets transmit or receive numerical data;**

- **the** purple **sockets transmit or receive data and values of vectorial type (mapping, height, relief, etc...).**

One could be think that only sockets of the same type/color can be interconnected. This is only partially true. In fact there often could be cases in which numerical values defines a color variation and similar cases.

181

Before analyzing one by one all the nodes, try to solve a simple exercise.

At its present state the cube under exam has set only the Diffuse color. In the following exercise we will make it glossy.

 EXERCISE N. 3: RENDERING OF A GLOSSY MATERIAL

For making glossy a material it is necessary to add a dedicated shader. This shader is said *Glossy*.

Once selected the cube in the 3D view, in the *Node Editor* the nodes determining the base color set by default will be visualized.

Add a *Glossy* node, chosen among the nodes contained in the submenu *Shader* and place it under the *Diffuse* node.

In this phase this new node cannot be connected to any other node such as to obtain a precise and logic meaning.

This because, if we look to the previous scheme, a node is missing for joining the two nodes.

We find it in the same submenu and is said *Mix Shader*.

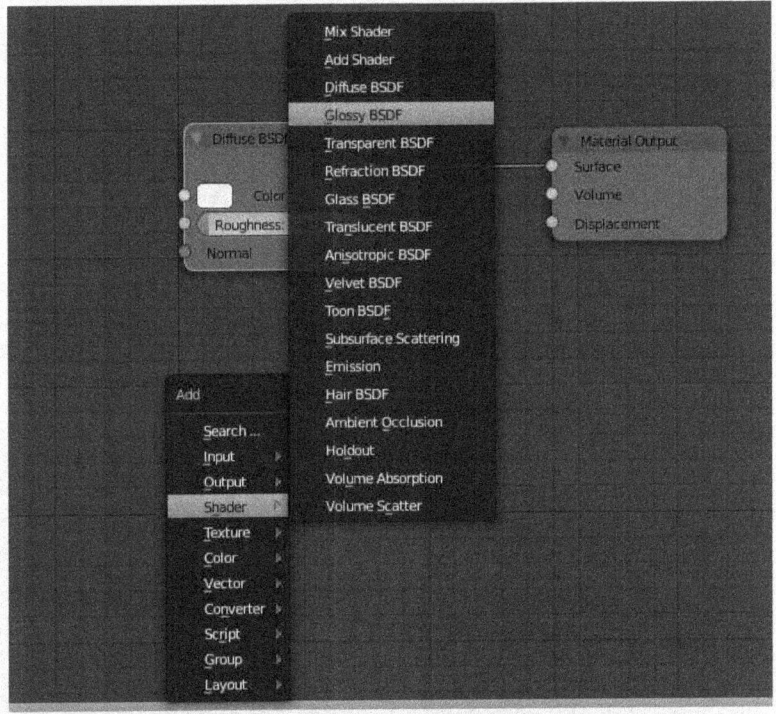

fig. 181 addition of a *Glossy* node

This node has two green *sockets* in input and one in output indicating that two nodes of shader type may be connected to it and mixed together in one output channel.

Getting the node close to the connection flux (the curve) between the *Diffuse* output and the *Surface* input of the *Material Output* node, this will become yellow, informing that by confirming the node insertion in that zone of the *Node Editor*, Blender will automatically operate the correct connection.

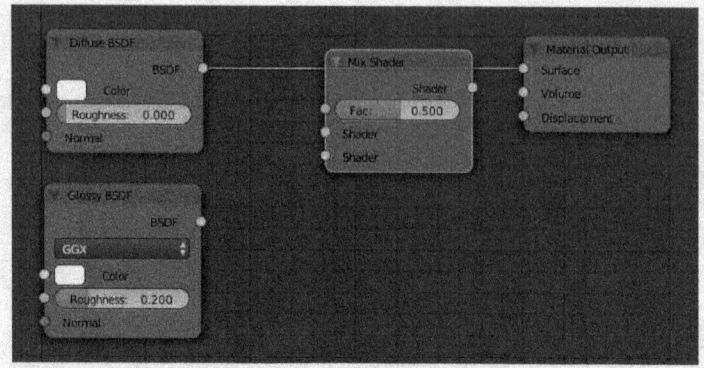

fig. 182 addition of a *Mix Shader*

Confirm the insertion. The *Mix Shader* node will be placed between the *Diffuse* and the *Material Output*.

Connect now the green output *socket* of the *Glossy* to the second input downward of the *Mix Shader*.

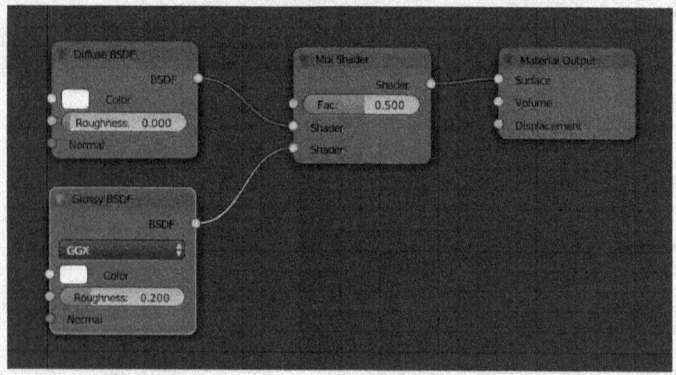

fig. 183 connection of two *shaders* to the *Mix Shader*

This procedure means that two *shaders* will be mixed at 50% by the *Mix Shader*, depending on the *Fac* parameter (balancing factor) of the latter.

It is possible to modify the balancing. For values tending to 0 the *shader Diffuse* will prevail, for values tending to 1, the *Glossy* will prevail.

Automatically, in the mean time, the node analytic representations will be updated and added to the *Surface* panel of the *Material* tab.

fig. 184 the updated *Surface* panel

Try to build our scene. The cube is now become more reflective to the light and the possible other objects.

fig. 185 rendering of the scene

Try to modify the *Fac* value to observe the outcome.

Like in *Render Blender* environment the *Preview* panel shows the chosen material preview.

fig. 186 the *Preview* panel shows a material preview

Analyze now the *Diffuse* node.

As we know, this represents the coloration (whether flat or complex) of the material.

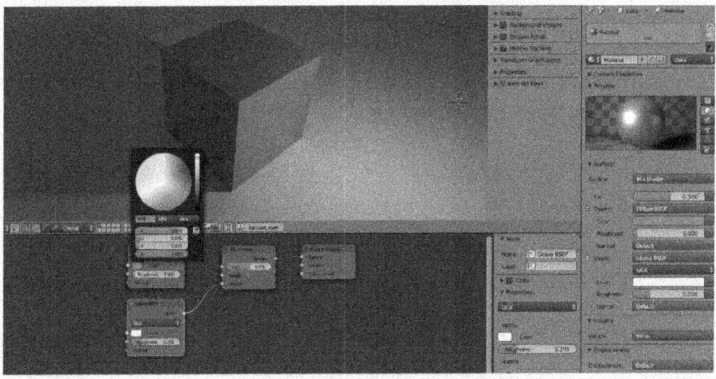

fig. 187 modification of the *Diffuse* color

We can observe in the scheme that a further node can be applied to the *Diffuse*, specifically determining the color. Then for determining and applying a color to the *Diffuse* we should add a node. However, in our case, dealing with a simple color, the addition of a node defining a *RGB* color is useless, since the color palette is already present in the node itself. Try to change the Diffuse color from white to red, by clicking in the white box and acting on the palette.

Obviously, a different procedure will be required in case we want to assign to the material (and so to the *Diffuse*) a *texture*, a particular color configuration suitably mixed or a procedural texture. We will see in the foregoing how this can be done.

As last step of this exercise, we want to make the balancing between two shaders not be defined by a simple percentage value (*Fac*), but by the index of refraction, value pertaining to any specific material. This value forces the material to reflect the light and the other objects depending on the light incidence and the point of view.

187

Larger angles of incidence will generate a larger reflection, whereas angles close to 90°, no reflection.

This effect is really realistic.

Add a **Fresnel** node, which belongs to the *Input* group and set an index of refraction (IOR) equal to 1,450.

Connect the *Fresnel* node output to the gray input of the *Mix Shader*, in correspondence of the value *Fac*. This operation will force Blender to consider the index of refraction as balancing value between the color (*Diffuse*) and the reflection (*Glossy*).

The reflection effect will appear even more realistic, blurred and directly proportional to the incidence angle.

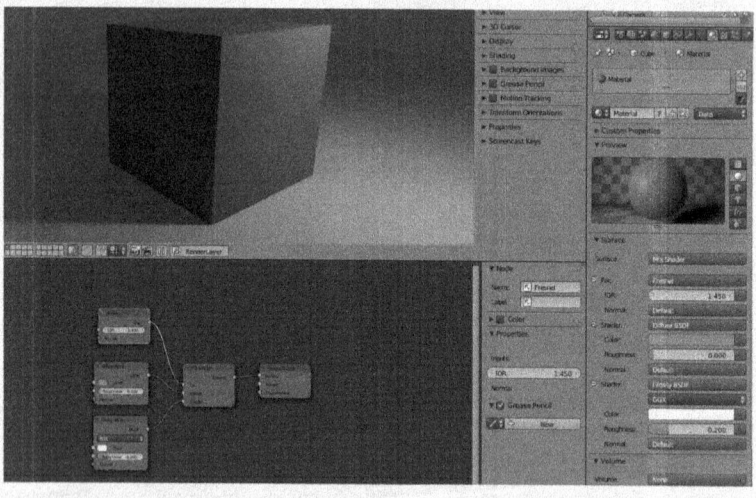

fig. 188 addition of the *Fresnel* node as balancing factor between color and reflection

At this time, you would have an idea of the node function.

In order to get a more detailed and complete understanding, we will discuss the nodes belonging to the Material environment, defined by the yellow cube icon in the *header* of the *Node Editor*, one by one, starting from the most important, that of the **Shaders**.

A) *SHADER* NODES

DIFFUSE

As already revealed this node represents the principal color of the material, i.e. the one, which is reflected among the color mixture contained in the light ray hitting an object.

This node is composed of three parameters and three input *sockets* associated to it:

- *Color* with a dedicated palette, on which set the color. A texture can be, for example, connected on the associated yellow socket;

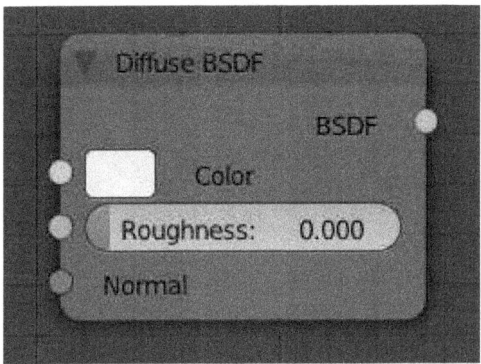

fig. 189 the *Diffuse BSDF* node

189

- *Roughness*, defining the material roughness. A mathematical type node (*Converter*) can be for example connected to the associated gray socket, defining the amount;

- *Normal*, whose value can be assigned by an external node of Vector type, connected to the violet socket, defining the relief.

The *Diffuse* node has a green color output, which can be usually connected to a *Mix Shader* node, for the mixing between two nodes, or directly to a node of the Output group.

GLOSSY

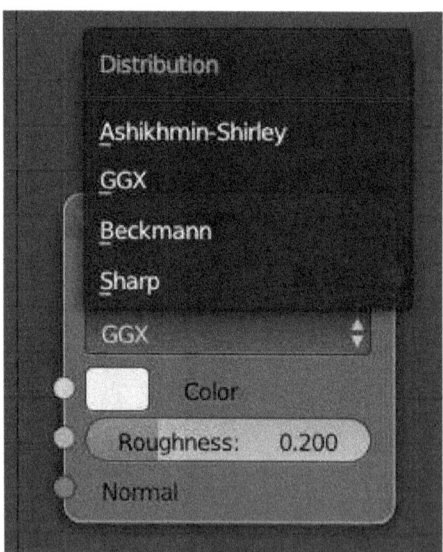

fig. 190 the *Glossy BSFD* node

Also the **Glossy** has been already analyzed in the previous exercise. That node defines what in *Blender Render* was represented by the *Mirror* and *Specular* shaders.

This node has the same parameters of the *Diffuse* except a drop-down menu, named *Distribution*, determining the algorithm generating the reflection effect.

Four algorithms are available: *Ashikmin-Shirley; GGX* (by *default*); *Beckmann; Sharp.*

TRANSPARENT

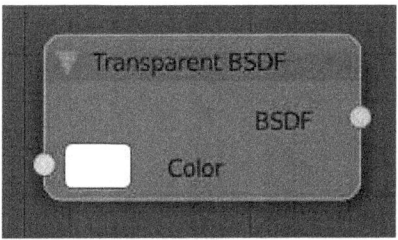

fig. 191 the *Transparent BSDF* node

fig. 192 the *Preview* of the *Transparent* node with red coloration

This node assigns a transparency to the material, eventually colored thanks to the only available parameter *Color* and its related color palette, or to the yellow *socket* on which connect nodes relevant to color.

Obviously this node is used for materials using the alpha channel.

191

The **Refraction** shader is endowed of parameters common to the *Diffuse* and the *Glossy* (*Color, Roughness* and *Normal*) and of the relevant input *sockets*.

Moreover it has a drop-down menu defining the computing algorithm with three options: *Beckmann, GGX* and *Sharp*; and a counter *IOR* in which to insert the index of refraction of the material.

The refraction represents the deviation of the light crossing a transparent medium like a fluid, the atmosphere itself or the glass. This deviation of the light ray is determined precisely by the index of refraction.

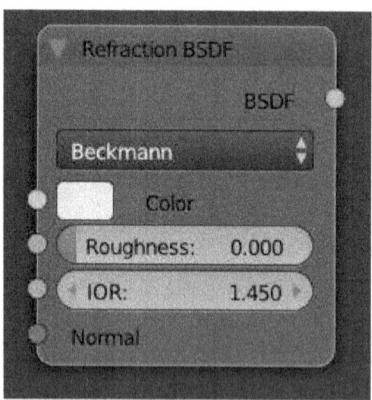

fig. 193 the *Refraction BSDF* node

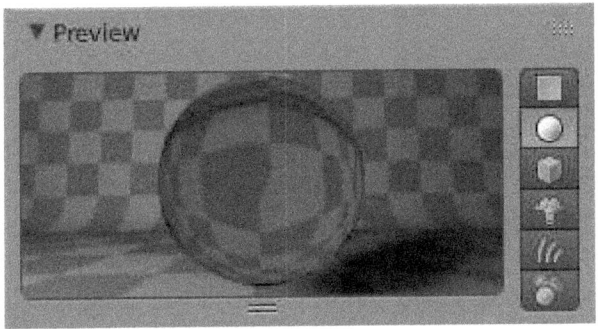

fig. 194 the *Preview* of the *Refraction* node

The parameters of the **Glass** shader are the same of the previous one, but the node is preset and optimized for simulating the behavior of a glass.

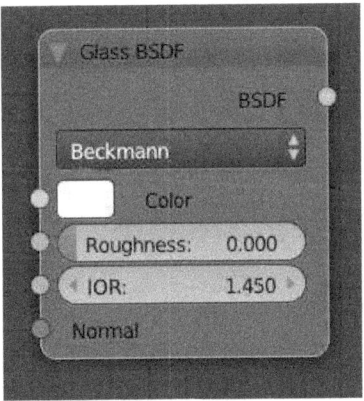

fig. 195 the *Glass BSDF* node

As a matter of fact, this *shader* is not sufficient for a correct and realistic simulation of this material and a mix is needed with other *shaders*, as we will see in the foregoing with a suitable example.

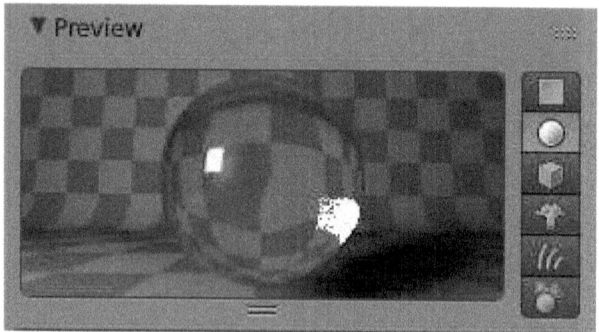

fig. 196 the *Preview* of the *Glass* node

TRANSLUCENT

This *shader* simulates the behavior of a semitransparent material, like for example a curtain, partially letting in the light.

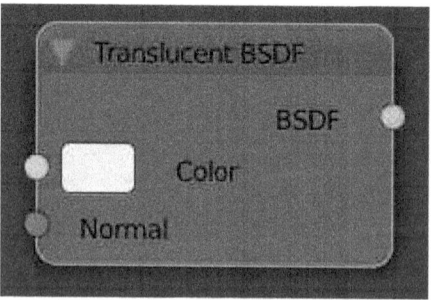

fig. 197 the *Translucent BSDF* node

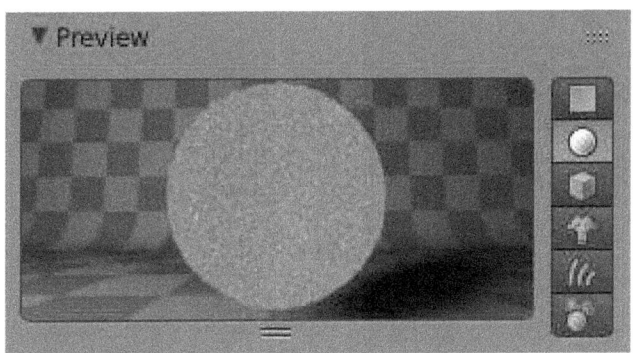

fig. 198 the *Preview* of the *Translucent* node

This node has at disposal two parameters only (and a same number of input *sockets*): *Color*, to which associate a color or a weave; and *Normal*, to which eventually associate a relief.

At the end of this chapter a practical example of application will be described.

ANISOTROPIC

This shader is particularly suitable to simulate metals, whose surface tends to deflecl light, describing the typical curves, often concentric. Think for example to the bottom of a pot or to a metal handle.

Anisotropic has the parameters (and socket inputs associated with them) *Color*, *Roughness* and *Normal*, besides the menu inherent to the computing algorithm of shading, where you can choose one of the options Beckmann, GGX and Ashikmin-Shirley. In addition to these the Rotation parameter is available, defining the rotation of the anisotropy effect and Tangent, on which associate an external node through the purple socket, presumably belonging to the Vector category.

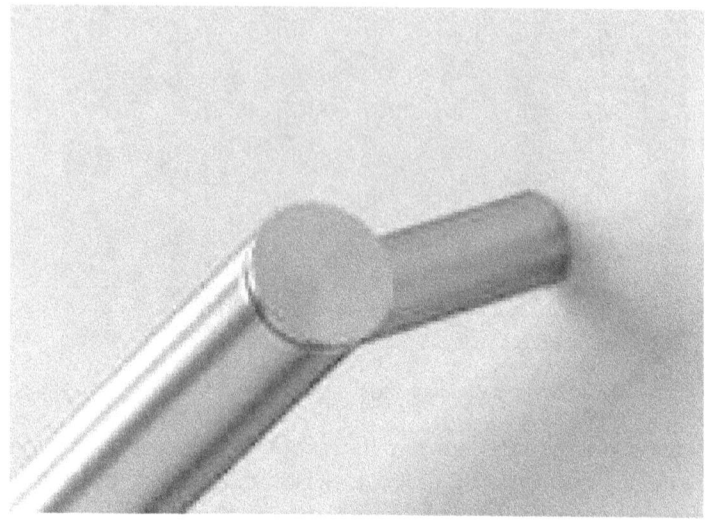

fig. 199 the effect of anisotropy on the cap of this handle section

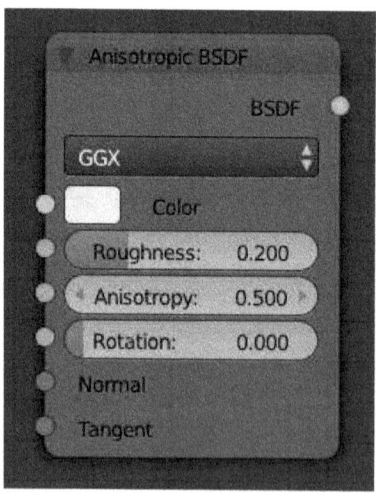

fig. 200 the *Anisotropic BSDF* node

fig. 201 the *Preview* of the *Anisotropic* node

VELVET

Usually mixed with a Diffuse, Velvet simulates the changing shadow of a velvet or a microfiber. Mainly useful for towels, bathrobes, sofa in *Alcantara*, the velvet itself, silk, this shader has only three parameters: Color, Sigma (which determines the intensity of the changing effect) and Normal.

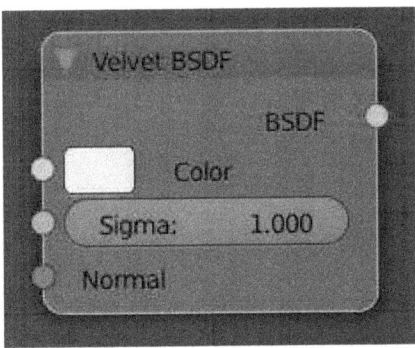

fig. 202 the *Velvet BSDF* node

197

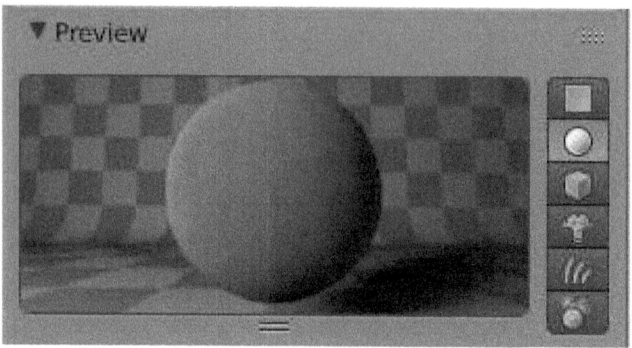

fig. 203 the *Preview* of the *Velvet* node, mixed with a *Diffuse* and set on the red color

TOON

This shader is used for rendering in cartoon style, with really sharp shadows, reflections and light strokes.

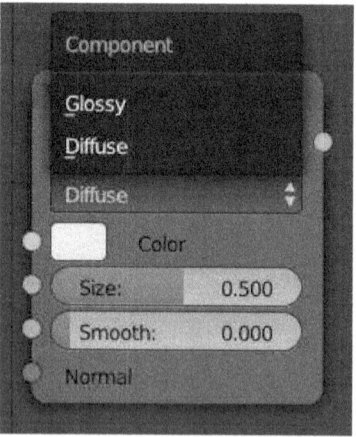

fig. 204 the *Toon BSDF* node

To properly simulate this effect in a 3D model, it is necessary that there is a very strong source of light to irradiate the object with this material applied, so as to help the shader to correctly perform its function of net color differentiation.

fig. 205 the *Preview* of the *Toon* node, set as *Diffuse* of red color

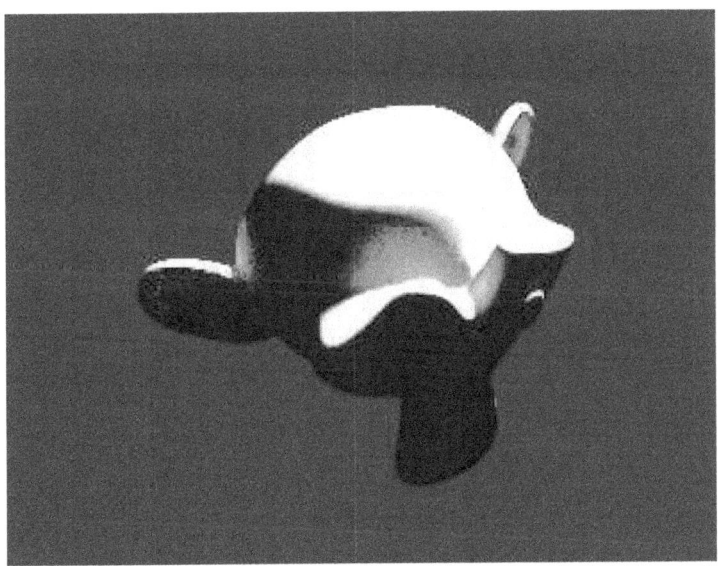

fig. 206 the *Toon* shader on *Suzanne*

Toon can be set as *Diffuse* or as *Glossy* into the specific *Component* menu.

Moreover it is possible to define the color (*Color*) and a possible relief (*Normal*).

Finally the parameters Size and Smooth, defined by the respective cursors with values ranging from 0 to 1, determine the size of the area subject to illumination and the bevel (or hardness) of the effect.

SUBSURFACE SCATTERING

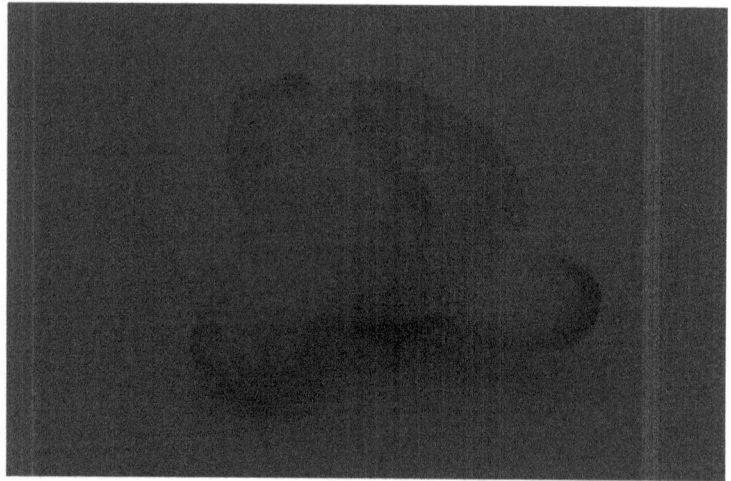

fig. 207 the *Subsurface Scattering* shader on *Suzanne*

As seen in the Blender Render environment, this useful shader simulates the translucence of some materials such as leather, wax and certain gelatinous materials.

The light can penetrate into the surface, partially illuminating the insides.

The effect looks more visible with light sources positioned behind the framed object.

Subsurface Scattering has many parameters ad disposal.

The falloff menu allows you to set the algorithm between Cubic and Gaussian. The first is the most simple, defined by the function $(r - x)^3$, where r is the radius and x the distance; the second causes a beveled decay of the interior lighting.

Color defines the material base color.

Scale controls the global factor relevant to the scattering radius.

Radius opens a drop down menu where the scattering radius for each RGB channel can be more precisely defined.

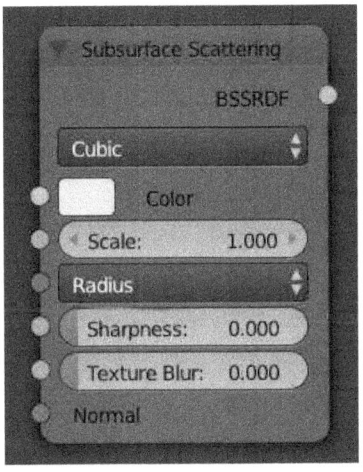

fig. 208 the *Subsurface Scattering* node

Sharpness works only with Cubic and, for values between 0 and 1, reduces unwanted dark areas.

Texture Blur allows you to mix the effect of scattering with an applied texture, that will result pasty, blurred and softened. Normal allows you to set a relief effect on the surface.

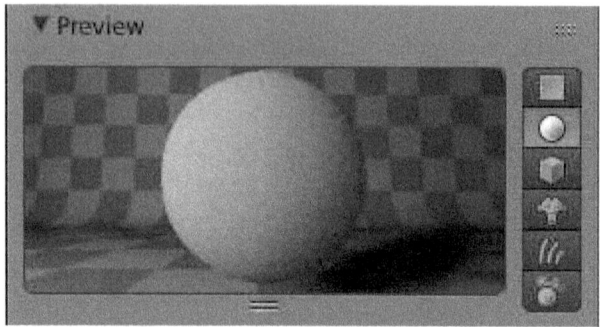

fig. 209 the *Preview* of the *Subsurface Scattering* node

EMISSION

fig. 210 the *Emission* shader allows *Suzanne* to produce light

Emission allows the object to produce light.

Useful for making luminous panels, illuminating the scene with an emitting background, lamps, signs, this shader can really find many applications and be mixed with other shaders.

This *shader* has the only parameters *Color* and *Strength*, determining the emission intensity.

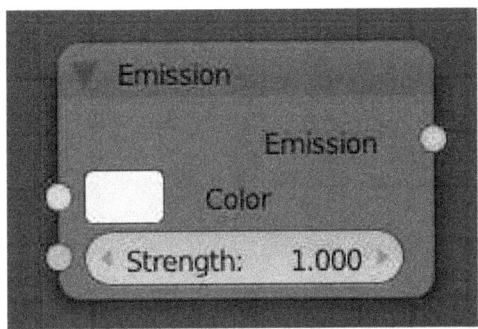

fig. 211 the *Emission* node

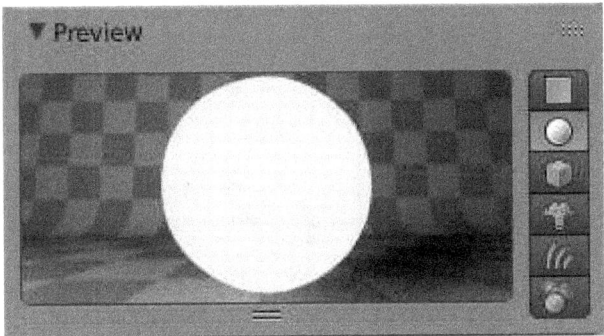

fig. 212 the preview of the *Emission* node

It can only be used for the Surface output of the World tab, connected to the World Output node (see below). It is ignored in all the other cases.

It is provided with two parameters: *Color* and *Strength*.

fig. 213 the *Background* node

The **Holdout** shader is useful for the *compositing*, for creating an "hole" in the image with the *alpha* transparency value equal to 0.

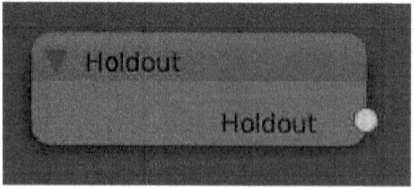

fig. 214 the *Holdout* node

If activated the check of the Ambient Occlusion panel in the World tab, this shader allows to influence the objects in which it is set, so to be shaded according to this algorithm.

Creating different materials with this node in different amounts, you can make sure that the various objects in the scene can be affected differently from general Ambient Occlusion.

This node is provided with only one parameter for color control (*Color*).

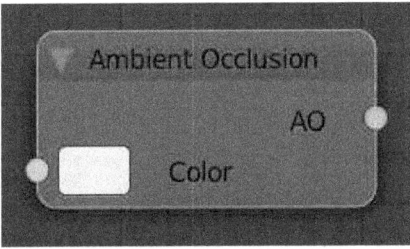

fig. 215 the *Ambient Occlusion* node

This node must be connected to the volume input of the Material Output node, because it allows you to generate a light ray dispersion within a volume, getting a smoky and nebulous look, useful, precisely, to create volumetric effects like clouds and vapors.

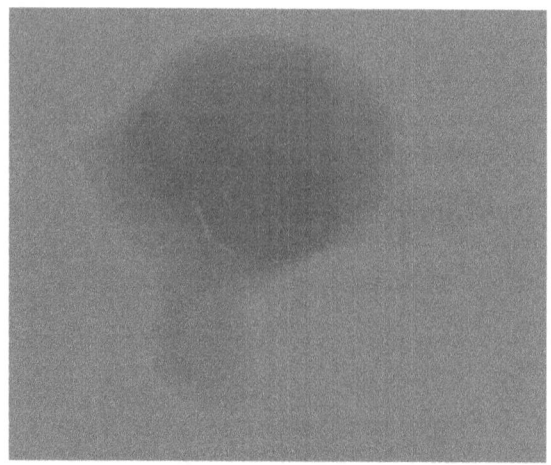

fig. 216 *Suzanne with the material created by Volume Scatter takes on a hazy appearance*

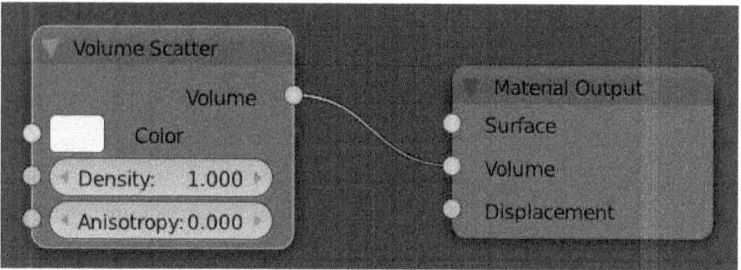

fig. 217 the *Ambient Volume Scatter* node

Note two parameters at disposal:

- *Density* defines the volume density, i.e. the resistance to be crossed by the light.

- *Anisotropy* regulates the light path analogously to what already explained for metals.

fig. 218 the *Preview* of the *Volume Scatter* node

VOLUME ABSORBPTION

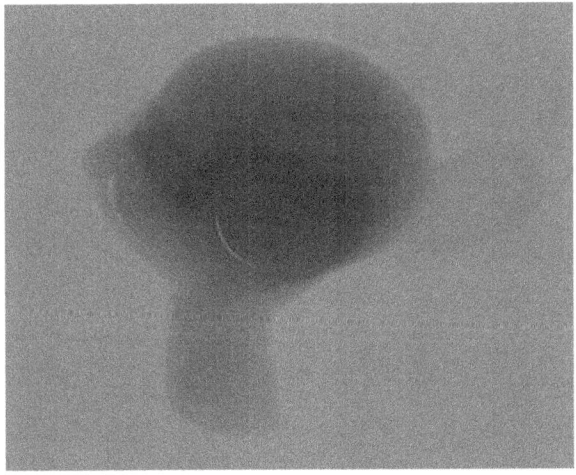

fig. 219 *Suzanne* with the material created by *Volume Absorption*

This node is very similar to the previous one and is able to absorb the light rays depending on the *Density* parameter and the *Color.*

Also this node can be connected only to the Volume input *socket* of the *Material Output* node.

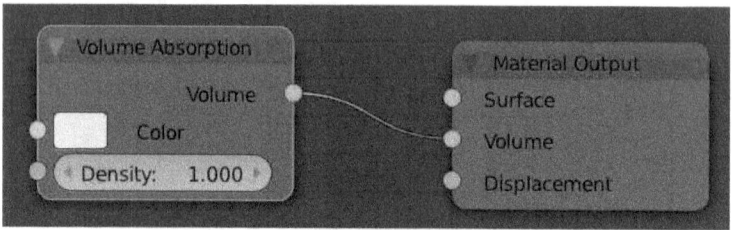

fig. 220 the *Ambient Volume Absorption* node

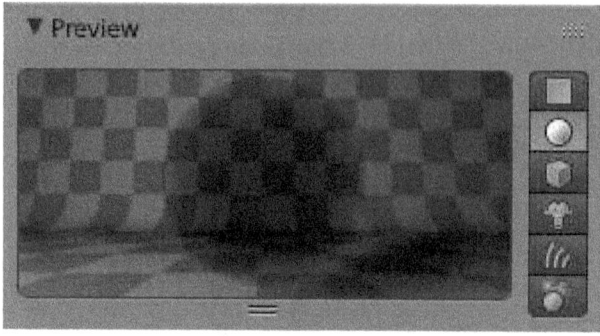

fig. 221 the *Preview* of the *Volume Absorption* node

HAIR

This node is used to control the filament material (hair, blades of grass...) generated by the Particle System (see below) on a mesh.

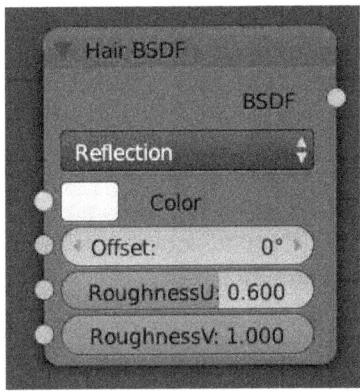

fig. 222 the *Hair BSDF* node

The node controls the light transmission and reflection on the hair.

We will analyze in more detail the particle system later.

fig. 223 *Suzanne* with an applied *hair* particle system

This node, as previously seen in the exercise, is of the outmost importance for mixing together many *shader* nodes.

The shader nodes connected in the two input sockets are mixed together according to a percentage balance parameter Fac or as defined by an external node that calculates the factor according to a given algorithm. In the exercise it was for example used the Fresnel node as a balancing factor.

To mix together many shader nodes you must add several Mix Shader nodes.

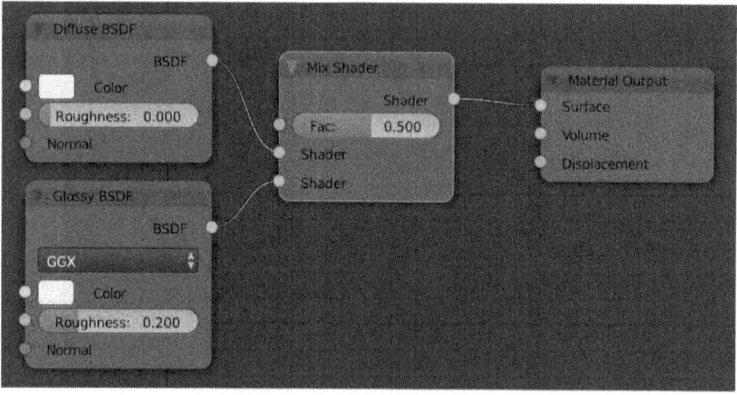

fig. 224 the *Mix Shade* node merges together two shader nodes

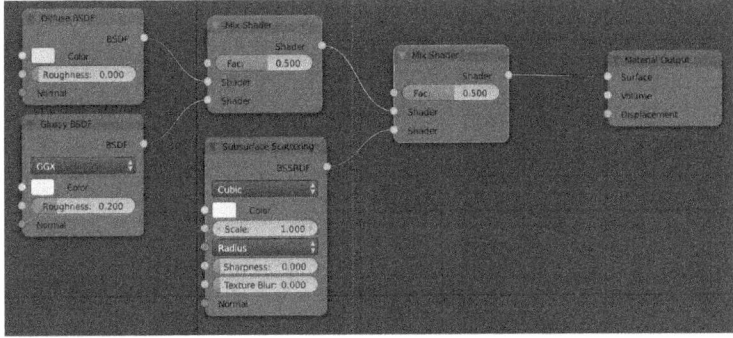

fig. 225 a more complex node composition through the use of three shaders and two Mix Shaders

Add Shader is similar to the previous one but, instead balancing together two shaders depending on a factor, add them with the same weight, thus does not have any specific control parameter.

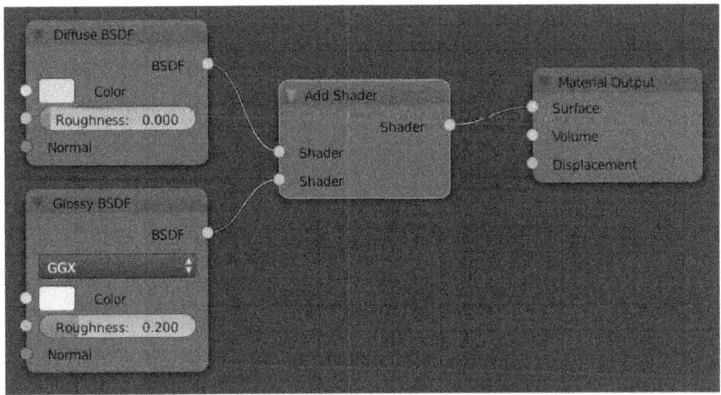

fig. 226the Add Shader node adds the effect of two shader nodes

211

B) *OUTPUT* NODES

This group is composed of only two nodes and represents the final result, the output channel of a system of interconnected nodes. In practice they display the final result of a material.

MATERIAL OUTPUT

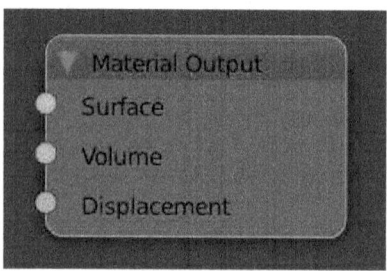

fig. 227 the *Material Output* node

The **Material Output** node collect all the information and data of a material.

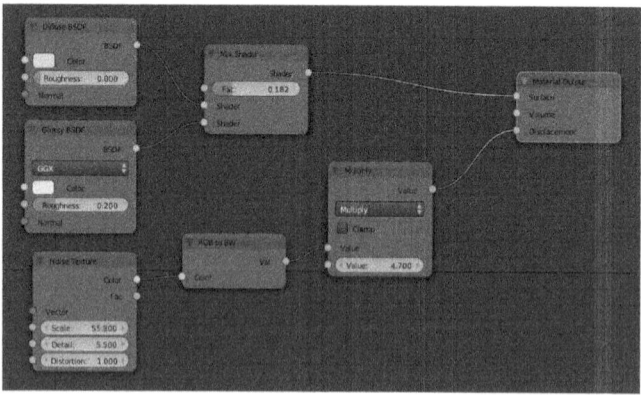

fig. 228 a complex node system, some of them determining the relief effect (*Displacement*)

It has at disposal three input *sockets* and, obviously, being an ending node, no output *sockets*.

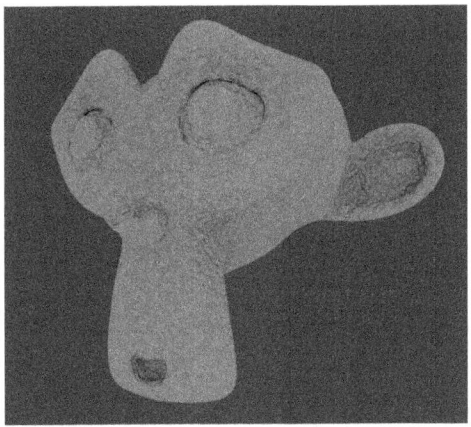

fig. 229 the material outcome relevant to the previous nodes

The input *sockets* are:

- *Surface*, on which all nodes determining the object surface material are connected;

- *Volume*, on which the nodes determining a volumetric effect are connected;

- *Displacement*, on which it is usually connected a texture or a mathematical - type node applying a relief to the material.

The **Light Output** node is related to the node configuration associated to a direct light source (*Lamp*).

213

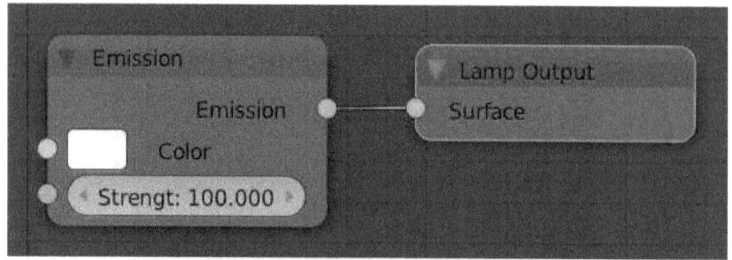

fig. 230 the *Lamp Output* node

C) *TEXTURE* NODES

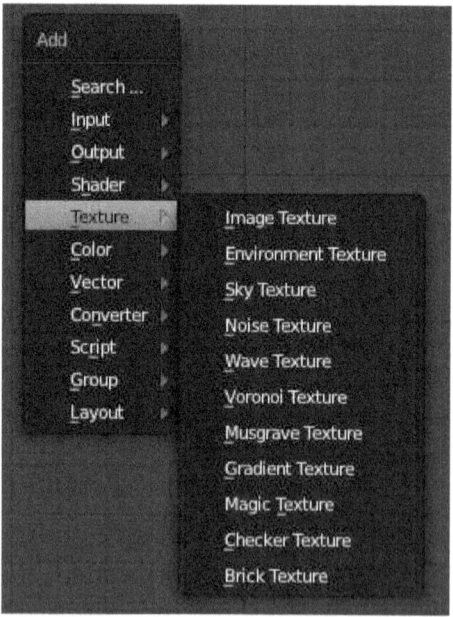

fig. 231 the *Texture* node group

This important group contains all the nodes related to a texture insertion to be associated to a *shader* node or to any other node

214

in such a way as to behave like a base factor for the range of colors, as we will see in the foregoing with specific examples.

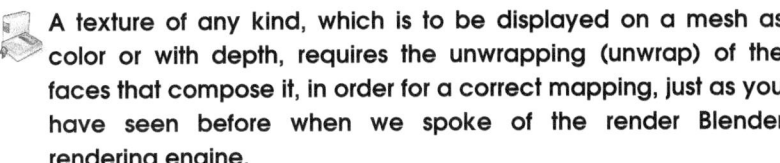 A texture of any kind, which is to be displayed on a mesh as color or with depth, requires the unwrapping (unwrap) of the faces that compose it, in order for a correct mapping, just as you have seen before when we spoke of the render Blender rendering engine.

IMAGE TEXTURE

Cycles works so very different than Blender Render. The inclusion of a texture no longer takes place through the tab of the Texture Properties editor (tab whose use is definitely reduced and marginal), but with the inclusion of a specific node connected to a shader.

We wish to clarify that texture does not mean "material", but only its colored component (Diffuse), or in some cases, a different component, such as the one that defines a surface relief (bump).

Let's stress once again, that **a material is the set of a number of components, of which the color (Diffuse) and the texture represent only a part.**

Image Texture allows one a *texture* to a *shader* and becoming part of a material.

 EXERCISE N. 4: APPLY A TEXTURE TO A MATERIAL COLOR

In this exercise we will explain, in few passages, how to apply a *texture* to a material and set it as main color (*Diffuse*).

215

After having assigned a new material to the mesh, insert an *Image Texture* node in the *Node Editor* pressing SHIFT + A.

Suppose that the *texture* represents the object diffuse color. We will need to connect the *Color* output of the node to the Color input *socket* of the *Diffuse shader*. The palette of the latter will disappear since the color will be defined by the texture only.

If we try to render the object, we will notice that the latter has become magenta.

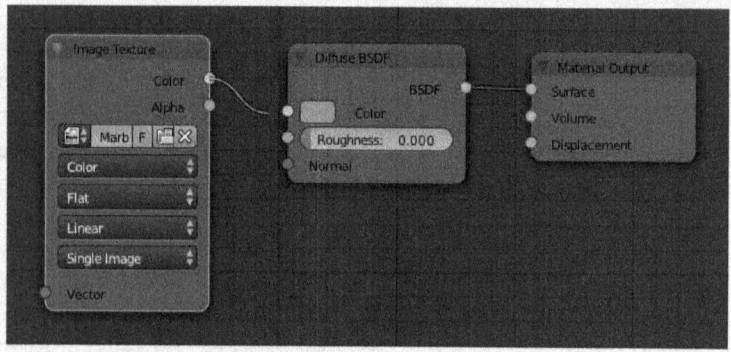

fig. 232 insertion of an *Image texture* node and connection with the Diffuse *shader*

This is because no image has been uploaded in the *Image Texture* node.

216

fig. 233 if no file is uploaded in the *Image Texture* node, Blender visualizes in magenta the rendered *mesh* indicating the file missing

By clicking on *Open* inside the *Image Texture* node, the browser will open from which it will be possible to upload the file chosen.

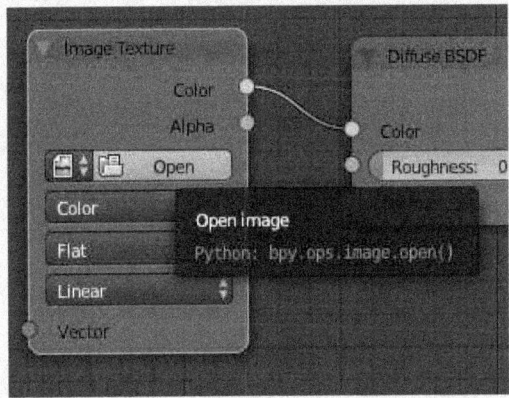

fig. 234 *file* upload in the *Image Texture* node

fig. 235 placement of the *texture* on the unwrapped *mesh in the UV/Image Editor*

Now, once selected the *mesh*, enter in *Edit Mode* and execute the *unwrapping*(key U) and choose the most suitable method depending on the mesh type, as previously explained in the chapter relevant to the *unwrapping*, possibly indicating some unwrapping lines with the command *Mark Seam* (key E).

Entering the *UV/Image Editor*, we can scale, rotate and correctly place the *texture* on the *mesh*.

Now the *texture* can be visualized and correctly applied to the *mesh*.

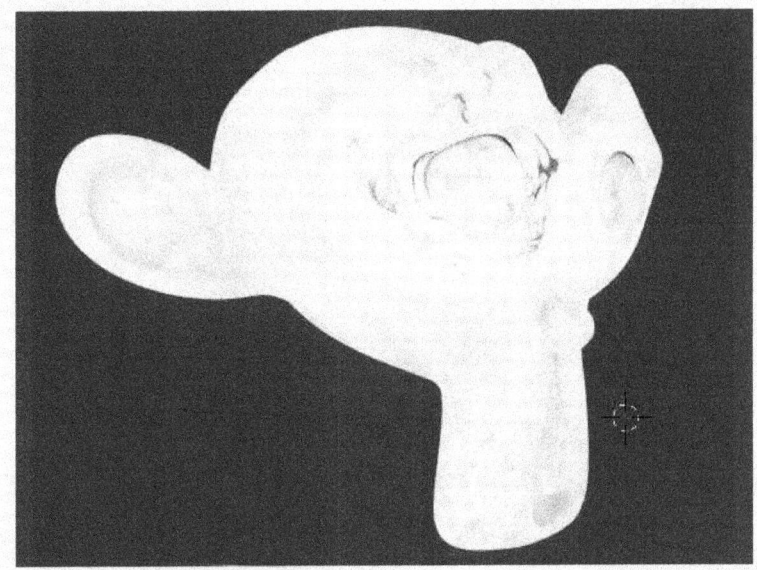

fig. 236 the *texture* applied to the *mesh*

Try now to modify the connection of the *Image texture* node with the node, by connecting it to the Displacement socket of the *Material Output* node instead to the *Color* of the *Diffuse*.

Add a *Math* node, which can be found in the *Converter* nodes, between the *Image Texture* node and the *Material Output*, and set it as *Multiply* from the drop-down menu, by greatly increasing the *Strength* value.

Set the *Image texture* node as *Non Color Data*, to make it monochromatic in gray scale.

What happened?

The *mesh* shows a displacement effect defined by the *texture* and, more precisely, depressions are visible in the areas where the *texture* is darker, whereas reliefs can be seen where the texture is clearer.

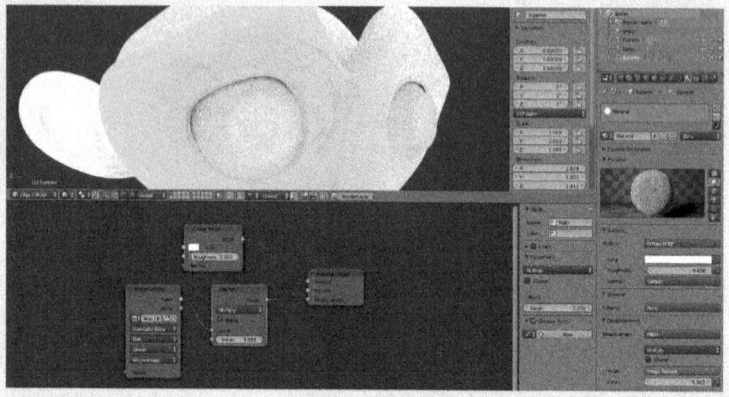

fig. 237 the *texture, connected to the* Displacement socket *of the* Material *Output* node, suitably increased with a mathematical node math *Multiply*, acts as a displacement factor on the mesh

In this case, the *texture* does not act as a color, but as balancing factor between reliefs and depressions.

The *Math* node, set as *Multiply*, multiply the effect intensity.

Now cancel the *Math* node and add a *Bump* node, chosen among the options of the *Vector* group.

Connect the output *socket* of the *Image Texture* node with the *Height* input *socket* and then the *Normal* output *socket* with the *Normal* input socket of the *Diffuse*.

An effect analogous to the previous one will be achieved, but with a slightly different logic meaning.

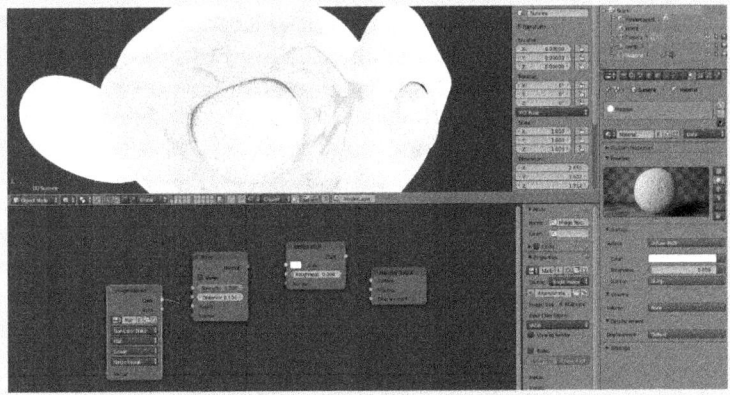

fig. 238 the *texture* connected to the height of the *Bump* vectorial node determines the relief height

The *texture*, with its gray scale, acts as a factor for the *Bump* vector height, which affects the *Normal* vector of the *Diffuse*.

These nodes will be examined in detail in the foregoing.

Analyze now the specific parameters of the *Image Texture* node.

The menu *Color Space* allows you to visualize the *texture* in colors (*Color*) or in gray scale (*Non-Color Data*).

The *Projection* menu defines the mapping method of the 2D image on the 3D model, choosing between *Flat* (standard projection method along the two axes *x* and *y*) and *Box* (acting in three different directions, depending on the value set by the dedicated *Blend* cursor).

The *Interpolation* menu regulates the pixel interpolation on the mesh and can be set as *Linear*, *Closest*, *Cubic* and *Smart*.

The last menu, finally, named *Source*, defines the file type that can be uploaded in the node, choosing between *Single Image*, *Image Sequence*, *Movie* and *Generated*.

fig. 239 the *Image texture* node

Image texture have only one input *socket*, of vector type (*Vector*) and two output *sockets*: *Color* (yellow), usually useful for the connection to a *shader* or to a factorial *socket*; and *Alpha*, recovering from the *texture* the information of the only transparent channel, if existing.

ENVIRONMENT TEXTURE

This node is associated to the 3D environment background.

Usually it is used to be connected to the input *socket* of the *Background* node, being part of the *Output* node group, and

222

can be activated entering the *World* environment (icon with the planet) in the *header* of the *Node Editor*, which we will analyze in detail at the end of the node description.

fig. 240 *Environment* of the *Node Editor*

In this node an image *file* can be uploaded (*Single* Image) representing a background, an image sequence (*Image Sequence*), a movie (*Movie*) or a box image generated by Blender.

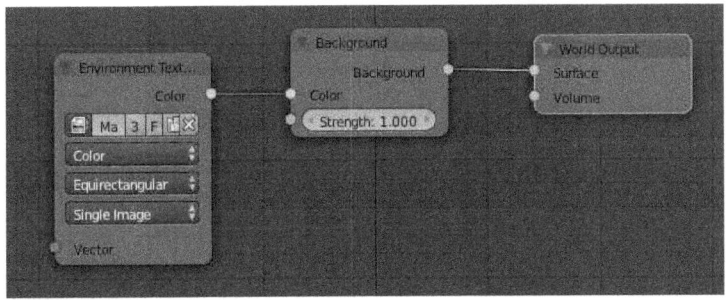

fig. 241 the nodes relevant to the *environment*

Selecting *Single image* you can insert an HDR *file*, of which we will discuss later.

The *Projection* menu allows you to choose the *environment* projection type, choosing between *Equirectangular or Mirror Ball* (or spherical image.

SKY TEXTURE

Sky Texture generates a sky, which is assigned as color to the *Background* node, like for the *Environment Texture*.

223

The settings of this node can be found in the **World** panel, in the *Surface* panel.

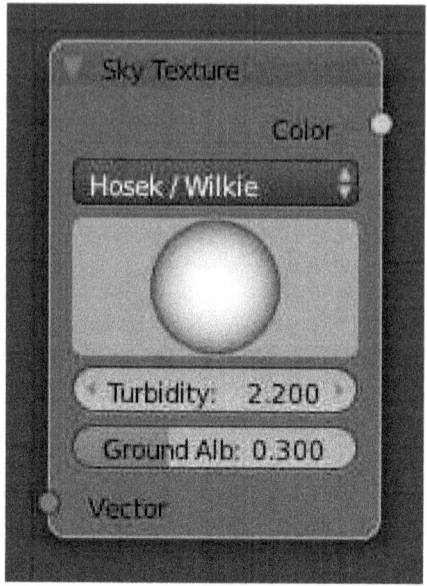

fig. 242 the *Sky Texture* node

It has an input vector *socket* and an output color *socket*.

The *Sky Type* menu define the sky type according to one of the two algorithms *Hosek/Wilkie* or *Preetham*.

Turbidity allows you to add a turbid air effect, with a red, desertic, almost Martian appearance, whereas *Ground Albedo* is a parameter adding to the atmosphere an effect of rarefied atmosphere, typical of the sunrise.

In the *Preview* editor of the node (or in the *Properties* panel of the *Properties sidebar*, or also in the *Surface* panel of the *World* tab of the *Properties* editor) it is possible to rotate the sky sphere to define the sun position, also in terms of *zenith* (height). The sky will adapt to the sun position, coloring accordingly.

fig. 243 regulation of the sun position in the *Sky texture* node

fig. 244 *preview* of the *Sky texture* in the *Properties* editor

The *Sky Texture* (like for the *Environment Texture*) will affect the illumination of the objects present in the scene depending on the *tab World* settings under *Cycles* in the *Properties* editor.

3.2.3. Tab World

The **World** tab is very similar to the *Material* tab associated to the objects.

However its parameters refer to the *environment*, i.e. to the environment surrounding the scene.

The *tab* is composed of a **Preview** panel, visualizing the sky effect, a **Surface** panel and a **Volume** panel, which, similarly to those contained in the *Material* tab, summarize the chain and the node and file composition associated to them.

In this modality, the *Background shader* acts as a *Diffuse* for the background, to which a color, a texture, an image sequence, a movie, a procedural texture or a gradient can be associated.

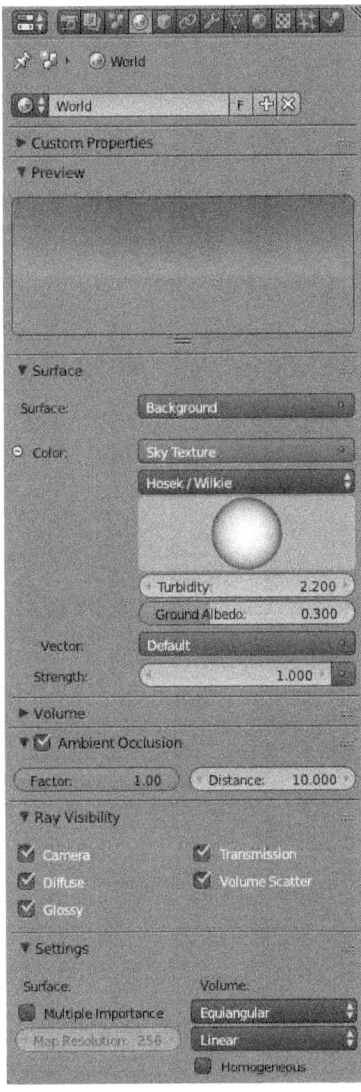

fig. 245 *tab World* of the *Properties* editor

227

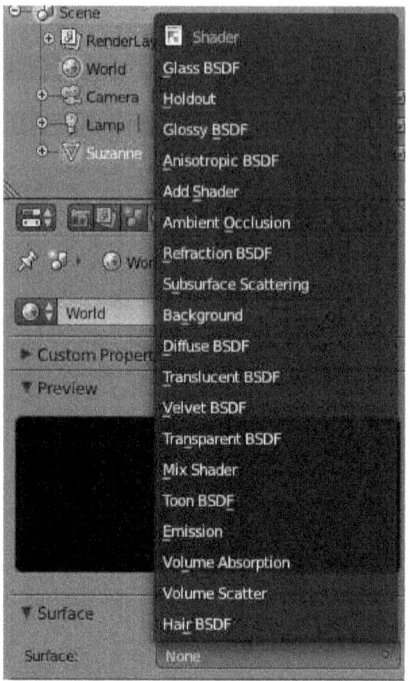

fig. 246 *shader* choice (likely a *background*) for the background surface

The **Ambient Occlusion** panel, if activated, adds this type of illumination (not projecting shadows) to the scene. The *Factor* and *Distance* values have the same function of those already analyzed for the same panel in *Render Blender* environment.

Ray Visibility is a very useful panel. Contains some flag options, similar to those present in the homonymous panel in the *Object tab* (referring to objects in the scene). It is used to make visible the background and, if the relevant flags are activated, to influence the illumination, the *Camera*, the object colors (*Diffuse*), the object reflection (*Glossy*), the transparence

228

transmission (*Transmission*) and possibly the volumetric effects (*Volume Scatter*).

Finally, the **Settings** panel allows you to act on some surface and volume settings, such as:

- *Multiple Importance* regulating the background sampling during the *rendering*;

- *Map Resolution* (which is activated by checking the previous option), determining the background resolution in pixel;

- the *Volume Sampling* menu determines the computation method of the color sampling on the volume. *Distance* is suitable in case of dense volumes with far lights; *Equiangular* in case of poorly dense volumetric effects and close illumination; *Multiple Importance* combines the previous two options;

- The second menu, *Volume Interpolation*, computes the shading interpolation method according to one of the two available options: *Linear* in case of poorly smooth volumes (faster computation); *Cubic* in case of volumes with high definition smoothing (slower computation);

- The flag on *Homogeneous* yields faster rendering time making the volume density uniform.

NOISE TEXTURE

In *Cycles*, the procedural *textures* are different with respect to those present in *Blender Render*. Some of the "old" *textures* can be used, uploading them from the *Texture* tab, for some functions, some modifiers and some simulation processes, but not in the nodes.

This is not a drawback, because in *Cycles* the new procedural *textures*, such as **Noise Texture**, are likewise versatile.

Noise Texture generates a very useful color procedural *texture* (not needing any file uploading).

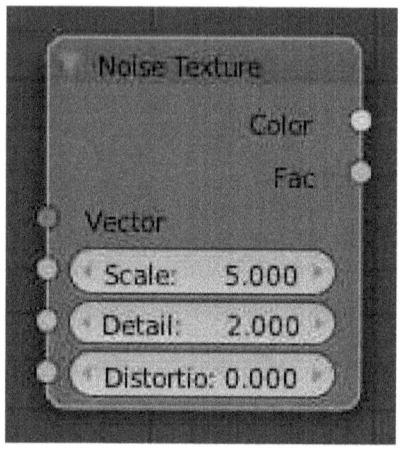

fig. 247 *Noise Texture* node

Like to *Clouds* it has three parameters:

- *Scale* sets the dimensions of the cloudy effect;

- *Detail* yields, for higher values, a greater image detail;

- *Distortion* applies a distortion to the image.

All the three parameters are connected to input *sockets* of mathematical type on which nodes can be connected.

Moreover there is an input *socket* of vector type (*Vector*), useful for defining the mapping of this texture on a mesh.

The node has, finally, two output sockets:

230

- *Color* for using *Noise* Texture as color, thus associating it usually to a *Diffuse* or to another *shader*;

- *Fac* for using the node as balancing factor, associating some values for light colors and other values for darker colors.

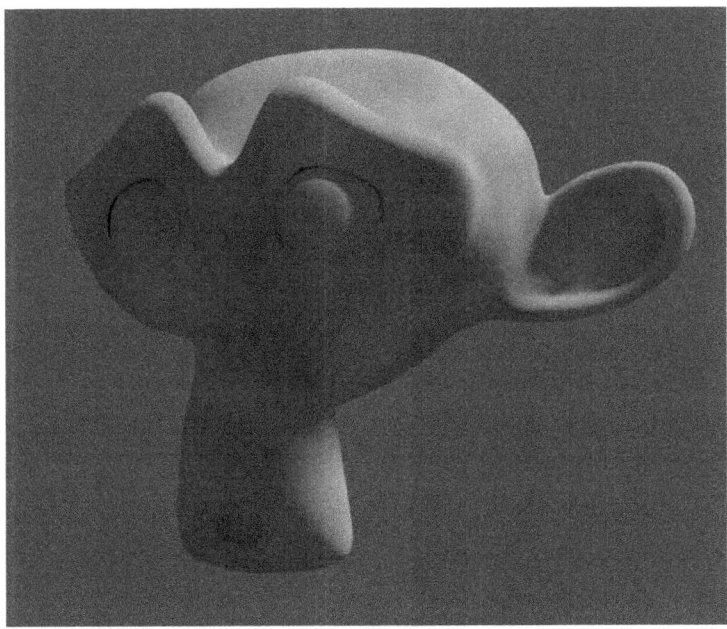

fig. 248 *Noise Texture* associated to the *Diffuse* colors the *mesh*

On the other hand, using *Noise Texture* as balancing factor between two colors, it will be conceived in black and white and, in correspondence of the areas tending to white will shift the mesh color toward the first *Diffuse*, whereas in correspondence of the darker areas, toward the second *Diffuse*.

231

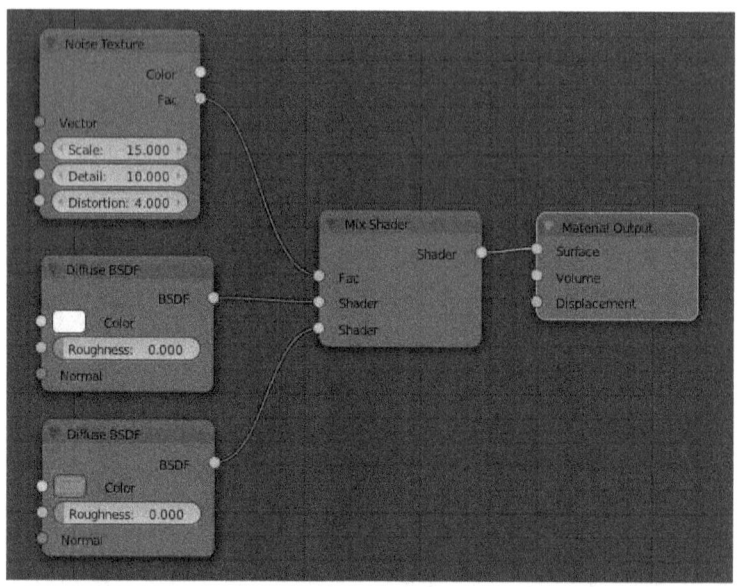

fig. 249 *Noise Texture* set as *Fac* between two *Diffuse* determines the balancing between the two colors

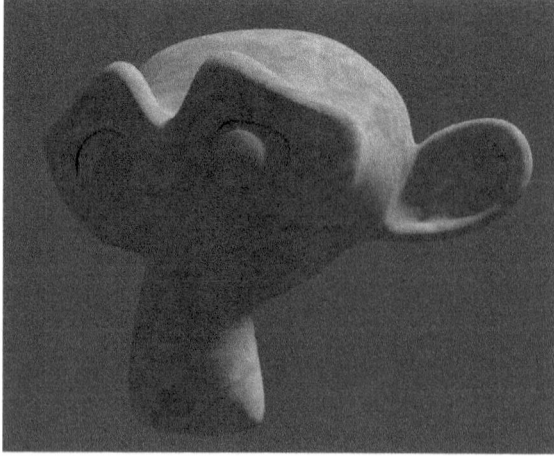

fig. 250 mesh rendering whose material is defined by the composition of the nodes above, in which *Noise Texture* acts as balancing factor between two colors

232

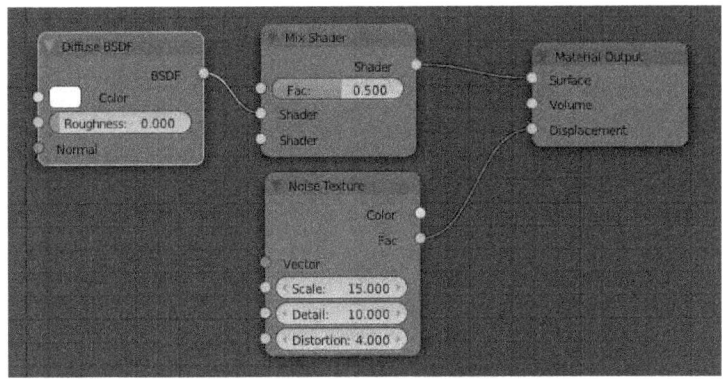

fig. 251 *Noise Texture* set as *Fac* of *Displacement* determines an relief effect

fig. 252 mesh *rendering* whose material is defined by the composition of the nodes above, in which the *Noise Texture* acts as relief factor

Obviously *Noise Texture*, such as any other procedural texture or image can be composed with analogous or different others, colors, achieving complex coloration, overlapped relief effects and many other possibilities of use.

233

fig. 253 the resin pavement of this setting has been obtained by mixing and overlapping procedural *textures* of different scales which behaved also as balancing factor between color tones, *Noise Texture* themselves and light *Bump* effects (relief). Image realized with Alan Zirpoli.

The procedural *texture* **Wave** generates a sequence of black and white bands or concentric rings, which suitably modified by specific parameters of the node, can simulate waves, wood veins and other effects with alternate behavior.

This node of *Cycles* substitutes *Wood,* among the procedural *textures* of *Blender Render.*

Let's see which are the available node parameters for the image manipulation.

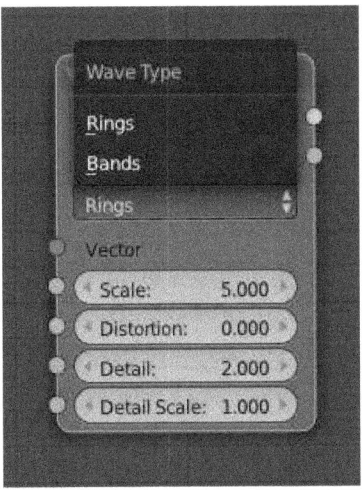

fig. 254 the *Wave Texture* node

The *Wave Type* menu allows you to choose if the base *texture* must be composed of black and white parallel bands (Bands) or concentric rings (*Rings*).

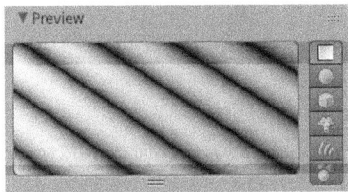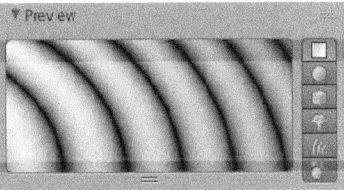

fig. 255 *Wave Texture* node preview set as *Bands* (on the left) and as *Rings* (on the right)

Like for *Noise Texture*, *Scale* resize the image. For larger values, the bands or rings will be more packed.

Distortion applies a distortion to the bands or the rings.

Detail adds a higher definition to the bands, whereas *Detail Scale* defines the detail maximum dimensions.

235

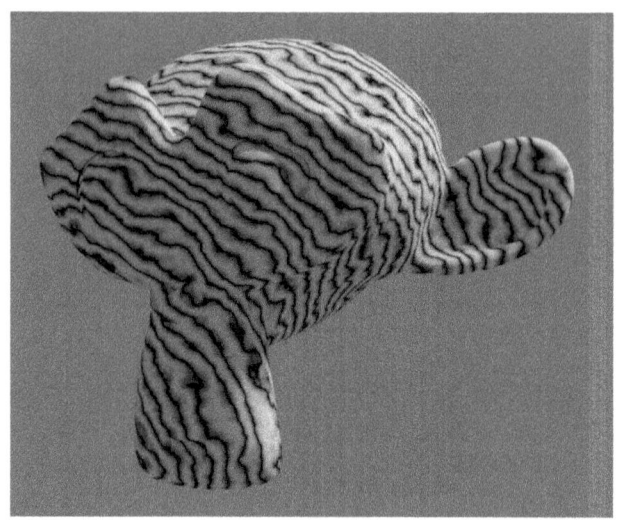

fig. 256 *Wave Texture* applied to the *Diffuse* with modified parameters *Scale* = 10; *Distortion* = 20; *Detail* = 2; *Scale Detail* = 1. A striped effect is achieved

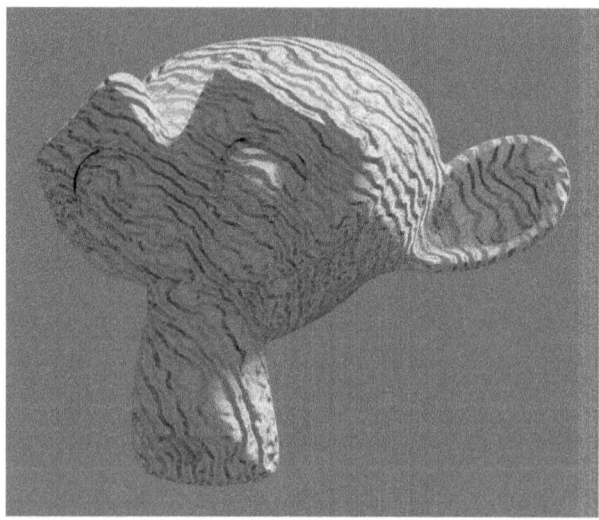

fig. 257 the same settings of the node connected by means of the *socket Fac* to the *Displacement* of the *Material Output* generates an relief with striped behavior

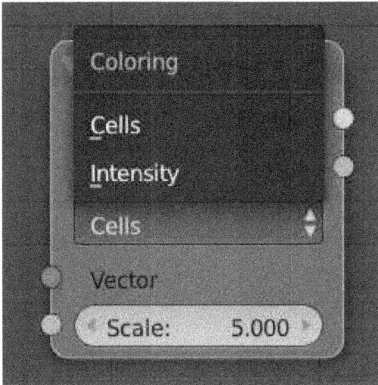

fig. 258 the *Voronoi Texture* node

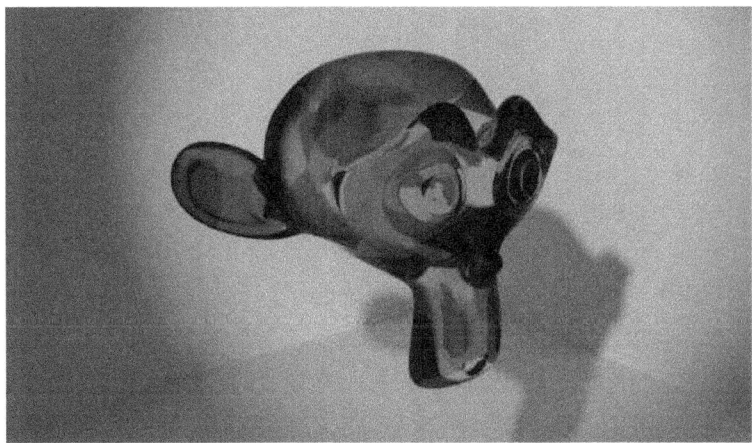

fig. 259 *Voronoi Texture* set as *Cells* and applied to the *Glass* node

This *texture* generates an irregular check effect similar to colored cells if the *Type* is set to *Cells*, or to a blurred black and white cell grid if set to *Intensity*.

It is much effective for creating psychedelic effects and colored glasses, and has the only parameter *Scale* determining the weave dimensions.

MUSGRAVE TEXTURE

Totally similar to the homonymous procedural *texture* of the *Blender Render* engine, **Musgrave** generates a fractal model in black and white, much useful to obtain, for example, the bovine pied mantle.

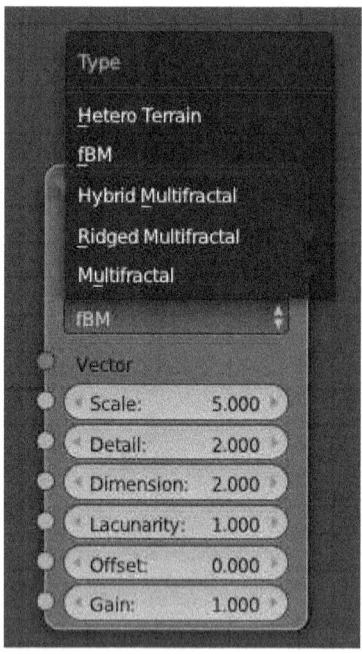

fig. 260 the *Musgrave Texture* node

The *Type* menu allows you to choose the fractal typology used by the node for generating the procedural texture. Five options

238

are available: *Multifractal, Ridged Multifractal, Hybrid Multifractal, fBM, Hetero Terrain.*

Scale defines the scale, the *texture* global dimensions, whereas *Detail* and *Dimension* represent, as for the previous cases, the detail level and the relevant dimensions.

Lacunarity, Offset and Gain regulates the space percentage left free by the fractal modulus.

fig. 261 *Musgrave Texture* applied to the *Diffuse*

GRADIENT TEXTURE

This node generates a procedural *texture* of gradient type.

For gradient we mean a smooth shift between a tone and another one (white and black, for example).

The gradient type can be chosen from the *Gradient Type* menu between *Radial, Quadratic Sphere, Spherical, Diagonal, Easing, Quadratic, Linear.*

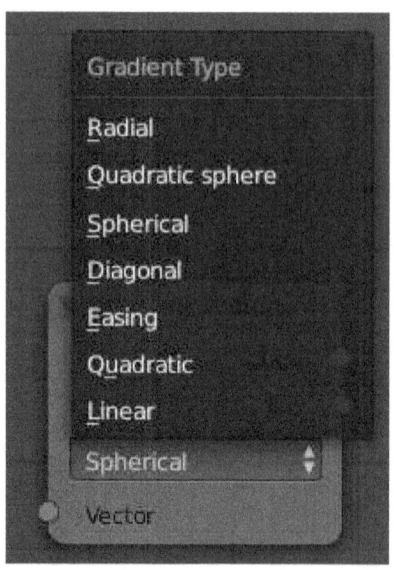

fig. 262 the *Gradient Texture* node

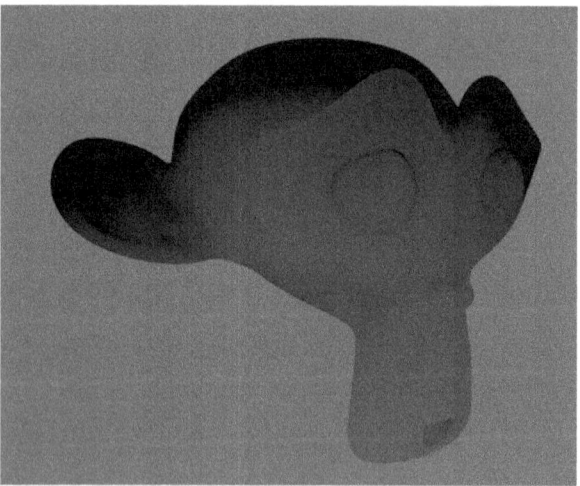

fig. 263 *Gradient Texture* applied to the *Diffuse*

The node has a Vector input *socket*, useful for defining the mapping coordinates, dimensions and rotation, and two output sockets: *Color* and *Fac*.

MAGIC TEXTURE

Magic Texture generates a colored psychedelic *texture*.

Depth regulates the turbulence of the generated noise, modifying the chromatic range.

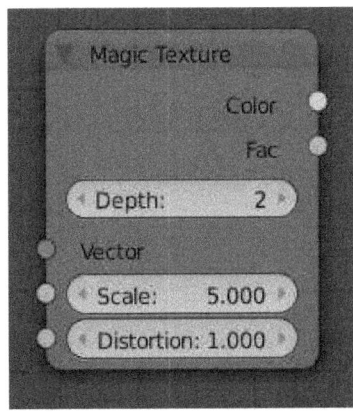

fig. 264 the *Magic Texture* node

Scale regulates the *texture* dimensions, whereas *Distortion* modifies the noise shape, by applying a distortion.

These two values can be set and regulated by external nodes by connecting them to the corresponding input *sockets* of mathematical type.

Moreover, in input the *Vector* socket is present, for the external control of the mapping.

The external *sockets* are *Color* and *Fac*.

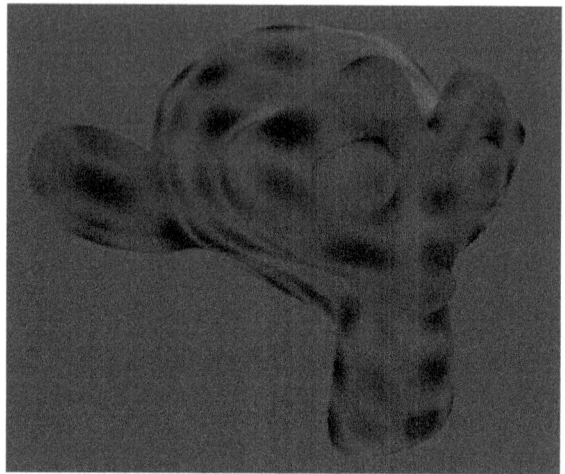

fig. 265 *Magic Texture* applied to the *Diffuse*

CHECKER TEXTURE

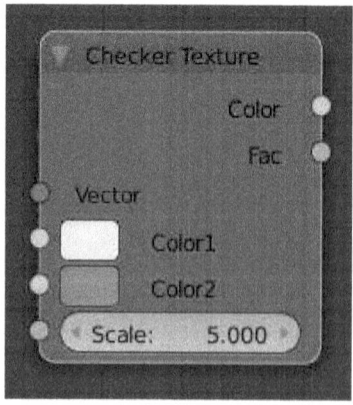

fig. 266 the *Checker Texture* node

The *Checker Texture* node generates a simple texture with two-color checks.

The colors can be defined in the two palettes (*Color1* and *Color2*) present in the node or defined by external nodes connected to the corresponding yellow *sockets* (*Color*).

fig. 267 *Checker Texture* applied to the background (a glass material has been assigned to *Suzanne*)

Scale defines the *texture* dimensions.

The input *sockets*, besides the two yellow *colors*, are *Vector*, for the mapping, and the gray mathematical node on *Scale* for managing the dimensions with configurations of external nodes.

Two output *sockets* are available: *Color* and *Fac*.

BRICK TEXTURE

This very interesting node produces a procedural *texture* useful for the simulation of bricks.

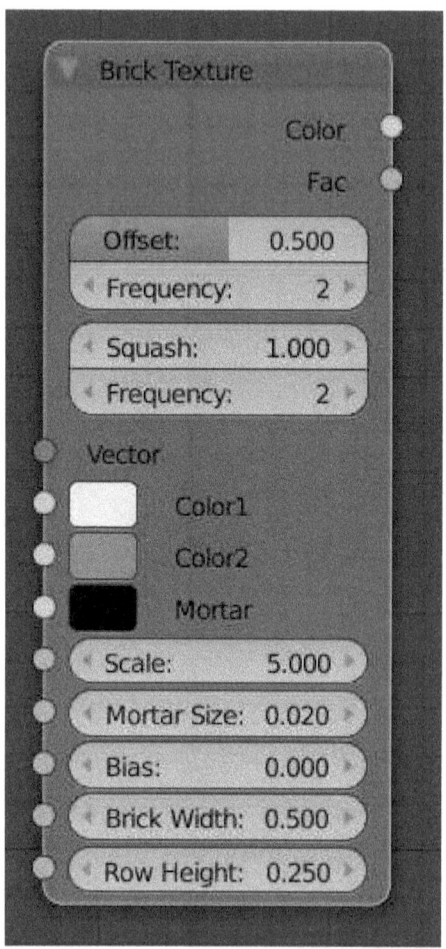

fig. 268*Brick Texture* node

It is based on parameters alternating three colors according to a scan along the *x* axis, one along the *y* axis and one reproducing the mortar layers.

Offset defines the displacement offset of a brick line with respect to the one above. The value 0.5 places a brick in

244

correspondence of the midpoint of the brick belonging to the line above.

Frequency defines the number of brick lines after which the new line must be translated of the *Offset* value (it is set to 2 by *default*, implying alternate brick lines).

The three palettes, *Color1*, *Color2* and *Mortar*, determine the two base colors for the bricks and the mortar. A yellow socket *Color* is associated to each of them for defining the color through external nodes.

fig. 269 the *Brick Texture* node set as Diffuse factor of a flat material

Scale defines the base dimensions of the *texture*.

Mortar Size the thickness of the mortar layers between two bricks.

Bias is a parameter defined in a cursor (with values ranging between -1 and 1) balancing the brick color between *Color1* and *Color2*, with intermediate steps.

245

Brick Width and *Row Height* regulate, respectively, the brick width and height.

Squash alternates the brick lines such as to obtain brick lines of different width. *Frequency*, like for *Offset*, defines the line pattern.

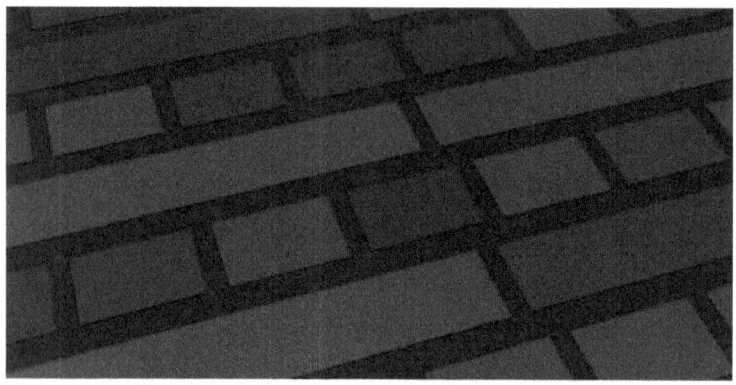

fig. 270 Squash *set to 0.5 assigns to consecutive lines different brick width*

Obviously this node can act not only like color and brick pattern, but also as vectorial factor of *Displacement* or *Bump*.

D) *COLOR* NODES

This node group is closely related to all the information regarding the color.

By using these nodes it is possible to mix colors or *textures*, modify the curves, regulate the luminosity and the contrast.

Let's examine the 7 available nodes belonging to this group, their functions and main applications.

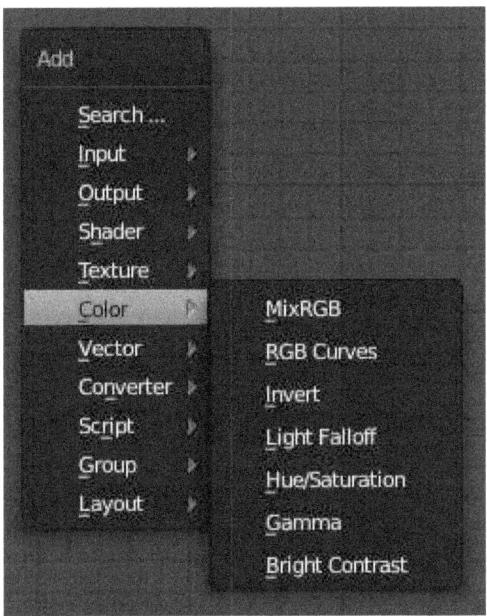

fig. 271 nodes of the *Color* group

MIX RGB

Differently from what the name of this node seems to suggest, **MixRGB** can be used not only for mixing two colors.

It is possible to choose between as many as 18 different algorithms: *Mix, Add, Multiply, Subtract, Screen, Divide, Difference, Darken, Lighten, Overlay, Dodge, Burn, Hue, Saturation, Value, Color, Soft Light* and *Linear Light*.

The mixing factor Fac related to the *Blend Type* algorithm can be numerically defined (ranging from 0 to 1, where 0 implies only color1 and 1 only color 2) or by means of external nodes connected to the corresponding gray *socket*.

Let's make an example to clarify its use.

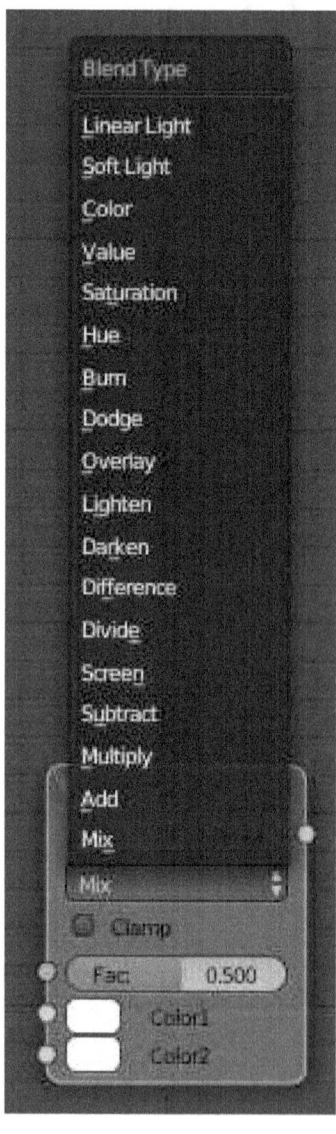

fig. 272 *Blend Type* of the *MixRGB* node

The drop-down menu *Blend Type* allows you to define the algorithm *Cycles* will use on the two colors (or on the *textures*) defined by the palettes or the *sockets Color1* and *Color2*

 EXERCISE N. 5: A MATERIAL DEFINED BY MIXING TWO COLORS

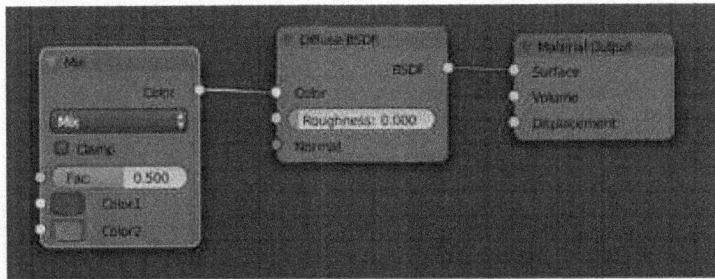

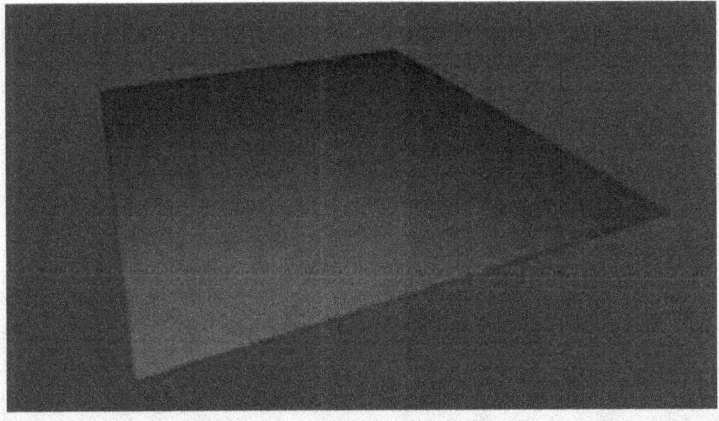

fig. 273 *mix* between two colors

Try to assign a new material to a *mesh* and apply the *MixRGB* node to the yellow input socket of the *Diffuse*.

Set a blue color on the palette relevant to *Color 1* and a red color on the palette of *Color 2*.

With a mixing factor set by default to 0.5 the resulting material color will be violet. An outcome perhaps a little be trivial, not very useful.

By modifying the *Fac* value to 0, the blue color will be obtained, whereas, with 1, the red color will be obtained.

But if we introduce, for example, a *Noise Texture*(by means of the Fac *socket*) as balancing factor between the two colors, a quite different outcome will be achieved.

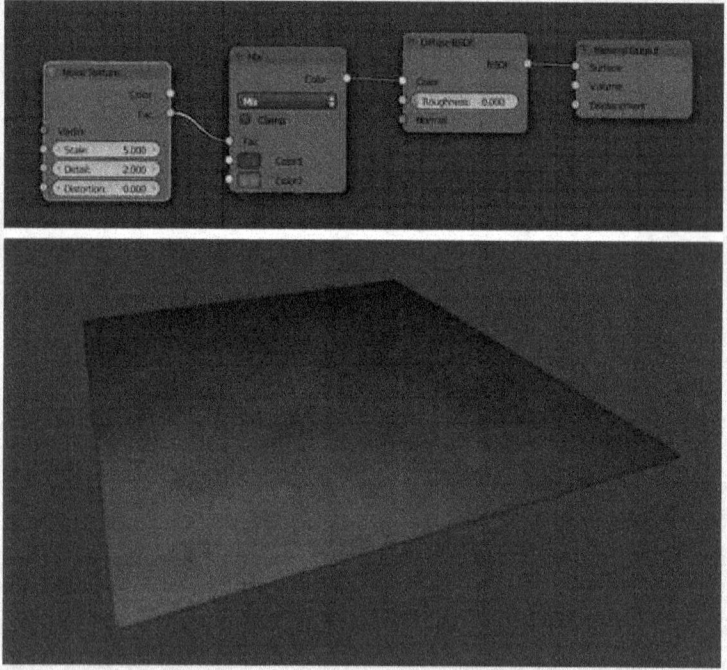

fig. 274 *mix* between two colors with a *Noise* Texture set as balancing factor

In the clearer areas of the *Noise Texture*, the dominating color will be blue (*Color 1*), whereas in the darker areas the red.

This node can be a useful and powerful tool for creating complex materials, in which different *textures* (or colors), mixed or overlapped, play a fundamental role for the realism.

RGB CURVES

This node is useful for graphically modifying a color or the tone of the *texture* by acting on the curves on the composite channel (C) or on the curves of the three RGB channels (red, green and blue).

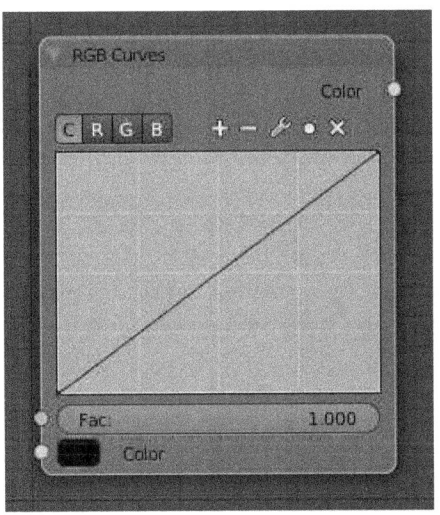

fig. 275 the *RGB Curves* node

You can act directly on the curve by clicking in the proper graphical space with the LMB. For each *click*, a new control point for the curve will be added.

Next to the colors, some buttons are present: + and – are used for regulating the zoom of the curve for a more fine control. The button with the monkey wrench icon (Tools) and that with the white ball icon (*Clipping Options*) add some functionalities to the point control. The X key cancels the selected control point.

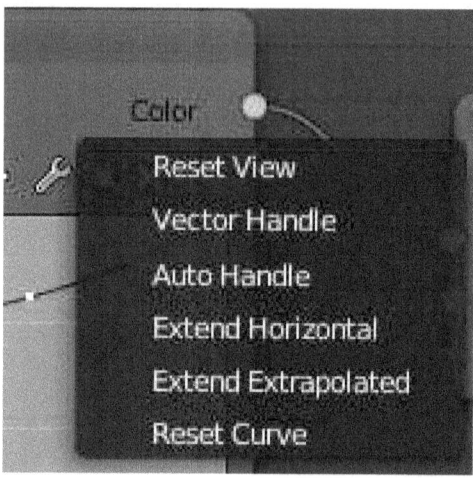

Fac determines the balancing value between the original color (or colors) and the one modified by the curves (element which can be defined also by external nodes connected to the gray *socket*).

The palette on the bottom defines the base color to be corrected or, if connected to the yellow socket, one or more external nodes at color complex definition, like for example a *texture*.

The *Color* output *socket* is usually connected to a *Diffuse*, but also to other nodes, like *Bump*, *Displacement*, or more complex configurations of nodes.

EXERCISE N. 6: CORRECTION OF A TEXTURE COLOR

Imagine you want to modify the color of a *texture*, connected to the *Diffuse* of a material.

Insert the *RGB Curves* node between the *Image Texture* node, containing the *texture* file, and the *Diffuse*, connected to the *Material Output* node.

 You can also drag the icon of the file directly on the *Node Editor* (such as into the *UV/Image Editor*). Immediately a *Texture* node with the file will be created.

By adding control points to the curve of the different channels, the *texture* color will change, obtaining the desired result.

fig. 277 the *texture* imported in the *Image texture* node

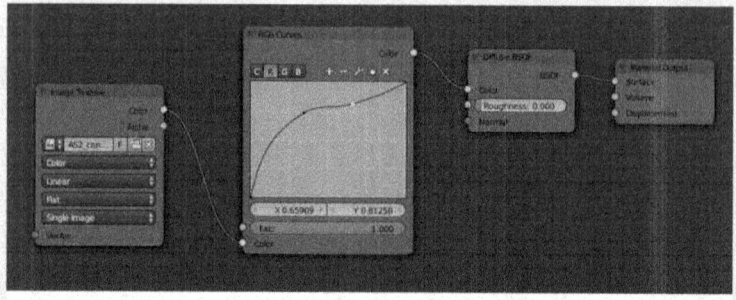

fig. 278 the *texture* modified by *RGB Curves* and rendered on the *mesh*

Invert inverts a color chosen in the palette (or the color or the *texture* connected to it by means of the yellow *socket*), according to the balancing factor *Fac*.

The gray *socket* on the left hand side of *Fac* can connect a node configuration acting as non-numeric factor.

The output *socket* is of *Color* type (yellow).

254

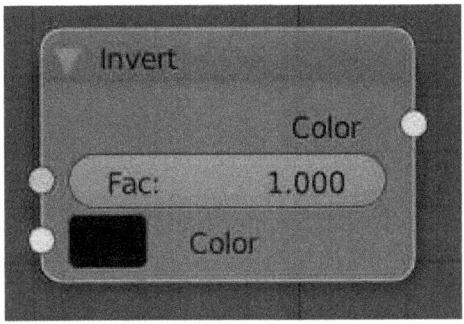

fig. 279 the *Invert* node

This node defines the way the light intensity decreases as a function of the distance.

3 preset typologies are available in output.

- *Quadratic*, reducing the quadratic light. This option does not modify the intensity if the *Smooth* parameters are set to 0;

- *Linear*, reducing the linear light, yielding a slower intensity decrease depending on the distance;

- *Constant*, reducing the intensity of the constant light.

Note that the use of *Linear* or *Constant* may favor more light to be introduced with each global illumination bounce, making the extremely radiant resulting image, especially if they were set many bounces.

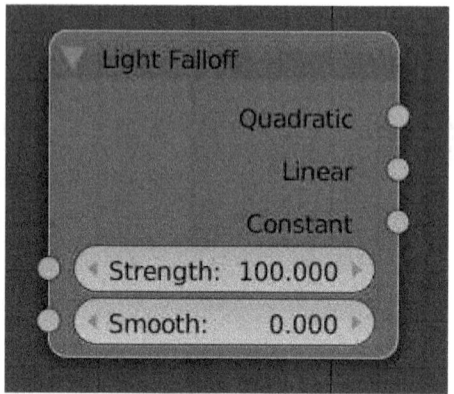

fig. 280 the *Light Falloff* node

Other parameters are:

- *Strength* Input: light strength before the damping is applied;

- *Smooth Input*: light intensity close to other luminous sources. It can avoid hard reflections, and reduce the global illumination noise. 0.0 corresponds to no damping; for higher values a larger damping will be achieved.

Obviously, it is possible to define these parameters by making use of external nodes connected to the gray sockets at the node input.

HUE/SATURATION

Hue/Saturation Value is a color regulation node alternative to a *RGB Curves*.

As an alternative to the decomposition according to the three *RGB* channels, in fact, a color can be thought as a mix between different tones, i.e. normalized values along the visible spectrum

256

between the infrared and the ultraviolet rays. The amount of added color depends on the saturation of that color: the larger the saturation, the more pigmentation will be added.

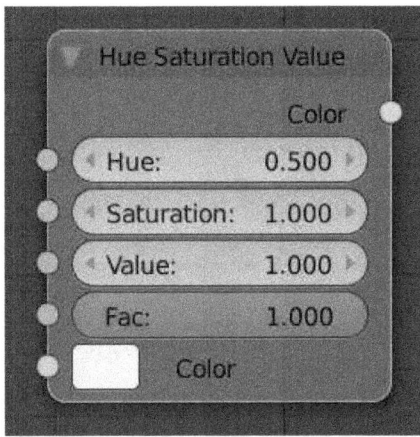

fig. 281 the *HUE/Saturation* node

This node acts on a color (palette or an input image)on which the tone parameters (*Hue*), the saturation parameters (Saturation) and the overall effect (*Value*), can be regulated, defined by the cursors with values between 0 and 1.

Fac determines how much this node affects the image or the original color. A factor 0 implies that the image or the input color is not affected by the settings, whereas a factor 1 totally shift the mixing toward the effect.

The 4 parameters may be defined by external nodes connected to the grey input numerical sockets, likewise the color (yellow *socket*) by a *texture*, for example.

The output yellow *socket* supplies a modified color, which can be connected, for example, to a Shader-type node.

The **Gamma** node acts as a multiplier of the input color and increases the intensity for the values defined by the *Gamma* cursor (between 0 and 1, where 0 yields the original color whereas 1 the modified color).

The input color can be defined through the *Color* palette or externally imported through the yellow *socket*, likewise the *Gamma* value can be defined by a node system of mathematical type determining a fixed or variable value.

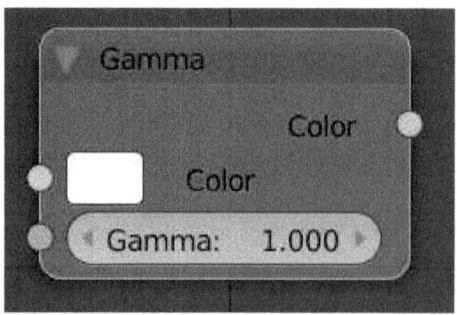

fig. 282 the *Gamma* node

The **Bright/Contrast** node allows you to modify an input color or texture (yellow *socket*) by acting on the brightness (*Bright* cursor) and on the contrast (*Contrast*). The cursors allow you to insert a value between 0 (minimum) and 1 (maximum), or, through the gray sockets, or values defined by external nodes.

The *Color* output supplies the modified color.

258

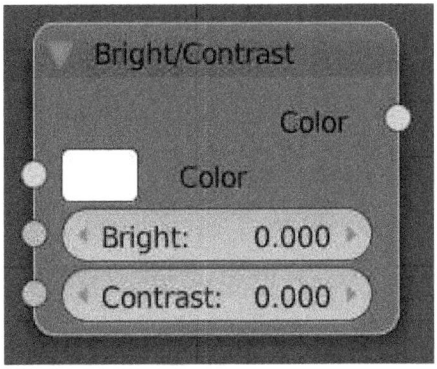

fig. 283 the *Bright/Contrast* node

D) *INPUT* NODES

These nodes define a parameter, a command or an initial value to be inserted at the beginning of a certain node chain.

These nodes supply, as to say, a starting pulse to the node they are connected to.

These node types define, for example, the coordinate system on which to base a mapping, a color, the index of refraction (*IOR*), the light path etc.

15 *Input* nodes are available: *Texture Coordinate; Attribute; Light Path; Fresnel; Layer Weight; RGB; Value; Tangent; Geometry; Wireframe; Object Info; Hair Info; Particle info; Camera Data* and *UV Map*.

Let us analyze them in detail.

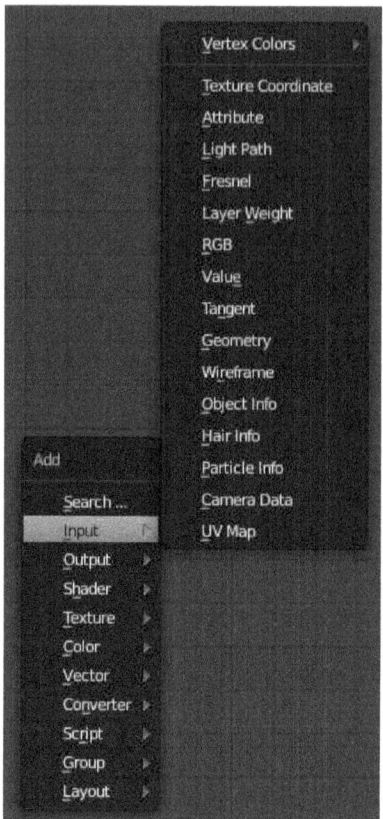

fig. 284 *Input* group nodes

TEXTURE COORDINATE

This node directs the coordinates of a *texture* along some predefined paths.

This node is usually connected by means of one of the output *sockets* to vectorial-type nodes (*Vector*).

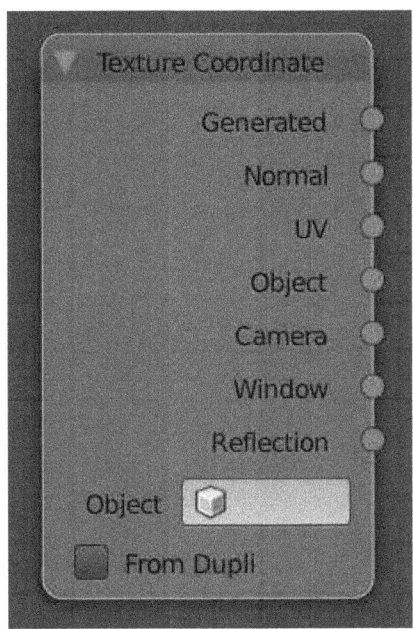

fig. 285 the *Texture Coordinate* node

- *Generated* automatically generates the texture coordinates without deformations starting from the vertex position, allowing them to keep always the same position during animations;

- *Normal* generates the texture coordinates keeping the normals to the mesh as fixed point;

- *UV*, perhaps the most used output channel, assigns as texture coordinates the *UV* defined in the *UV/Image Editor*;

- *Object* allows you to upload an object chosen among those present in the scene and defined in the underlying field, and to generate the texture coordinates depending on the position of the object itself;

- *Camera* determines the coordinates according to the spatial position of the active camera;

- *Window* determines the coordinates depending on the view in the current window;

- *Reflection*, usually used in case of environmental maps, generates the texture coordinates along the reflection directions;

The flag *From Dupli* uses the object duplicate, if available.

Let us consider an example of use.

We learned how to modify the coordinates, the scaling and the rotation of a texture in the *UV/Image Editor.*

By directing the node flux with *Texture Coordinate*, connect the *UV* output to the *Vector* input of the *Mapping* node which can be found between the nodes of the *Vector* group and that we will see in the foregoing. For now let's limit ourselves to insert it in the *Node Editor.*

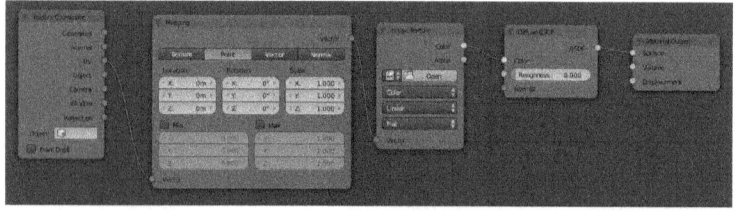

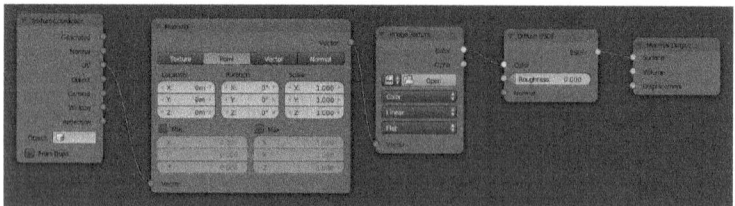

fig. 286 use of the *Texture Coordinate* node

262

This node chain represents the action executed by hands in the *UV/Image Editor*. We can read these nodes: *the material is determined by a texture, connected to the Diffuse (color), whose scaling, position and rotation are defined by the Mapping node, depending on the UV coordinates of the assigned texture file.*

ATTRIBUTE

Attribute restores the data (attribute) associated to the object or to the mesh. Presently *UV* maps and colors can be restored in this way correctly inserting their names in the *Name* text box.

A practical use of this node will be presented in the foregoing when we will learn how to generate fire and smoke.

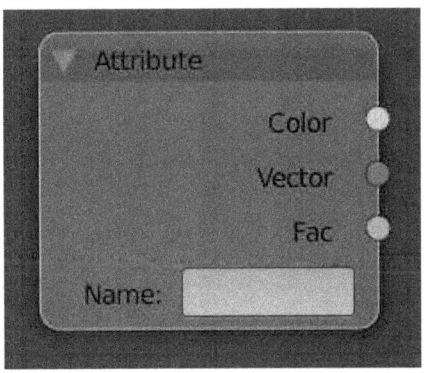

fig. 287 the *Attribute* node

LIGHT PATH

This node allows you to determine the light ray type, which can affect the *shader* of an active material.

263

One or more options among those available can be assigned to the light path (*Is Camera Ray, Is Shadow Ray, Is Diffuse Ray, Is Glossy Ray, Is Singular Ray, Is Reflection Ray, Is Transmission Ray, Ray Length, Ray Depth, Transparent Depth*) and can be eventually added together by means of one or more *Math* nodes.

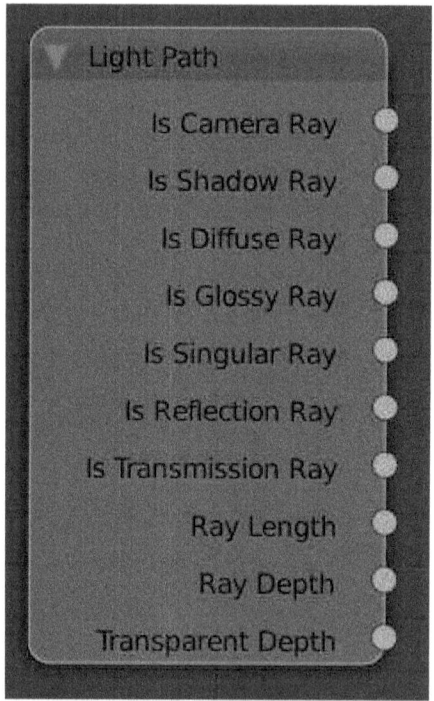

fig. 288 the *Light Path* node

The node operation, in practice, defines which component of the luminous rays must influence the shader it is connected to.

While describing the *shader Glass* node we anticipated that, though faithful enough concerning the glass simulation, it could not be suitable for correctly reproducing certain light paths, for example the glass behavior under shadow and reflection conditions, implying light paths that, added together, will make the glass less or more transparent.

 EXERCISE n. 7: A GLASS SHEET

Create a plane and give it a thickness with the *Solidify* modifier (remember that each object has a thickness and in particular the glass, to be able to suitably respond to the refraction effect, must have a thickness).

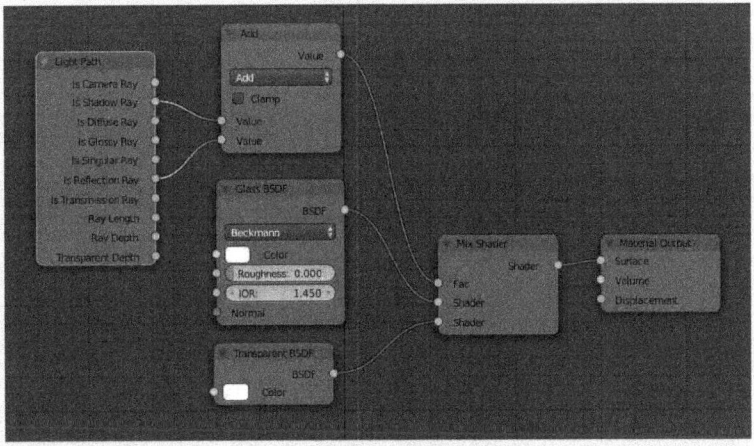

fig. 289 The glass material by using the *Light Path* node

Select the mesh, previously lighted and placed in a "room", and create a new material, substituting *Diffuse* with *Mix Shader* and connect to its input a *Glass* and a *Transparent* node.

Add a *Math* node from the *Converter* group, set it as *Mix* and connect it to the *socket Fac* of the *Mix Shader*, such as it acts as balancing factor between the *Glass* and the *Transparent* shader.

Connect the two output sockets *Is Shadow ray* and *is Reflection Ray* of the *Light Path* node to the two values *Value* of the *math* node.

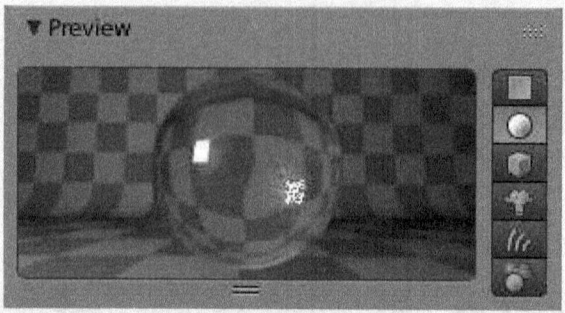

fig. 290 the material in the *Preview* panel

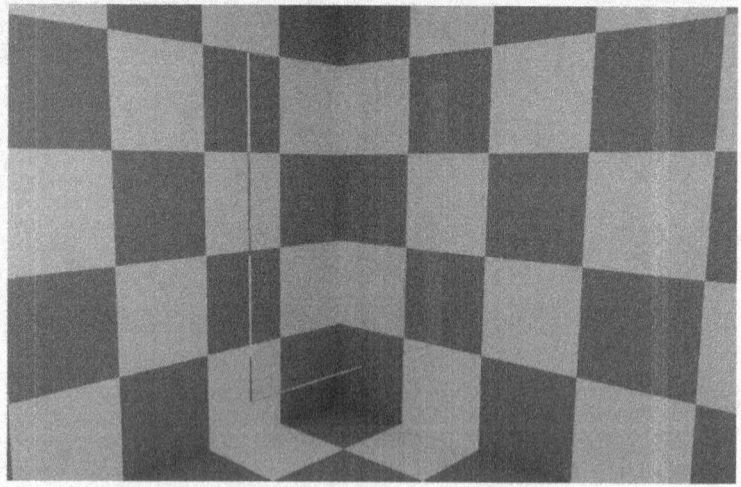

fig. 291 the glass *rendering*

This node configuration will simulate the correct glass behavior, which under certain shadow and reflection conditions will be more transparent and less subjected to the index of refraction proper of the *Glass* node.

266

It is recommended to save into a folder the node configuration reproducing the glass material.

FRESNEL

The **Fresnel** node is very important and must be used almost for all the materials requiring a balancing between a color (*Diffuse*) and a reflection (*Glossy*).

In the real world, the reflection depends on the light incidence.

For very small incidence angles the object will appear essentially white, almost totally reflecting, as a mirror, whereas for incidence angles almost equal to 90° the reflection will be very low.

Each material reflects depending on its specific index of refraction (*IOR*) represented by the *Fresnel* node.

Think for example to the "wet street" effect in perspective or to the desert mirage.

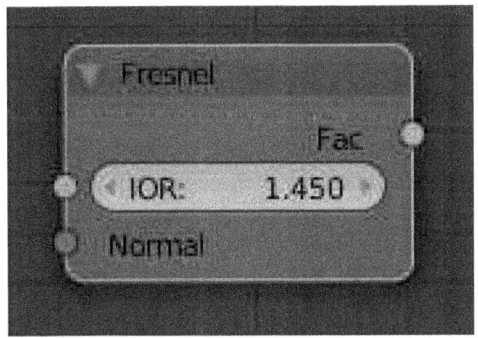

fig. 292 the *Fresnel* node

In order to clarify its operation we will show a practical example.

EXERCISE n. 8: A LACQUERED GLOSSY PANEL

If you have the possibility, go to see from close how one of your glossy lacquered shutters of your kitchen or of the book shelf in the living room is made.

It is a panel first painted and then brushed by hand, 19 mm thick and with variable dimensions.

Insert a cube in the scene and rescale it in such a way its dimensions are:

$$x = 60 \text{ cm}; \quad y = 1.9 \text{ cm}; \quad z = 72 \text{ cm}.$$

Reset the scale with CTRL + A.

Add a *Bevel* modifier with a 3 mm radius and 3 segments to the *mesh* such as to create a light and rounded grinding as in the reality.

Apply a material and insert the main nodes, such as it is determined by the balancing (*Mix Shader*) between a color (*Diffuse*) and a reflection (*Glossy*). We can color the *Diffuse* with red, for example.

Add a *Fresnel* node (set as *IOR* 1.450).

Launch the *rendering*: the shutter will correctly reflect the light and the objects depending on the light incidence.

By the way if you look to the shutter from the real you will notice that, having been brushed and polished by hand, it will reveal some small imperfections. It will appear, looking at it backlight, lightly rounded.

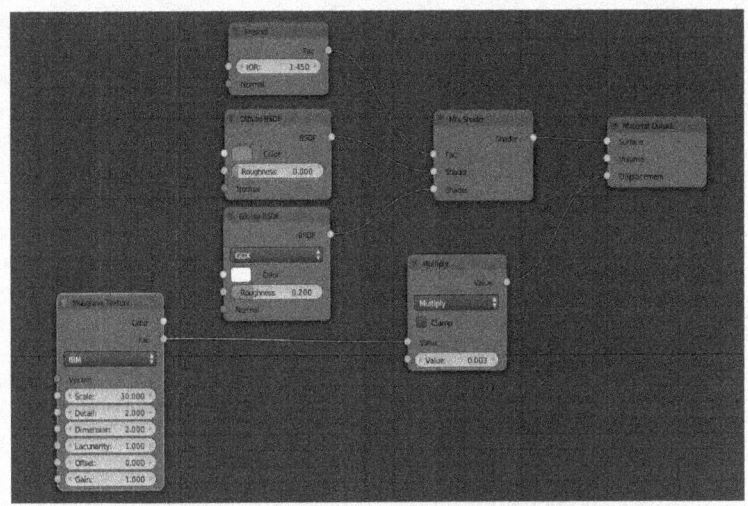

fig. 293 node configuration defining the material "lacquered glossy"

fig. 294 *rendering* of the lacquered glossy shutter

In order to reproduce this effect, add a *Noise Texture* node, scale it at 30 units, and connect the *Fac* output *socket* to the top input *socket Value* of a *Converter Math* node, set on *Multiply*. Assign 0.03 to the second node value. This will multiply the values belonging to the texture by the constant value 0.03 (i.e. 3%). Connect the *Math* output to the *Displacement* input *socket* of the *Material Output*.

Launch again the rendering. The outcome will be definitely improved.

LAYER WEIGHT

This node, quite similar to the *Fresnel* one, is usually associated to the *shader* and is used to associate to those a specific *layer*.

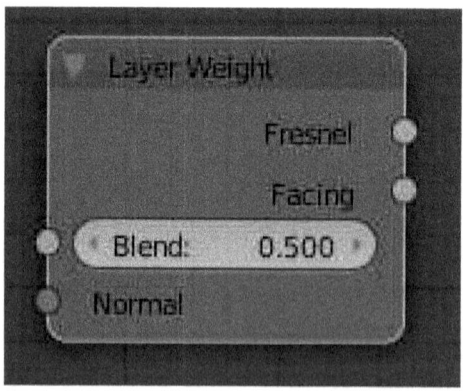

fig. 295 the *Layer Weight* node

It has the only parameter *Blend* used to mix, depending on a parameter (between 0 and 1) two *shaders*. This value can be assigned by taking it from an external node configuration connected to the gray socket.

The *Fresnel* output socket is useful, for example, to create a plastic material obtained from the two shaders *Diffuse* and *Glossy*.

The *Facing* output socket determines the balancing between the two *shaders* to which it acts as factor with respect to the current view and as a function of the oblique angle.

RGB

The **RGB** node is a simple palette in which to define a color and to direct it, by means of the output *socket Color*, to a *shader* or to a color managing node (*Color* group) or mathematical (*Converter*), like for example *Mix RGB* or *RGB to BW*.

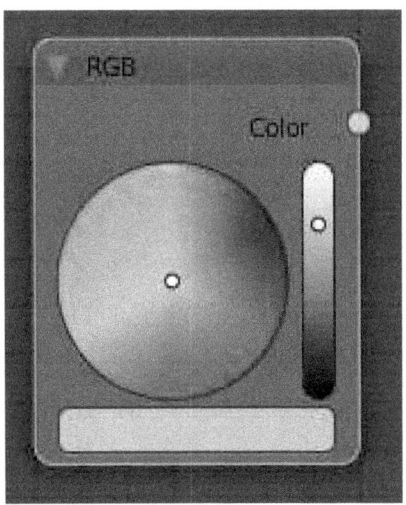

fig. 296 the *RGB* node

271

Value is a node used only for assigning a value (*Value*) to be connected by mean of the output socket *Value* to any other node requiring the insertion of a certain value (*Bump, Math...*).

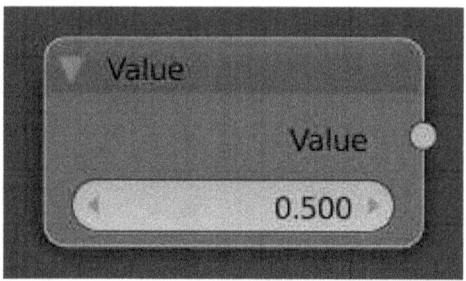

fig. 297 the *Value* node

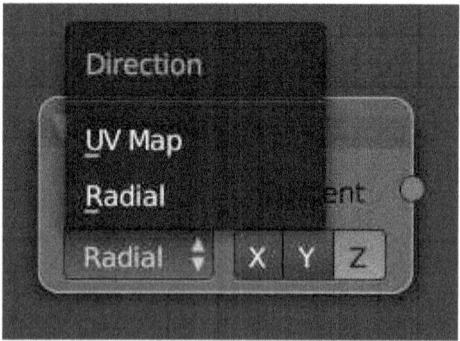

fig. 298 the *Tangent* node

Tangent, usually associated to the *shader Anisotropic* node, generates a tangent in correspondence of the surface along the direction defined by the menu *Direction* menu (*UV Map* or

Radial) and according to the reference axis chosen among *X*, *Y* and *Z*.

The *Tangent* output is of vectorial type since it indicates a direction.

Geometry yields geometrical information on the current *shading* point. All the vectorial coordinates are in *World Space*.

Several outputs are available depending on the information.

- *Position* gives information concerning the position of the shading point;

- *Normal* gives information on the *shading* normal to the surface (included the normals on smooth surfaces and *bumps*);

- *Tangent* gives information concerning the surface tangent;

- *True Normal* gives information concerning the flat surface;

- *Incoming* gives information concerning the vector directed toward the *shading* point from which the object is viewed;

- *Parametric* gives information concerning the parametric coordinates of the shading point on the surface.

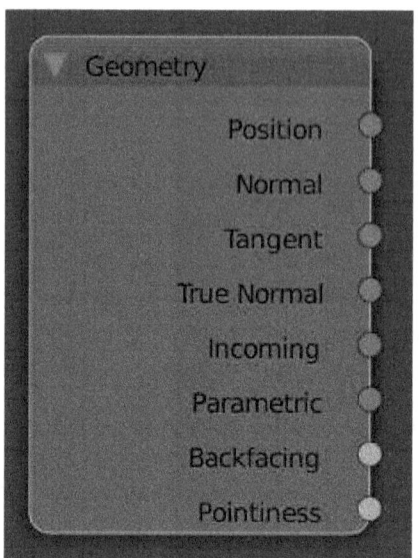

fig. 299 the *Geometry* node

- *Backfacing*, if connected to a *shader*, gives information regarding the faces directed from the opposite side of the view point;

- *Pointiness* yields an approximation of the mesh curvature. Lighter values indicate convex angles, darker values indicates concave angles.

These latter two are related to output *sockets* of mathematical type instead of vectorial type, like for the others.

WIREFRAME

This node is useful to be associated to a *shader* for a visualization, during the rendering, of the edges (for now only for the triangulate geometry).

274

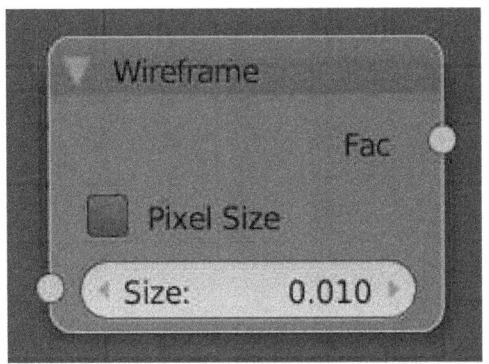

fig. 299 the *Wireframe* node

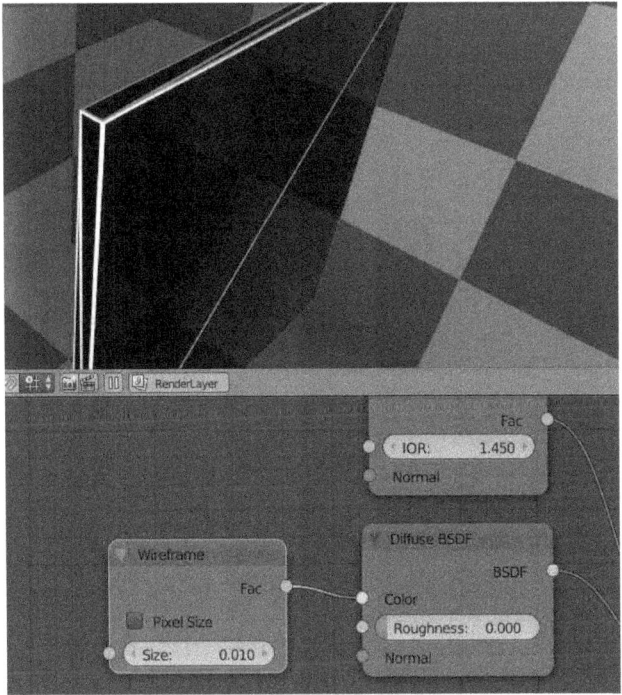

fig. 301 the *Wireframe* node connected to the *Color* of the *Diffuse* shows the rendered solid edges

275

By checking *Pixel Size* the screen pixel is used as unit.

Size defines the wireframe thickness.

The node has an output of numeric type *Fac*.

Object Info gives information concerning an object linked duplicate (ALT + D).

This node can be useful for yielding some variation of a single material assigned to many linked duplicates, through the object index (*Object Index*) or of a material (*Material Index*), based on the location (*Location*) or randomly (*Random*).

For example, the same *Noise* Texture can yield random colors is associated to different indices.

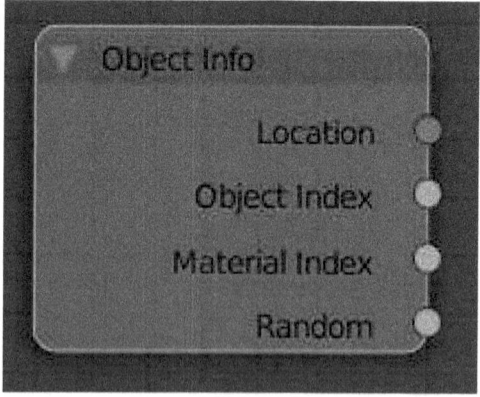

fig. 302 the *Object Info* node

276

These two nodes yield information on the particle system and for now they will not be discussed.

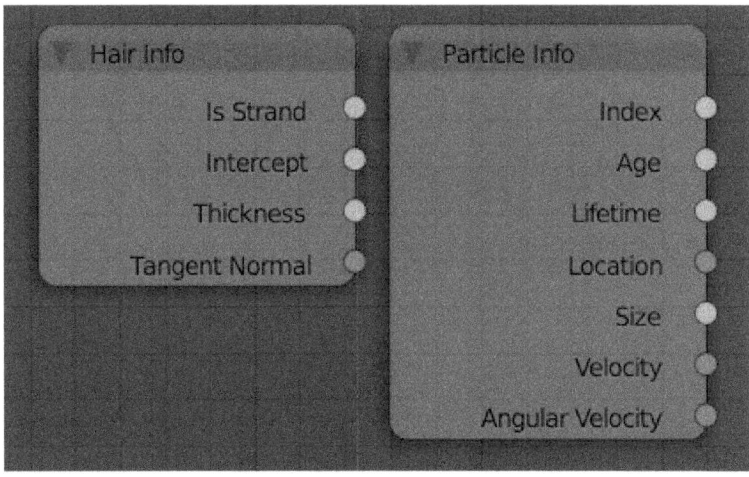

fig. 303 the *Hair Info* and *Particle Info* nodes

CAMERA DATA

Camera Info gives information on the active camera it is associated to, in particular:

- the camera vectorial space from view point;

- the depth of the normal to the framing (Z);

- the distance between the camera and the connected shading point.

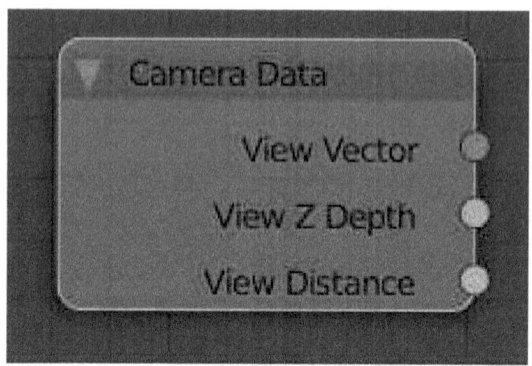

fig. 304 the *Camera Data* node

UV MAP

This last node of the *Input* group yield vectorial-type information on a map depending on the *UV* coordinates.

The available coordinate type (*UV*) can be inserted in the box.

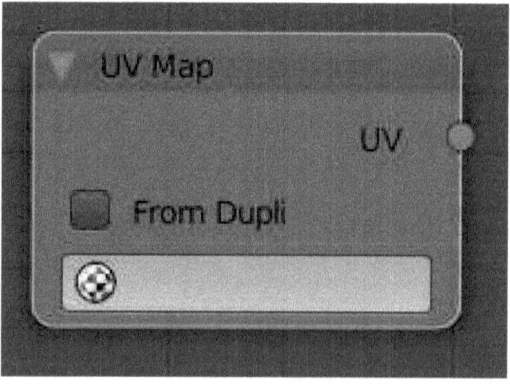

fig. 305 the *UV Map* node

278

E) *VECTOR* NODES

The nodes belonging to this group are used to direct the vectorial-type information connected to them.

Vectorial is referred to all what concerns position, direction, scaling and rotation.

They are used, for example, for determining a texture mapping on a mesh or for yielding information regarding a surface relief.

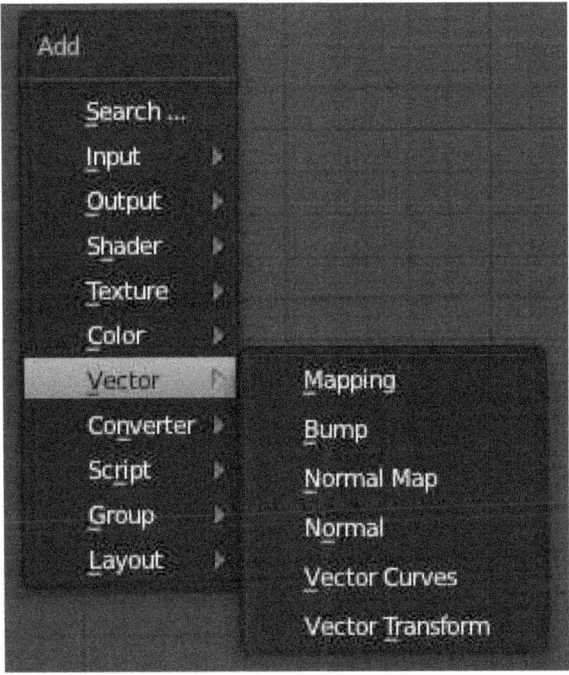

fig. 306 the nodes of the *Vector* group

6 vectorial-type nodes are available.

It is the most important vectorial node.

It contains all the information and parameters relevant to a texture mapping.

This node is usually connected to an input vectorial-type *socket* (indigo color) of a *texture*, such as to define its position, rotation and scaling along the three reference axes.

This node, however, requires an upstream further information, i.e. which reference coordinates must be taken into account. This means that a connection flux with a *Texture Coordinate* output must be connected to the input socket, usually of *UV* type.

This operation corresponds to the transformations, which are manually executed with the *textures* and the unwrapped *meshes* inside the *UV/Image Editor*.

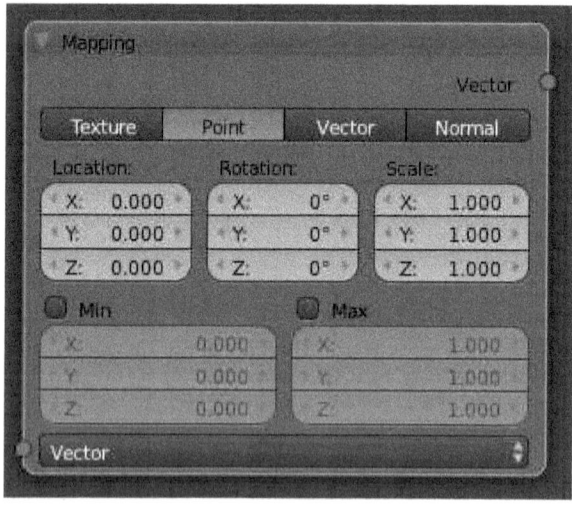

fig. 307 the *Mapping* node

The mapping transformation occurs along the *x*, *y* and *z* coordinates of the *texture* position with respect to the *mesh* (*Location*), of the rotation around the axes (*Rotation*) and on the scaling along the axes (*Scale*).

The **Mapping** node will transform the position, rotation and displacement according to the method described by the four switches on the top:

- *Texture*: *texture* transformation;

- *Point*: point transformation;

- *Vector*: vectorial direction transformation;

- *Normal*: transformation of a vector normal to a surface.

The flags *Min* and *Max* enforce a clipping, i.e. an interruption, of the mapping starting from the values defined in the underlying counters *X*, *Y* and *Z*.

 EXERCISE n. 9: A CONCRETE CUBE

Try to create a material simulating the concrete and apply it to the default cube, which you have previously unwrapped (*Unwrap*, U key).

Illuminate the scene with a *Lamp Sun* and assign a new material to the cube.

As usual a *Diffuse* and a *Glossy* color will have to be mixed (*Mix Shader*, balanced depending on the index of refraction (*IOR*).

Apply a color texture (*Image Texture*) to the *Diffuse*. Copy the *Image Texture* node and set it as *Non-Color Data*. Add a *Bump* node (see in the foregoing), which can be found among the

281

Vector node group and connect the *Color* output *socket* of the *Image Texture* in black and white (*Non-Color Data*) to the input *socket Height*.

Connect the Bump vectorial output socket to both the Vector input sockets of the *Diffuse* and the *Glossy*.

In doing so the relief effect (*Bump*) will act both on the color and the reflection.

Add a *Texture Coordinate* node and connect the UV output socket to a Mapping node, set as *Texture*, whose *Vector* output must be connected to the Vector input *sockets* of the two *Image Texture* nodes.

If the *textures* are equal, or anyway one is derived from the other one (*Image Texture* and *Bump Texture*, for example) it is recommended to check that the scaling, the positioning and the rotation occur on both the textures at the same time and in the same way.

This is why the *mapping* output is connected with two flux lines to both the nodes.

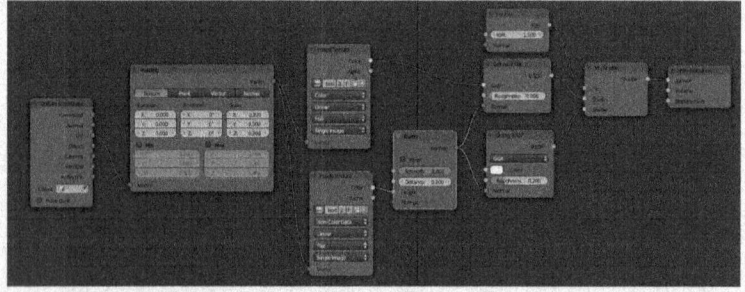

fig. 308 node configuration defining the "rough concrete" material

We can fine regulate the Mapping *Location*, *Rotation* and *Scale* values for regulating, respectively, the position, the rotation and the scaling of the textures related to it.

The rendering outcome is very realistic.

fig. 309 concrete cube *rendering*

BUMP

This node directs the vectorial information relevant to a mesh relief effect, usually influenced by the black and white chromatic range of a dedicated texture.

As we have many times repeated and anticipated, the gray scale *textures* are used by Blender to collect numerical information to be assigned to a certain function, for example the balancing between two nodes and the quote itself of the vertices.

In the case of the *Bump* simulating the relief effect on a surface, for tones close to white, in that area a surface relief will be assigned, whereas, for darker tones, a depression effect.

Bump simulates the relief, perfectly reacting to the incident light and the reflections, but technically does not move the vertices.

If we would like, for example, to simulate the relief of the wood veins, we need a color *texture* to be connected to the Color *socket* of the *Diffuse* node and a Bump *texture* (or *Disp*), perfectly coinciding with the previous one, in gray scale, to be assigned as height factor (*socket Height*) to the *Bump* node.

> **NOTE:** The *Bump* texture it is not the black and white version of any color *texture*. In fact, not necessarily the gray tones arising from the original texture color encoding return in the various pixels the exact gray tone and, consequently, the relief quote.

Let us make an example to better clarify this concept.

 EXERCISE n. 10: TEXTURE BUMP

fig. 310 *texture_diffuse* of a plank

Try to render a wooden plank.

The *texture* here depicted reproduces the veins of a wooden plank.

Now make a copy and convert the file in black and white.

The same image in gray tones will be achieved.

fig. 311 *texture_bn* of a plank converted in black and white

If we used this *texture* as a *Bump* factor, for sure we would get an relief effect, but not necessarily in correspondence of the correct areas.

Think for example to those very dark modern parquets, whose veins, treated and brushed, result clearer than the base color. By converting in black and white the *texture* of such a wood we would get even an opposite relief effect, with veins and grout spacing in relief (clearer).

Insert a plane in the scene, previously lighted, execute the *unwrapping* in *Edit Mode* and assign a material to the *mesh*.

As usual add the nodes necessary for the base configuration of a material, by mixing *Diffuse* and *Glossy* and balancing the two shaders with a *Fresnel* node.

285

Assign the *texture_diffuse* (in colors) to the *Diffuse* and the *texture_bn* (converted in black and white) to the *Height* socket of the *Bump*.

Finally, connect the *Normal* output socket of the *Bump* node to both the *Normal* input sockets of the *Diffuse* and the *Glossy*.

This should be the rendering outcome.

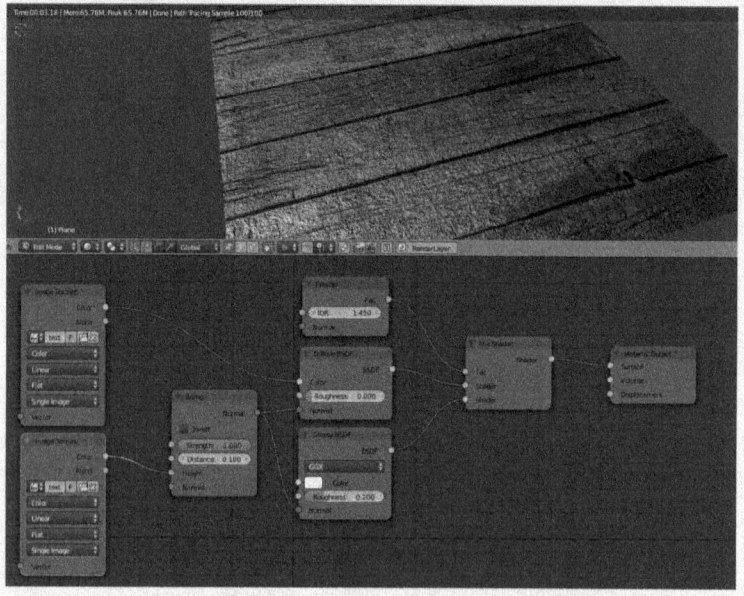

fig. 312 node configuration and *rendering* with the black and white *texture* as relief factor

The effect is not very bad, but too large and not desirable reliefs of the material can be noted.

In the black and white *texture* there are dark areas belonging to the original color and not corresponding to areas where a depression should appear.

fig. 313 *texture*_bump of a plank

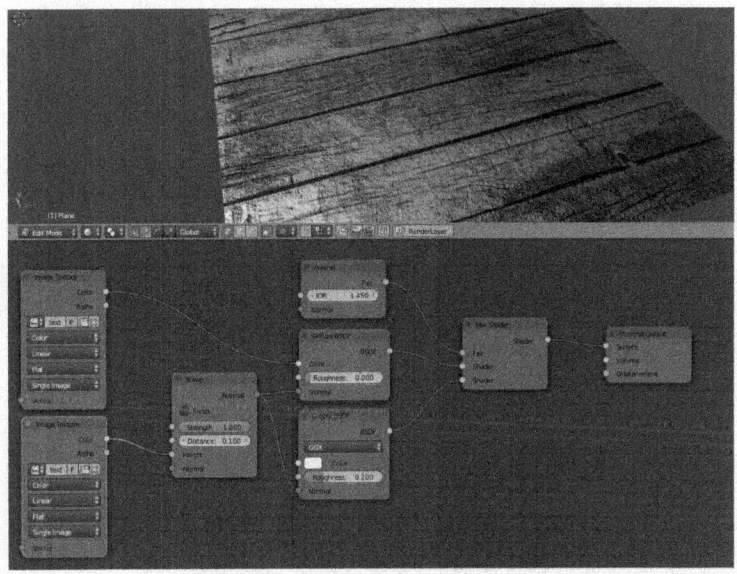

fig. 314 node configuration and *rendering* with the *Bump* texture as relief factor

287

Two solutions can be found to the problem:

1) using professional *texture* packages, in which the corresponding *texture Bumps* (named also *Disp*) are included, already regulated and corrected;

2) modifying with a photo editing *software* the black and white *textures*, modifying the contrast and luminosity and by eliminating too dark areas not corresponding to zones in depression.

This is the *Bump* texture adapted to the original *texture*.

Thus using this *texture_bump* in place of the black and white version, the relief effect will be much more accurate and realistic.

Let us then start the description of the *Bump* node.

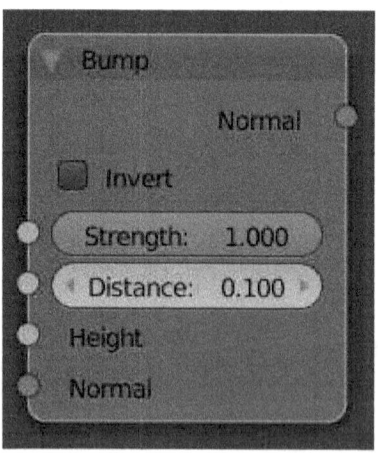

fig. 315 the *Bump* node

Bump has 4 parameters, two of which numerically settable or by means of external nodes (*Strength* defining the strength and *Distance* setting a further fine regulation of the relief strength as

288

a function of the distance from the observer) and parameters which can be managed only by external nodes (*Height* on which to set a value or a *texture* regulating the behavior of the relief height and *Normal* on which a vectorial node can be connected).

The flag *Invert* allows you to invert the colors of the applied *texture*.

The *Normal* output socket is used to connect the *Bump* node to one or more vectorial input nodes, usually *shader* nodes, such as *Diffuse* and *Glossy*.

NORMAL MAP

Differently from the *Bump Maps*, the *Normal Maps* are images storing a direction, that of the mesh normals and directly represented by the image RGB values. These *textures*, always used for generating a relief effect, are much more precise than the *Bump Maps*.

One of the methods for generating a *Normal Map* is the *baking*, i.e. a rendered image freezing. This topic will be analyzed at the chapter end.

These maps appear with a soft coloring ranging from blue to violet.

Many software are available on the market and in internet (*Crazy Bump*, *PixPlant..*), converting original *textures* and exporting in the dedicated formats the variations *Bump*, *Displacement* (*Normal Map*) and, in some cases, also *Specular*, which we will see in the foregoing.

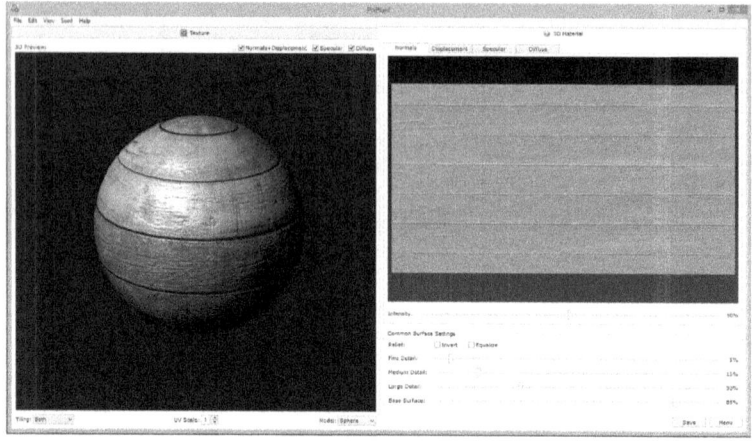

fig. 316 the *Pix Plant* software

Here is the *Normal Map* generated by the plank *texture*.

fig. 317 plank *normal map*

The procedure is almost identical to the previous one.

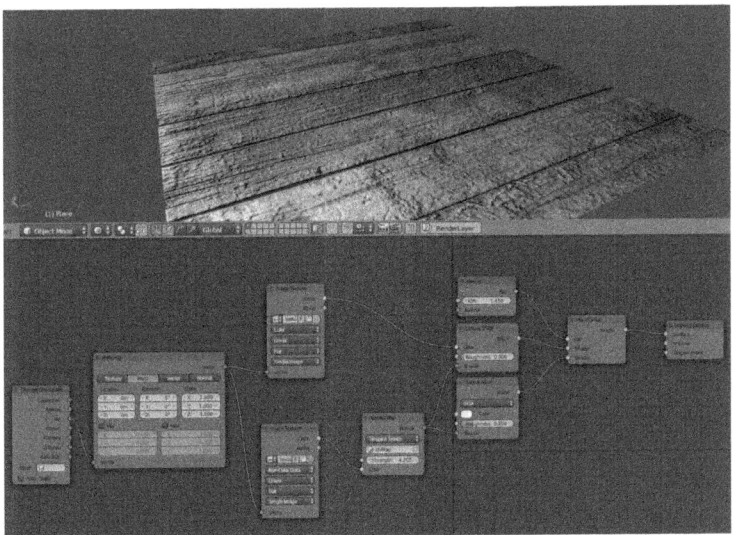

fig. 318 node configuration and *rendering* using the *Normal Map* as relief factor

Let us see which are the parameters and sockets of this node.

The *Space* menu defines depending on which vector the node must act.

- *Blender World Space*, depending on the scene global coordinates, compatible with the *Blender Render Baking*;

- *Blender Object Space*, depending on the object coordinates, compatible with the *Blender Render Baking*

- *World Space*, depending on the scene global coordinates;

- *Object Space*, depending on the object coordinates;

- *Tangent Space*, with reference to the tangency point.

291

fig. 319 the *Normal Map* node

UV Map states that the relief must occur depending on the texture *UV* coordinates.

Strength determines the strength and *Color* the color of the *Normal Map*, usually regulated by a suitable *Image Texture* node.

> **NOTE:** *Normal Map* must not be confused with the *Displacement* modifier which, as already seen, regulates the vertex height of a mesh it is assigned to, according to what has been defined by a *texture bump*.

292

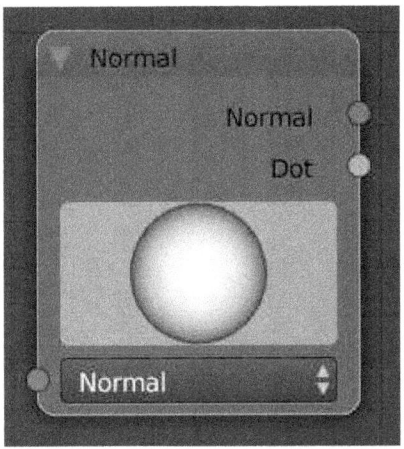

fig. 320 the *Normal* node

The **Normal** node generates a normal vector and a dot product. The normal direction can be defined by clicking and dragging on the sphere.

This node can be used for introducing a new normal vector in the node system. For example, this node can be used as input for a color node, through the image input socket.

VECTOR CURVES

This node work identically to *RGB Curves*, but refers to the graphical representation of a vectorial path, along the *x*, *y* and *z* directions.

The parameters are identical to *RGB Curve*.

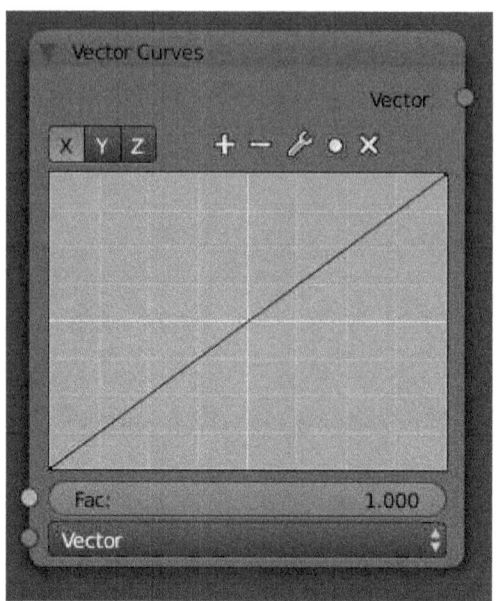

fig. 322 the *Vector Transform* node

VECTOR TRANSFORM

This node allows you the conversion of a vector, point or normal among the coordinates World - Camera - Object.

The *Type* switch specifies the input / output type: vector, point or normal.

The following two menus allow you to change the coordinates, respectively, from and to: *World*, *Object* and *Camera*.

The *Vector Input* menu defines the coordinates manually inserted or by means of an external node, whereas the *Vector* output socket returns the transformation to be connected to input vectorial sockets of other nodes.

294

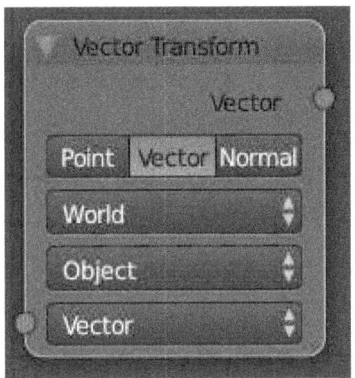

fig. 322 the *Vector Transform* node

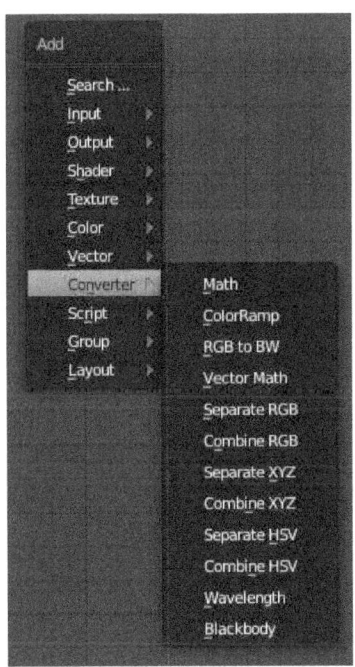

fig. 323 the *Converter* group nodes

295

F) *CONVERTER* NODES

These nodes of mathematical type process and convert the nodes they are connected to in numerical values, returning values determined by proper mathematical operations.

Let us analyze them in detail.

The **Math** description has been already reported. This node makes one of the expected operations between the values defined by the nodes connected to the *Value* inputs.

19 operations between the two inserted values are possible; the most used are *Add* (adding the values), *Subtract* (subtracting the values) and *Multiply* (multiplying the values).

The use of this node is thus much broad, being a mathematical node able to add, multiply, divide, raise, mix two sources, either numeric, texture or parametric.

The outcome of this operation will affect a material relief, such as for example the plank considered in the previous exercises.

Vector Math works in the same way, with the difference that the latter makes operation between vectorial nodes, such as for example adding two *Bump* nodes for getting two overlapped reliefs.

A classic example is given by the overlapping of the veins in relief of the scratched wood.

Vector Math executes less operation than the previous node, like for example the sum (*Add*), the subtraction (*Subtract*), the average (*Average*) etc. and allows you to export the vector generated by the operation (Vector socket) or a numerical value (*Value*).

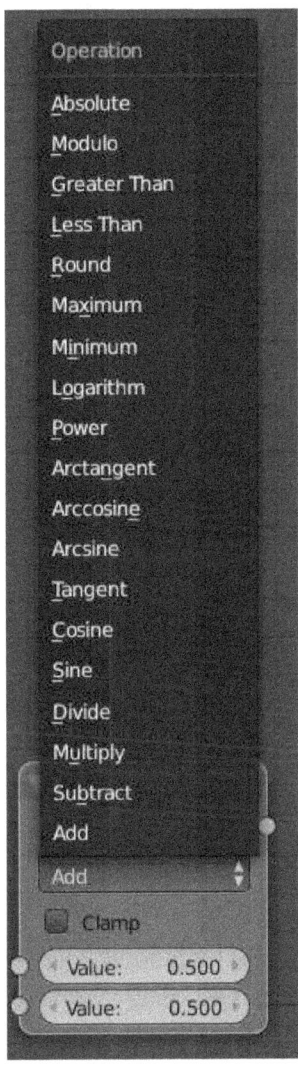

fig. 324 the *Math* node

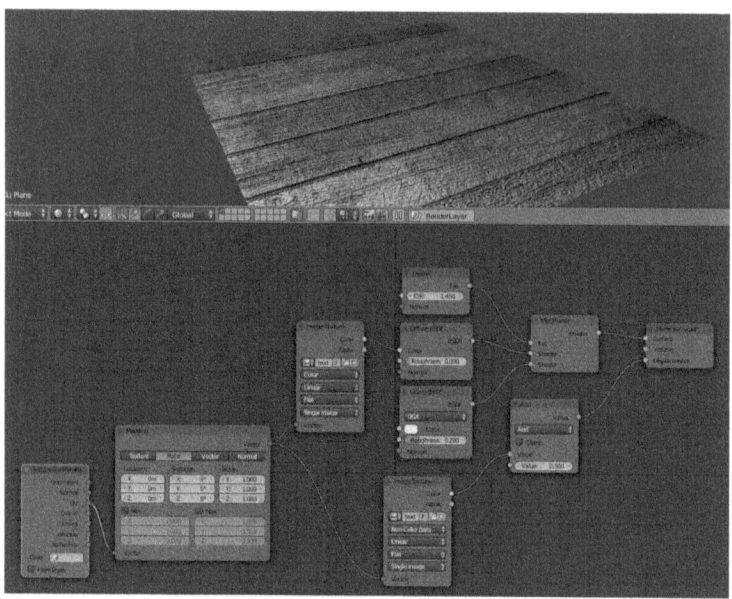

fig. 325 node configuration and *rendering* with the Math node used as multiplier of the *texture_bump* and connected to the *Displacement* socket of the *Material Output* node

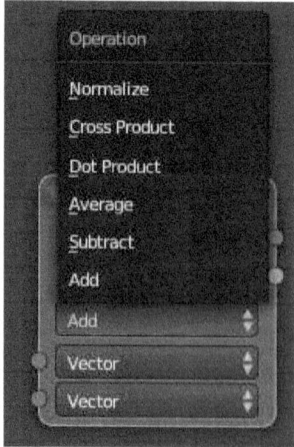

fig. 326 the *Vector Math* node

298

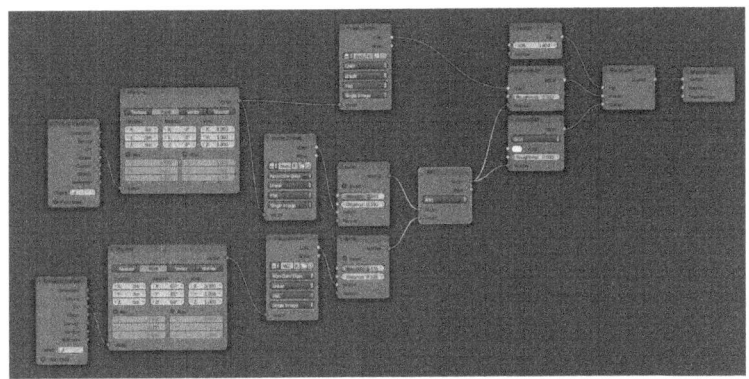

fig. 327 node configuration in which two *Image Textures* regulates two *Bumps* added with a *Vector Math* node set as *Add*

fig. 328 the veins in relief and the scratches of the wood are clearly visible in this image

In the previous image, this node configuration has been used to generate a wood veneer of a very thick *snack*.

Note the veins along a direction and the polishing and scratches along the opposite direction.

COLOR RAMP

The operation of this node is identical to that of the **ColorRamp** panel already seen in *Blender Render*.

This node allows you to modify the intensity, the color or other related parameters by acting on a ramp of two or more control points defining a color.

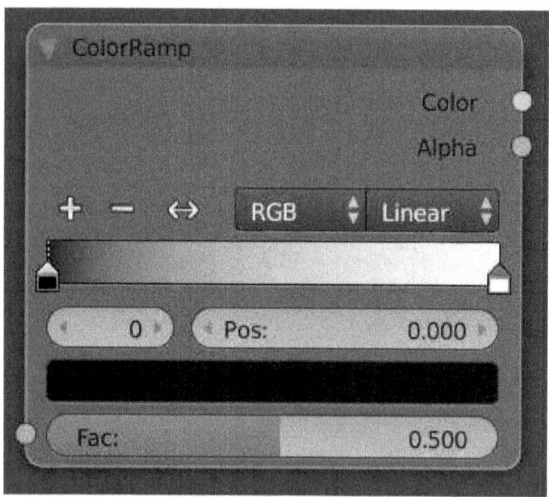

fig. 329 the *ColorRamp* node

By *default*, *ColorRamp* uses two control points of black and white color at the opposite side of the color spectrum. For modifying a color, select it on the underlying *color band*.

For adding or removing other color points, click + or -. A new inserted points can be placed in the *ColorRamp* dragging it with the LMB. The distance between two control points determines the transaction between the two colors.

Fac determines the balancing between the color or the original value (or the *texture*) inserted in the corresponding input *socket*.

An example of use of the *ColorRamp* on a *texture* is shown in the following figure. The *texture* appears colored according to the colors defined in the node.

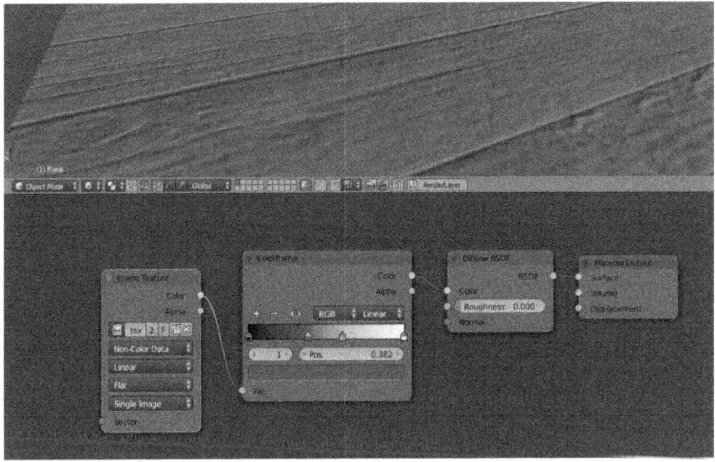

fig. 330 node configuration with the *ColorRamp* placed between an *Image Texture* and the *Diffuse shader*

RGB TO BW

This very simple node only converts in black and white a color image connected to its input socket.

301

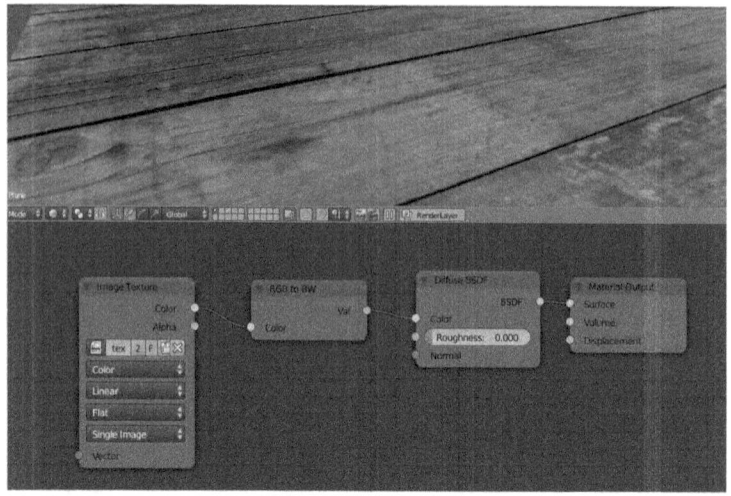

fig. 331 convert a *texture* in black and white with the *RGB TO BW* node

SEPARATE RGB and COMBINE RGB

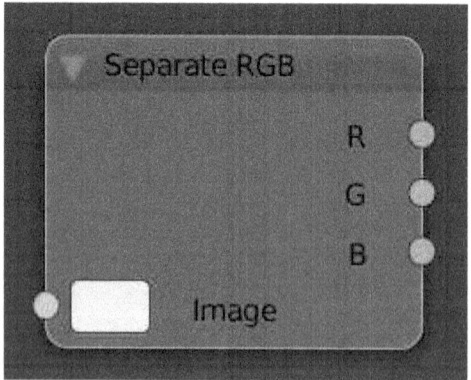

fig. 332 the *Separate RGB* node

302

Separate RGB divides the three *RGB* channels (red, green and blue) of an input source and allows the separate output of the three channels.

Combine RGB executes the opposite function, combining the three channels separated in input and yielding as output a single color channel.

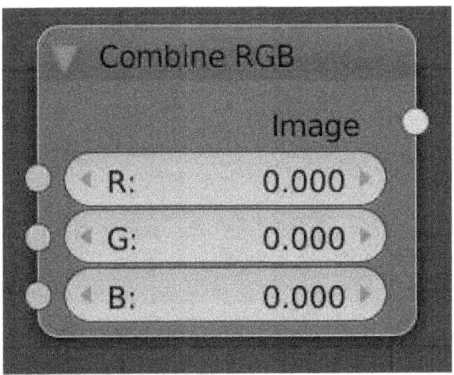

fig. 333 the *Combine RGB* node

SEPARATE HSV and COMBINE HSV

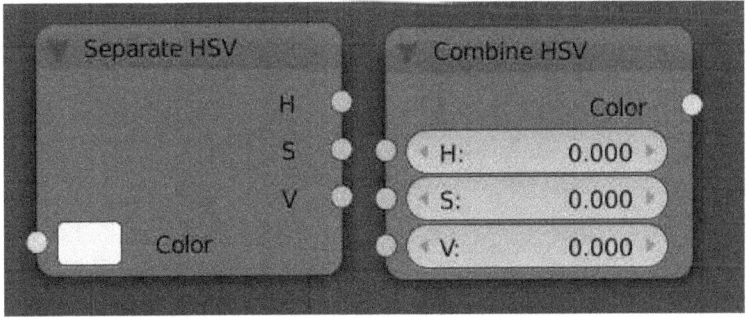

fig. 334 the *Separate HSV* and *Combine HSV* nodes

The nodes **Separate HSV** and **Combine HSV** operate in an identical way, separating or combining the *HSV* channels of a color.

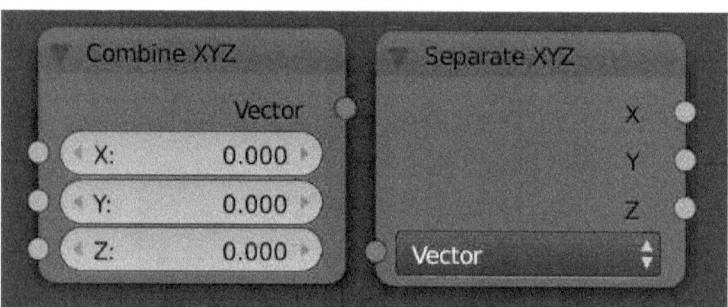

fig. 335 the *Separate XYZ* and *Combine XYZ* nodes

These two nodes separate and combine, respectively, the *x, y* and *z* coordinates of a vector connected to their input or output, respectively.

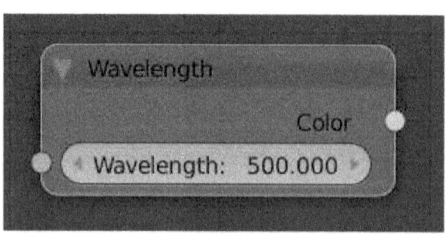

fig. 336 the *Wavelength* node

Wavelength converts a value expressed in nanometers into RGB coordinates, i.e. a color.

BLACKBODY

Useful if associated to a light source (Lamp), the **Blackbody** nodes converts a temperature expressed in *Kelvin* into a *RGB* color.

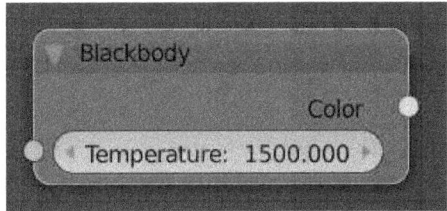

fig. 337 the *Blackbody* node

G) *SCRIPT* NODE

SCRIPT

This node allows to insert a *Script* in the *Node Editor*.

fig. 338 the *Script* node

These are not nodes but functions allowing you to group (CTRL + G) or ungroup (ALT + G), if already grouped, the nodes selected in the *Node Editor*.

The *Node Editor* will enter a new modality, with light green color, where the nodes not belonging to the group can be seen in translucence.

In the *Node Editor* normal modality, the node group appears included into a specific node *(Node Group)*.

The icon on the node top right part is used for expand it and entering inside the group to perform possible changes.

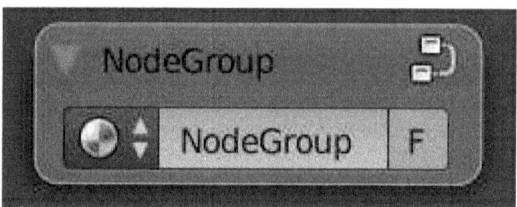

fig. 339 *Node Group*

This system is useful for reducing the dimensions of a complex and apparently confused, not easily readable, node configuration.

For opening and closing the *Node Group* press the key TAB.

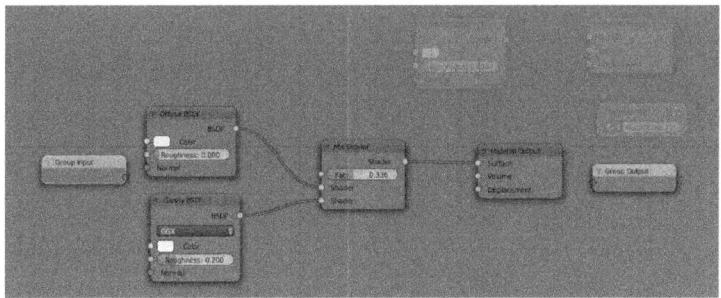

fig. 340 *Group* modality

H) LAYOUT

This node group is composed of two only elements: **Frame** and **Reroute**.

FRAME and REROUTE

Frame allows you to group and graphically organize some nodes inside a frame of the *Node* Editor.

Frame does not make any change in the node operation.

It is useful, for example, for grouping nodes of the same kind, or a node chain having a complex logical meaning.

First of all, it is needed to create a frame, inserting a *Frame* node.

Then, after having selected first the nodes and then the frame, press CTRL + P.

307

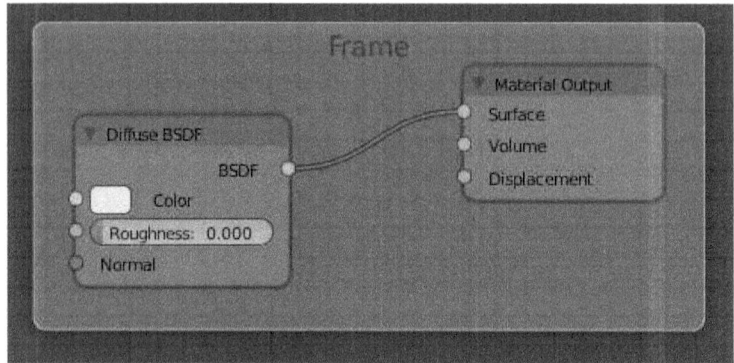

fig. 341 the *Frame* node

Automatically the nodes will be tied to the frame dimensions, which can be color or modified with the commands in the *Sidebar* panel at the right of the *Node Editor*.

fig. 342 renaming and coloring nodes and *frame*

For opening and closing the *Node Group* press the key TAB.

Reroute inserts a junction in the flux between two connected nodes, thus creating a path doubling toward another node.

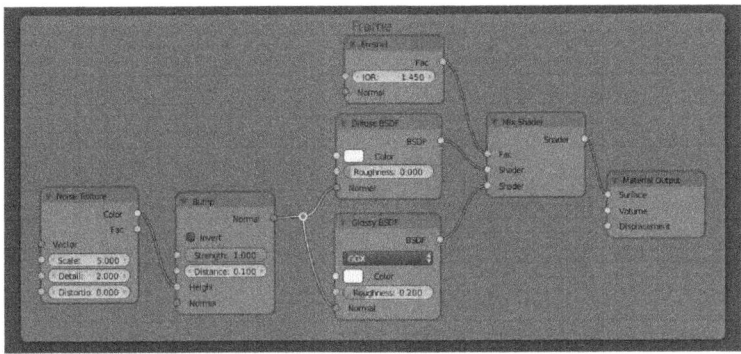

fig. 343 *Reroute* between the *Bump* node and the two *Vector* sockets of the shaders

 For directly connecting the input and output sockets *of the same kind* (yellow with yellow, gray with gray, etc.) between two nodes you can press the key F. With multiple pressures, also the following sockets of the same kind will be connected.

 For rapidly disconnect two nodes, on the other hand, thus *"cutting"*, breaking the flux, it is possible to use, instead of separating the link from the output channel, a method similar to the *knife*, holding pressed CTRL (or CMD for Mac) and dragging at the same time with the LMB pressed, across the link line.

3.2.4. Specular Map

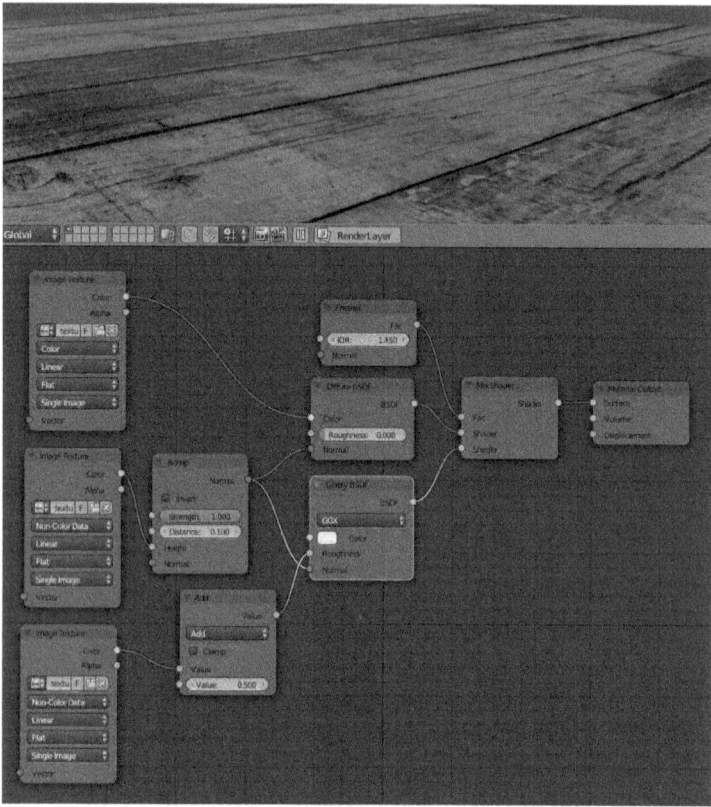

fig. 344 complete node chain of a plank, controlling the roughness with a *Specular Map*. You can also connect a *Specular Map* as *Fac* balance on the *Mix Shader*, possibly also multiplied (with a *Converter Math* node set as *Multiply*) with the *Fresnel*

The **Specular Map** is a kind of *texture* in gray scale, useful to define the specular effect intensity (i.e. the reflection) of a material.

The *texture* assigns the larger reflection intensity to the areas tending to white and the other way around for the darker areas.

This *texture* can be used, for example, as roughness factor of a *Glossy* shader, acting on the reflection.

To better clarify the concept, it is not true that all the parts of a material represented by a texture evenly reflect. Think for example to a grid of ceramic tiles, where the tiles will reflect the light whereas the grout spacing will be opaque.

The *Specular Map* will appear white in correspondence of the tiles and black (or dark gray) in correspondence of the grout spacing.

3.2.5. *The Alpha channel*

Some *shaders* and other nodes allow you to manage the *alpha* channel. To promptly explain the concepts and the methodology, we will propose a dedicated exercise.

 EXERCISE n. 11: A LEAVE

It is not true in general that modeling a leave is the best and quickest method, especially if a good *texture* is available (there are many in internet) reproducing the leave inside a transparent or black and white *background*.

METHOD 1

If you have at disposal the *texture* of the leave and the corresponding *texture* with the leave in black of white and the background inverted (white or black), you can adopt this first method.

fig. 345*diffuse*texture of the leave and *texture* of the leave contour on flat background

Insert a plane and rescale it. Enter in *Edit Node* and perform the *unwrapping*.

fig. 346 settings and rendering of a leave according to the first method

Assign a new material to the plane.

The material will be composed of a mix between a *Diffuse* node and a *Transparent* node.

312

The color leave *texture* will be applied to the *Diffuse*, whereas the black and white *texture* will act as balancing factor between the *Diffuse* and the *Transparent*. In particular, *Cycles* will render the color leave in correspondence of the black area of the black and white *texture* and will make transparent the remaining part corresponding to the white area.

METHOD 2

fig. 347 settings and rendering of a leave according to the second method

If on the other hand you have at disposal a *texture* with a color leave with transparent background and the *alpha* channel active (*.png), then you can use the *Alpha* output socket of the *Image Texture* node itself as *Fac* balancing factor between the transparency(on the Mix Shader input *socket*1) and the *texture* itself (on the *socket* 2).

 EXERCISE n. 12: TILES

In this exercise, we will create a surface covered with tiles.

First of all find a good *texture_diffuse* and the relevant *bump* and *specular*.

fig. 348*tiles*texture: from left to right, *diffuse, bump* and *specular*

Create a plane in *Edit Mode* and execute the *unwrapping Project from View* with *Top* view (7 NUM).

Then assign a new material to the *mesh* clicking on *New* of the *Material* tab of the *Properties* editor.

As usual create a node configuration performing the mix between the *Diffuse* shader (on which connect in input the *texture_diffuse*) and a *Glossy* whose roughness will be managed by the *texture Specular*, assigning low reflection to the grout joints and to some veins and higher reflection to the rest of the surface.

The index of refraction (*Fresnel* node) will control the global quantity of reflection according to the incidence angle, and connect the texture (*Non-Color Data*) *texture_bump* to the *Height* socket of the *Bump*, connected both to the *Diffuse* and the *Glossy*. Set hence the *Height* parameter to 0.3 to avoid too large reliefs.

fig. 349 node configuration for the rendering of a tile material

![ship icon] **EXERCISE n. 13: A CERAMIC CUP**

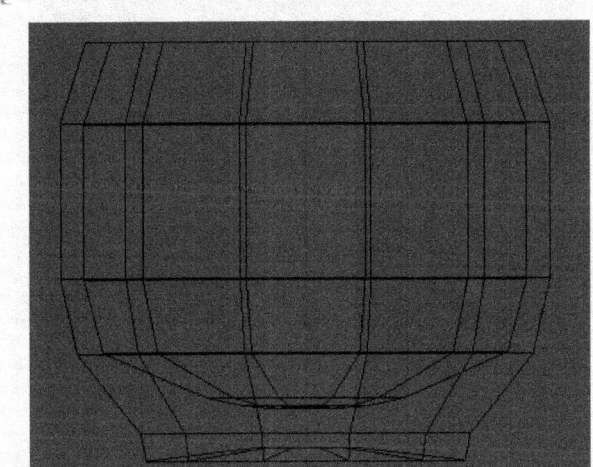

fig. 350 modeling of the cup body

315

In order to model a ceramic cup you can use one of the methods previously seen for the glass, i.e. by performing a sequence of extrusions and by rotating a profile, either generated by the *Screw* modifier or by the *Spin* tool.

Add the needed *loops* and select the faces directed along the *x* axis for creating, by extrusion, the handle.

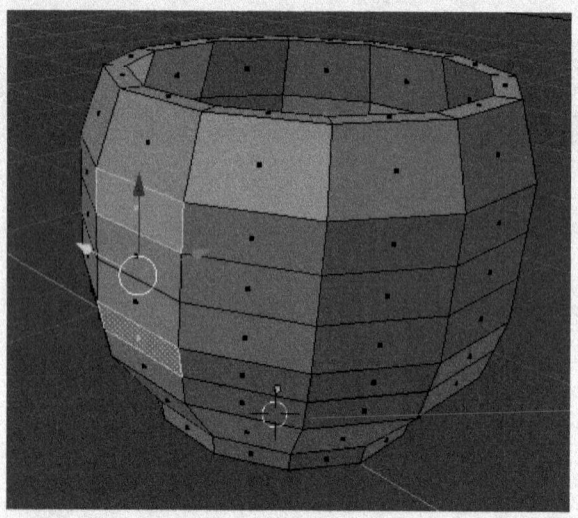

fig. 351 the faces to be extruded for making the handle

Extrude many times the two faces with *Extrude Individual*, regulating every time the rotation and position, till to get an arch shape.

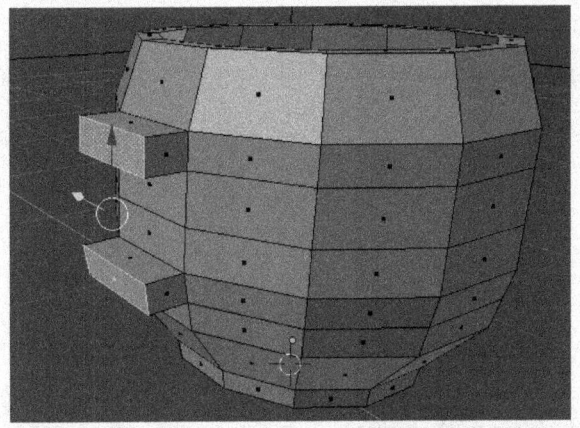

fig. 352 individual extrusion of the faces

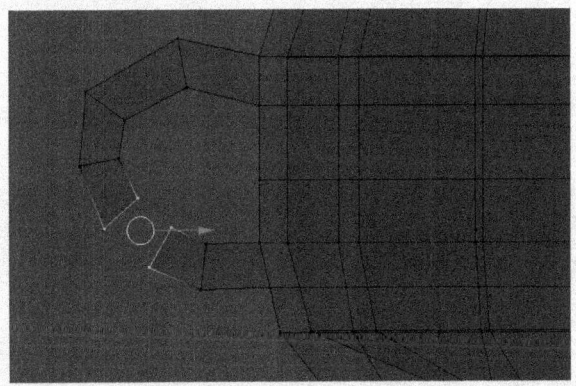

fig. 353 selection of the ending faces

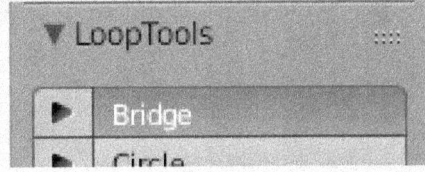

fig. 354 *Loop Tools*

317

Finally join with *Bridget* he two ending faces.

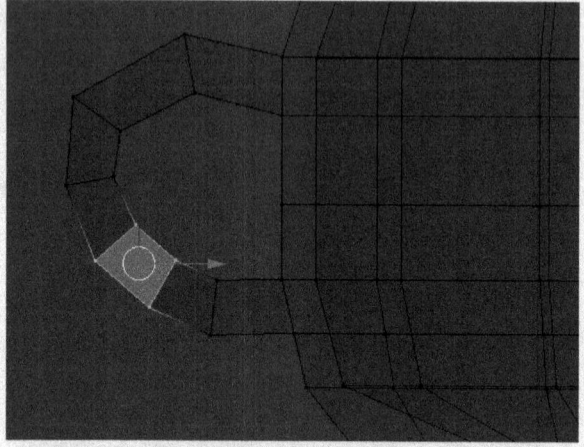

fig. 355 joining the two ending faces with *Bridge*

Regulate the handle thickness along the *y* direction with *Scale* (S, Y).

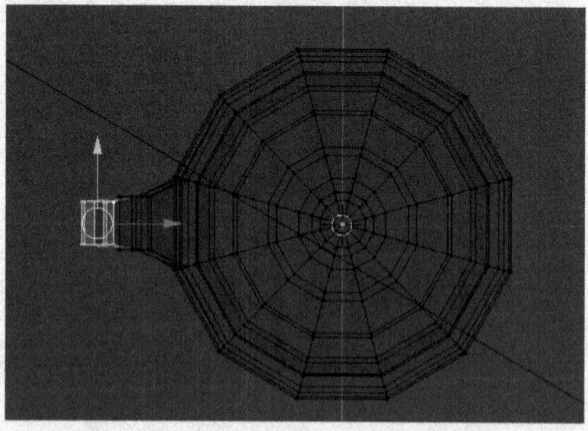

fig. 356 rescaling of the handle thickness

Add a *Subdivision Surface* modifier with three divisions to the mesh, and then a *Smooth*.

fig. 357 complete modeling of the cup

Select now one of the circular loops inside the cup. Duplicate it with SHIFT + D and drag it out of the mesh with P.

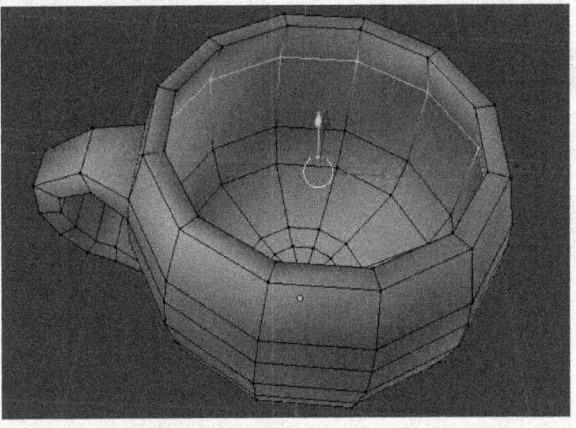

fig. 358 selection of the cup internal *loop*

319

Now select the circle of the new *mesh* and, with F, create a face. Add some *Insets* and finally apply to that surface the *Subdivision Surface* modifier.

fig. 359 the new *mesh*

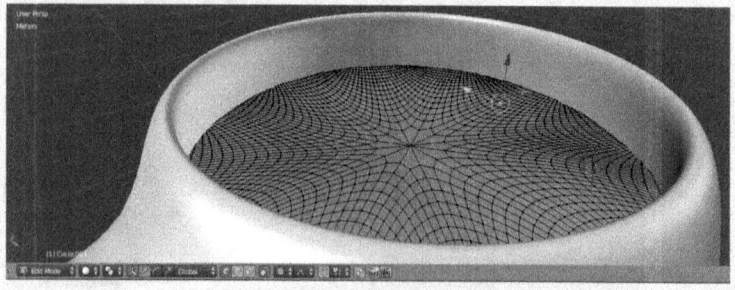

fig. 360 *Proportional Editing* during the position modify of some vertices of the "coffee" mesh along the z axis

This *mesh* will represent the coffee inside the cup. If you like you can obviously define the quantity depending on the chosen loop.

320

Rename the meshes *"cup"* and *"coffee"*.

Now enter in *Edit Mode* of the coffee and raise and lower some vertices with the *Proportional Editing* active, such as to obtain some little waves on the liquid surface.

Find now the *texture* of an espresso coffee (or of the dark beverage you prefer).

fig. 361 *texture_diffuse* (on the left) and *specular* (on the right) of the espresso coffee

Perform the *unwrapping* of the *"coffee"* mesh in modality *Project from View*, after having set the *Top* view (7 NUM).

Assign to *"coffee"* a new material and rename it *"coffee"*.

This material will be composed of a mix between a *Diffuse* to which the *texture_diffuse* is assigned, and a *Glossy*. Neglect the index of refraction, and simply balance the *Fac* setting a value equal to 0.1.

Connect an *Image texture* node (with the *texture_specular* uploaded) to the *Roughness* of the *Glossy* node, such as the bubbles reflect less than the rest of the surfaces.

fig. 362 node configuration for the coffee rendering

fig. 363 node configuration for the ceramic rendering

Finally create a material for the cup. This ceramic material is very simple. It can be composed of a simple mix of two *Diffuse* and *Glossy* shaders with balancing factor equal to 0.3.

322

EXERCISE n. 14: A KITCHEN CABINET: CREATING THE MATERIALS WITH CYCLES

Recover the kitchen cabinet you have already worked on with *Render Blender*.

Now assign the corresponding materials (wood and laminate) rendering them with *Cycles*.

Upload the file previously saved containing the kitchen cabinet and change the *rendering* engine.

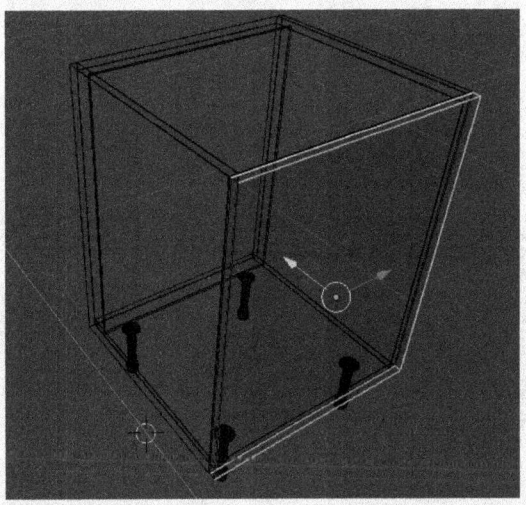

fig. 364 *unwrapping* and *Mark Seam* of the *mesh*

Select the shutter and apply a new material clicking *New*. Rename it "*wood*"

Set the standard node configuration.

In *Edit Mode* execute the *unwrapping*, but first mark the unwrapping edges with CTRL + E, *Mark Seam*.

Now the shutter faces can be mapped into a plane by a *texture* such as the wood veins be longitudinal on the edges and vertical on the faces.

The wood type we want to model is a gray durmast with polishing at 90°, much used nowadays, referred to as "*tranché*" wood.

Insert in the *Image Texture* node the file *gray durmast wood_diffuse.jpg*.

fig. 365 *texture diffuse* of the wood

Set as index of refraction *IOR* of the *Fresnel* node the value 1.650 and as *Roughness* of the *Glossy* 0.2, such as not to achieve too large reflections.

fig. 366 first step of the node configuration

The first step is done.

We will work a lot on the node complexity related to the *Bump*.

This node configuration is based on the mixing between different *texture* types representing scratches and other veins.

fig. 367 *texture wood2.jpg*to be used as *Bump*

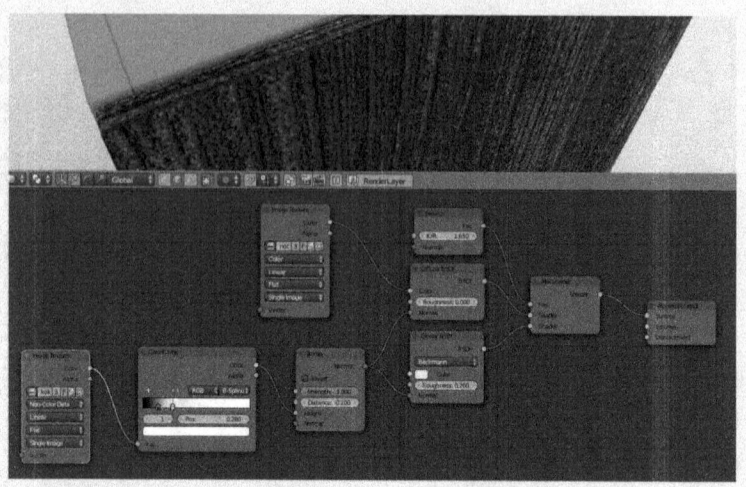

fig. 368 insert *wood2.jpg* like first *texture* of *Bump*

fig. 369 *texture Metal Scratches1.jpg* to be used as second texture for the Bump

Upload in an *Image Texture* node (in *Non-Color Data*) the file *wood2.jpg*and assign it to the *Height* input socket of the *Bump*, this latter connected both to the *Diffuse* and the *Glossy* shaders.

Regulate the texture dynamic range by inserting a *ColorRamp* node between the *texture* and the *Bump*.

Add a new image to be mixed to the previous one with the *Bump*: *Metal Scratches1.jpg*.

This *texture*, depicting from the real the frosting of a brushed metal, can be successfully used for creating the desired *tranché* effect in the wood, in opposite direction with respect to the natural veins.

Finally insert a third *texture* to be mixed to the other two: *Metal Scratch2.jpg*.

fig. 370 *texture Metal Scratch2.jpg*to be used as third texture of the Bump

Work on the dynamic range of the last two *textures* with the *ColorRamps* and add them together with a *Color MixRGB* node set to *Add*, to which the two *textures* are connected through the Color input sockets, as depicted in the figure.

327

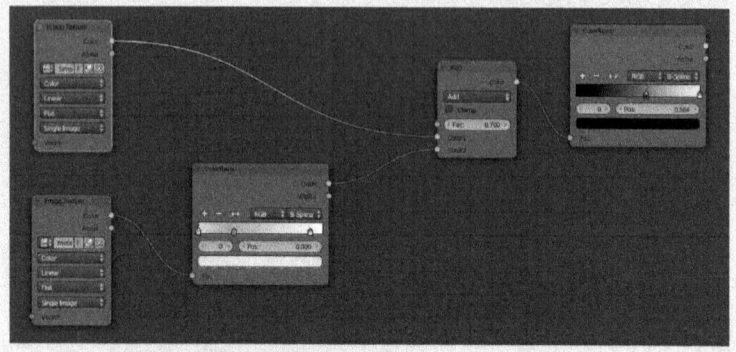

fig. 371 node configuration for the sum of *Metal Scratch1* and *Metal Scratch2*

Scale with a *mapping* node (*y* = 15) these two *textures*.

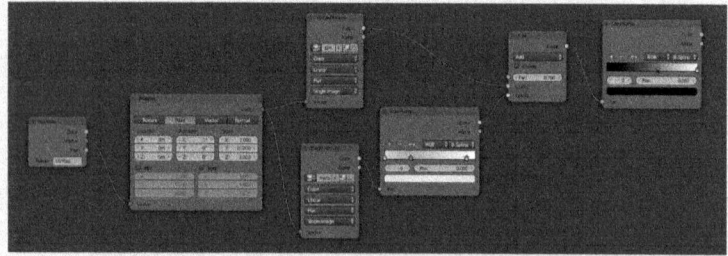

fig. 372 *Mapping* of the two textures *Metal Scratches1* and *Metal Scratches2*

Hence inserting a *Math Multiply* node multiply the *texture legno2.jpg* by the sum of *Metal Scratches 1* and *2*.

You can possibly use *Group Node* the node visualization.

328

fig. 373 node configuration reproducing a "*tranché*" wood

The outcome is definitely satisfying.

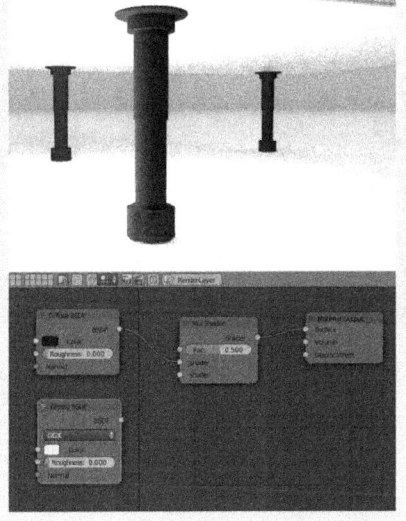

fig. 374 the cabinet feet

Define now the color of the feet and of the shell.

The feet will be simply black and semi glossy.

Create a new material and add to the diffuse a black color *Glossy* with balancing factor equal to and a *Roughness* on the *Glossy* set to 0.0 or to 0.1.

The shell will be gray semi glossy. The node scheme will be analogous to the previous one, with the light gray color set in the *Diffuse* and the *Roughness* of the *Glossy* set to 0.2.

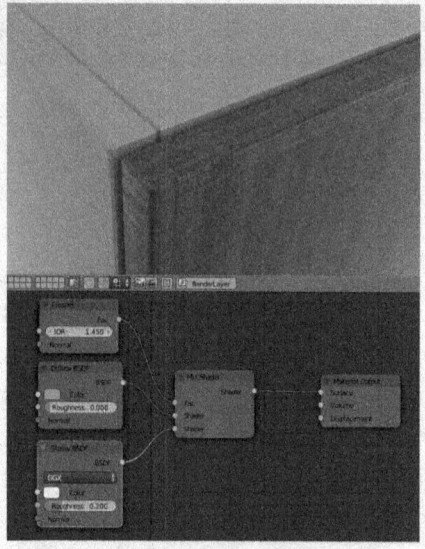

fig. 375 the gray shell

For now don't worry too much about the illumination, which will be separately discussed. Insert two emitting panels (two planes with *shader Emission* assigned) and place them in diagonal at the two cabinet sides such as to produce much wide shadows.

You can use the attached file *Light Setup Scene.blend*.

Finally place the camera and launch the rendering.

fig. 376 final *rendering* of the kitchen cabinet with *Cycles*

 EXERCISE n. 15: A TEXTURED FINISH WALL

To make a masonry more interesting for whom, to be appreciate your rendering, it is helpful to make the wall surface not too much smooth.

The simplest method could be to apply to the material *Bump* a *texture* reproducing a textured finish. However the use of one or more procedural textures could yield more interesting results.

Create the wall and apply a new material. Then set the base node configuration.

If you want to use an image *texture*, enter in *Edit Node* and execute the *unwrapping*, possibly marking with *Mark Seam* the cut edges.

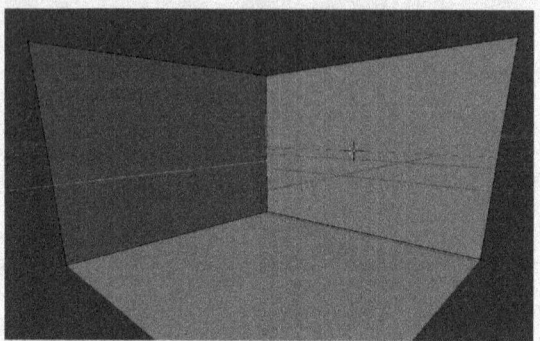

fig. 377 wall modeling and *mesh* unwrapping

Add a *Noise Texture* and connect the *Fac* output to the *Height* input of the *Bump* node.

Regulate the grain of the *Noise Texture* such as it is very fine (for example *Scale* = 500).

Set the strength (*Strength*) of the *Bump* to 0.05.

You can color the wall such as in addition to the textured finish it appears also cloudy, by mixing two colors (for example two gray tones, or other colors as you like) with a second *Noise Texture* acting as balancing factor (*Fac*) between the two *RGB* colors inserted in a *MixRGB* node.

You can further increase the textured finish complexity, by mixing two or more procedural *textures*, working on the *ColorRamp* to generate a less or more detailed relief.

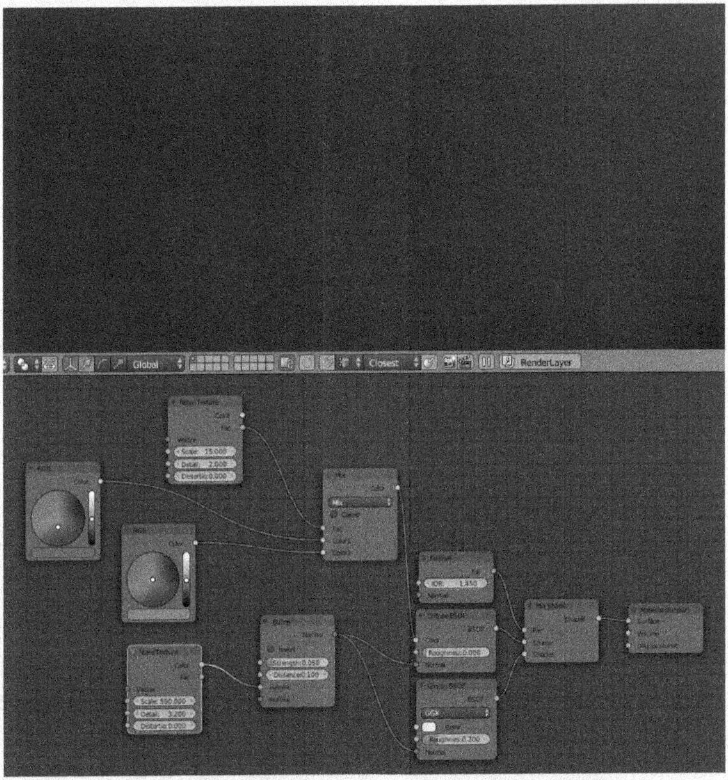

fig. 378 node configuration and *rendering* of a textured finish wall

3.2.6. Node reshaping and minimization

Each node has a small gray triangle at the top-left corner. If pressed, the node will minimize such as to occupy less space as possible in the *Node Editor*. To restore the original dimensions click again on the triangle appearing now rotated by 90°. Moreover, each node can be reshaped dragging its edges with the LMB.

fig. 379 Node collapse

3.2.7. Personalize the nodes: the *Sidebars* of the *Node Editor*

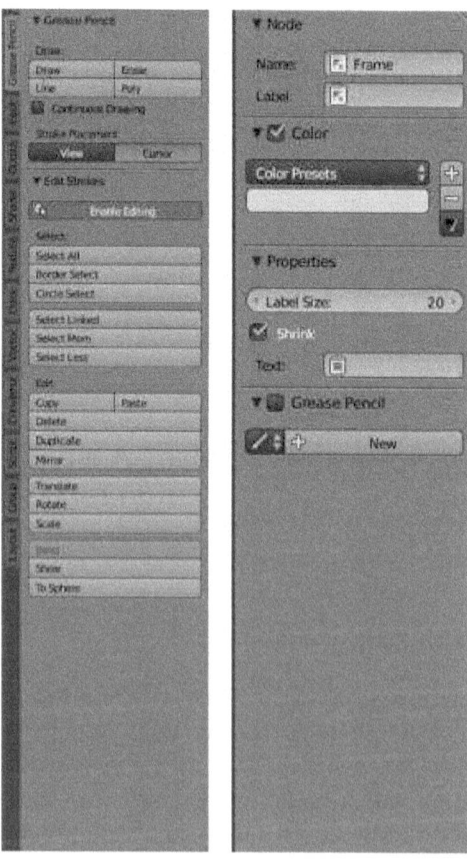

fig. 380 the two *Sidebars* of the *Node Editor*

Identically to the 3D view, also the *Node Editor* has two *Sidebars*, one *Tolls Shelf* on the left which can be enabled and disabled with the T key and a *Properties Bar* on the right, which can be enabled and disabled with the *N* key.

The **Tools Shelf** is divided in as many *tabs* as are the nodes. It is possible to add a node directly from this *Sidebar*.

In addition to the *tabs* relevant to the nodes, another tab is available, named **Grease Pencil**, useful to draw inside the working window and take notes, identical to the homonym panel in the *Properties Bar* of the 3D view, which will be described in the foregoing.

The **Properties Bar** contains some panels useful for personalizing the nodes.

In the **Node** panel two items are present. *Name* allows you to visualize and possibly rename a selected node (active). In the *Label* text box further information or labels can be added, relevant to the node.

fig. 381 the *Node* panel

In the **Color** panel it is possible, if checked, to modify the node background color (*Color* palette). The functions are useful, like the groups, to color the nodes of a specific chain like, for example, all the nodes relevant to the *Bump* of a material.

335

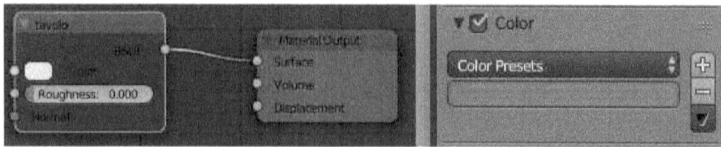

fig. 382 modifying the node background color

In the **Properties** panel all the information relevant to the node are contained: the parameters, the colors and the input and output sockets.

The **Grease Pencil** panel will be analyzed in detail in the next section.

3.2.8. The *header* of the *Node Editor*

fig. 383 the *header* of the *node Editor*

Like any editor, also the *Node Editor* has a *header*, in which the main commands and functions relevant to the nodes are summarized, the visualization, the selection, the working environments and other modalities.

The first menu is **View** in which all the functions relevant to the visualization are present.

The options are exactly the same as those already described relevant to the homonym menu of the 3D view header.

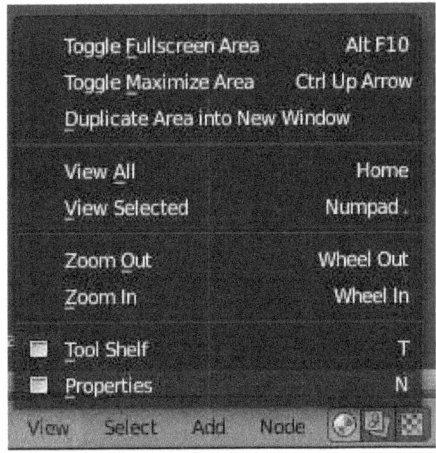

fig. 384 the *View* menu

The second menu, **Select**, contains all the commands relevant to the node selection.

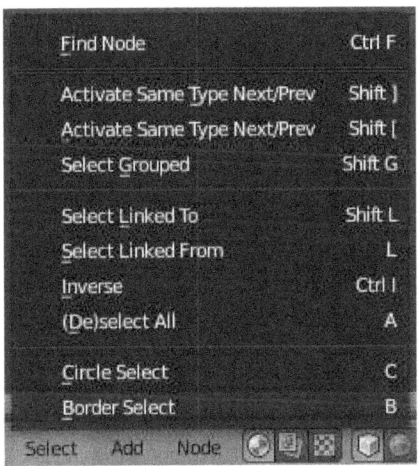

fig. 385 the *Select* menu

337

Find Node(CTRL + F) activates a window in the node working area, where the node list is present, from which a node can be selected. The selected node will be also graphically active at the same time.

fig. 386the *Find Node* editor

Activate and View Same Node Type, Step by Step allows you, once a node has been selected, to select, one by one with the command repetition, all the nodes having the same nature of the selected one.

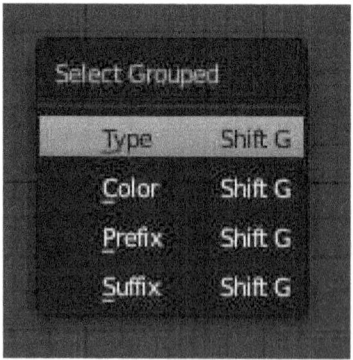

fig. 387 the *Select Group* menu

Select Grouped (SHIFT + G) groups the nodes depending on one of the menu options: *Type, Color, Prefix, Suffix.*

Select Linked To (CTRL + L) allows you to select the nodes connected to the active node output.

Selected Linked From (L) selects the nodes connected to the active node input.

Inverse (I) inverts the node selection.

(De)Select All (A) selects or deselect all the nodes in the *Node Editor.*

Circle Select (C) and *Border Select* (B) make a circular of rectangular selection analogously to the selection operation in the 3D scene.

From the **Add** menu a node can be inserted. The nodes are grouped by kind and functionality.

The **Node** menu contains all the tools relevant to the node functionality and their transformations.

Collapse and Hide Unused Sockets allows you to hide all the sockets of a node not connected, thus reducing the node dimensions.

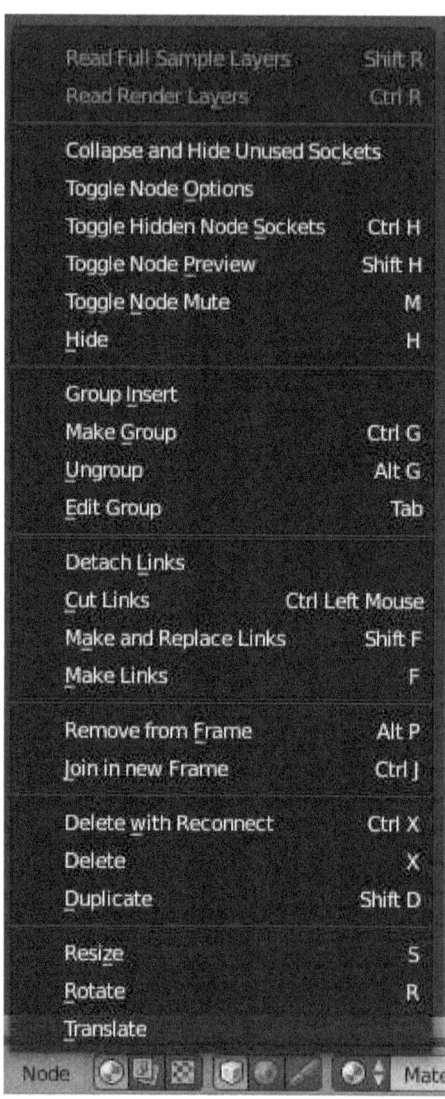

fig. 388 the *Node* menu

340

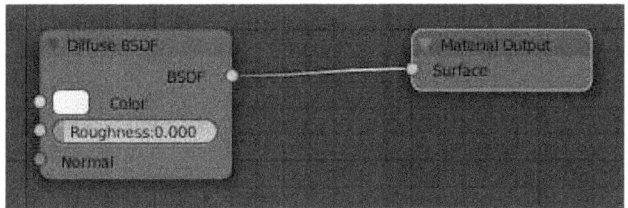

fig. 389*socket*collapse in the *Material Output* node

The following *Toggle* options are needed to expand the nodes.

Group Insert allows you to insert one or more selected nodes into a group of existing nodes, whereas *Make Group* (CTRL + G), *Ungroup* (ALT + G) and *Edit Group* (TAB) allow you, like for the nodes *Group* (SHIFT + A), to group nodes, drag them out of a group or entering a group.

Detach Links delete al the connection links between selected nodes.

Cut Links (CTRL + LMB) allows you to break a flux.

Make and Replace Links (SHIFT + F) creates links between selected nodes automatically connecting input sockets with output sockets of the same kind (color).

Make Links (F) connects two *sockets* by a link.

Remove from Frame (ALT + P) remove any parent relation of the node with the frames, whereas *Join in New Frame* (CTRL + J) relate the node with the current frame.

Delete with Reconnect (ALT + X) cancels the nodes selected in a chain, automatically connecting the two nodes net to the selection ends.

Delete (X or CANC) cancels the selected nodes.

Duplicate (SHIFT + D) duplicates selected nodes creating identical nodes.

Resize (S) scales the dimensions of a node selection widening or narrowing the fluxes.

Rotate (R) rotates the position of selected nodes around the selection center.

Translate (G) translates the selected nodes.

The three following icons refer to the **Node Tree**, i.e. the environment related to the node system.

This can be chosen among *Material* (for creating, as already seen, materials with the nodes), *Compositing* (for working in post processing on a *render,* method which we will analyze in the foregoing, when we will discuss the vast topic of compositing) and *Texture* (not so much used in *Cycles*).

fig. 390 *Node Tree*

The next three commands group (**Type of Data**) states if the *Node Editor* refers to the data of an object on which a material is applied, to the *environment* (*World*) or to the *Line Style* (for defining the contour line thickness for the *Freestyle* modality).

fig. 391 *Type of Data*

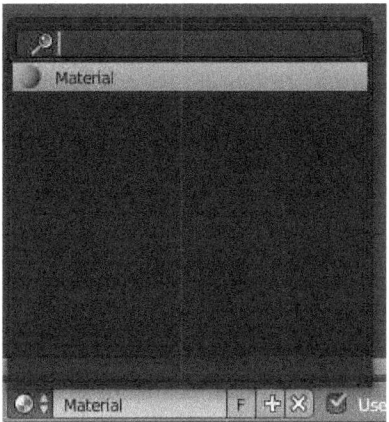

fig. 392 *browser*

The **Browser** allows you to upload or select a material or a image (in the *compositing* case), for performing changes on the nodes.

F allows you to duplicate the selected material, + to create a new material and X to cancel a material.

The flag **Use Nodes** enables or disables the node visualization and editing on a material or an image in *compositing*.

The icon button with the pin, allows you to introduce a *pinning*, i.e. to mark as important a node configuration.

The button with the arrow resends to the parent relationship of the active node chain, if existing.

The two **Snap** buttons act as those in the 3D view, allowing you to clasp and align the nodes.

343

Finally the two buttons **Copy** and **Paste** copy and paste the selected nodes in the *clipboard.*

fig. 393 Snap, Copy and Paste

3.3. Grease Pencil

The **Grease Pencil** is a technique allowing you to draw directly in the working area, clamping the perspective of the freehand drawing on the current view or on the objects, depending on the cases and the needs.

The tools and configurations of this pen can be found in the panels named **Grease Pencil**, placed in the *Tools Shelf* and in the *Properties Bar* inside the 3D view of the *Node Editor* and of all the windows allowing the freehand drawing inside them.

NOTE: the described *Grease Pencil* functions are almost identical to those relevant to the various windows, whose parameters and tools can be found inside the relevant and analogous *sidebars*.

3.3.1. *Tools Shelf*

The *Grease Pencil* tab placed inside the **Tools Shelf**, is divided into two panels:

- **Grease Pencil**, containing the base tools for drawing (*Draw*, *Erase*, *line* and *Poly*); a flag *Continuos Drawing* to draw a continuous line of some kind; and the *switch Stroke Placement* clamping the drawn lines on the *viewport* (*View*), on the *3DCursor* (*Cursor*), on the *mesh* surface (*Surface*) and with respect to the line itself (*Strokel*), these two last options available only in the 3D view;

- **Edit Strokes**, containing the tools for editing the vertices comprising the dashed line. The command *Enable Editing*

345

activates all the editing tools, identical to those present in the *Tools Shelf* of the 3D view.

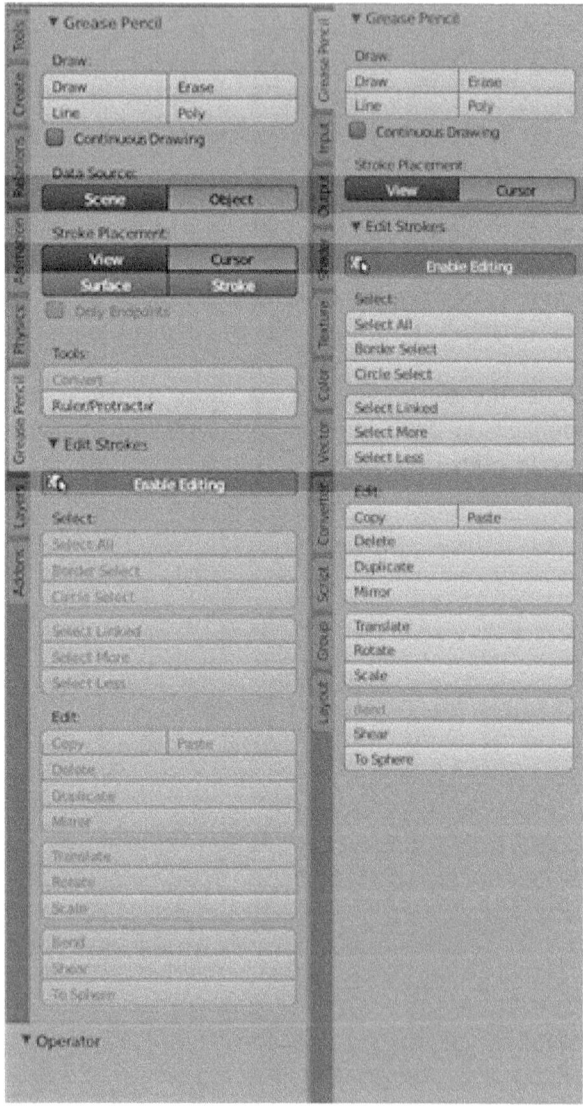

fig. 394 the *Grease Pencil* panels relevant to the *Tools* Shelf of the 3D view and to the *Node Editor* show little differences

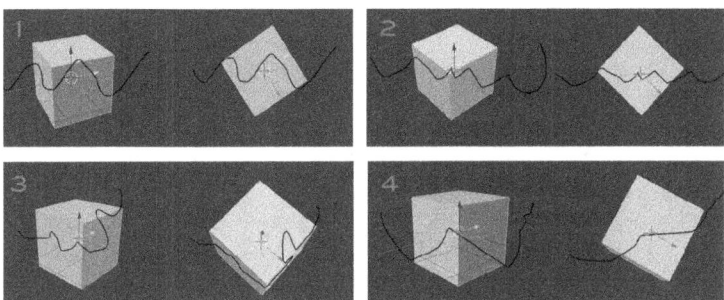

fig. 395 different outcomes of the *Stroke Placement* in the 3D view. 1) *View*: the line say still with respect to the current view; 2) *Cursor*: the line follows the coordinates of the *3D Cursor*; 3) *Surface*: the line in printed on the object surfaces, like it is drawn over them; 4) *Stroke*: the scene rotation and panning depend on the line

Once selected the line type you want to use from the *Grease Pencil* panel, you only need to drag with the LMB inside the working area to get a drawing.

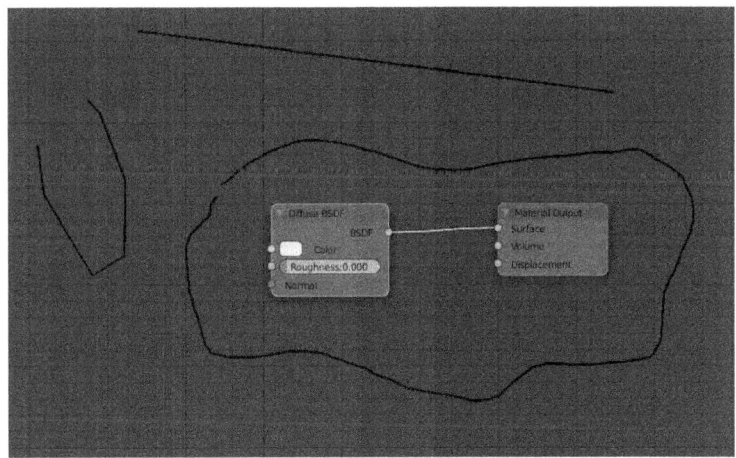

fig. 396 drawing with *Grease Pencil* inside the *Node Editor* working area

Each line drawn, as already said, can be edited, by selected, and moving the vertices belonging to it. Each selected vertex is colored orange.

All the selection methods previously seen for the object selection can still be used.

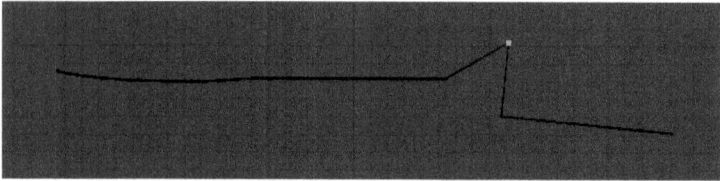

fig. 397 line *editing*

3.3.2. *Properties Bar*

The **Grease Pencil** panel placed in the **Properties editor** contains all the information relevant to the lines drawn in the working area of the *Node Editor* through the drawing tools previously described, and in particular:

- the *preset* name relevant to the *Grease Pencil*. It is possible to insert new ones or canceling the existing ones.

- The *layer* the line is belonging to;

- the color (*Stroke*) of the line and of the possible region delimited by closed loops (*Fill*) and the relevant opacities.

- the line thickness (*Thickness*);

- the possibility of drawing in front of the nodes, checking *XRay*;

- the possibility, checking *Volumetric*, to draw a dotted line with the dot distance depending of the drawing rapidity;

348

- the possibility to clamp the current *frame* to the *Grease Pencil layer* and thus creating and animation of a freehand drawing.

fig. 398 the *Grease Pencil* panel of the *sidebar Properties*

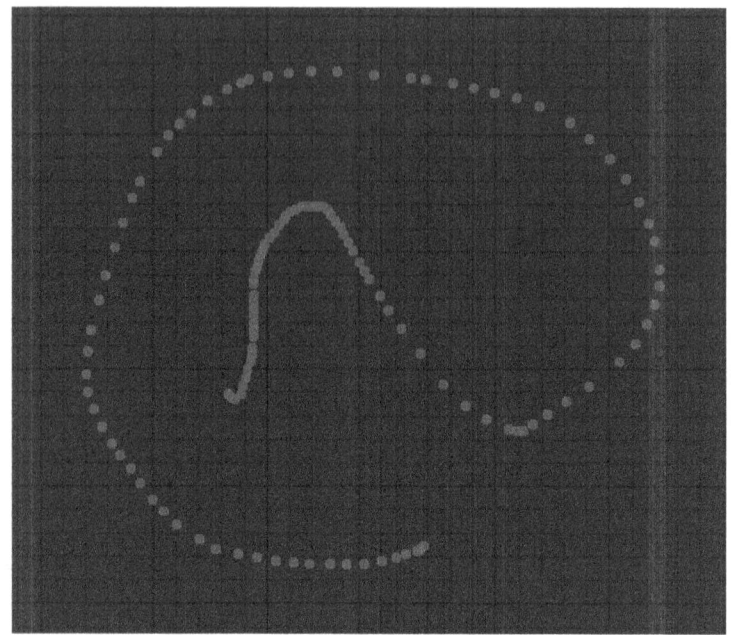

fig. 399 outcome of the *Volumetric* option

The last panel, **Grease Pencil Settings** enables again the *Stroke Placement* function and the *Proportional Edit* applied to the vertex transformation of the selected line.

Note: In the 5th volume, the *Grease Pencil* functions will be explain more in detail.

350

3.4. Illumination

From a technical and conceptual point of view, the illumination works exactly in the same way with any *rendering* engine of *unbiased* type. This means that what has been already discussed for *Render Blender* is valid also for Cycles, unless some parameters and interfaces characteristic of *Cycles*.

As it is well known, *Cycles* uses nodes for creating materials. The nodes, however, are used also for what concerns the illumination.

The various illumination typologies possible in Blender light the scene with *Cycles*, by means of a node chain. This holds for the *Lamps* like for the *environments*, being them emitting images, *HDR* images, procedural sky.

3.4.1. *Tab Lamp*

In this *tab* the nature of the *Lamp* object inserted in the 3D can be defined.

Like for *Render Blender*, 5 kinds of lights are available: *Point*, *Sun*, *Spot*, *Hemi* and *Area*.

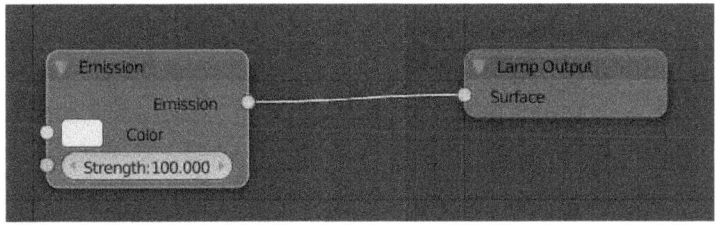

fig. 400 *standard* node configuration for a light source

351

The radiating effect of any *Lamp* is thus defined by an *Emission* node (on which a color is usually associated, defining the light temperature) connected to a *Lamp Output* node.

The *Emission* node defines, in addition to the color, also the light intensity (*Strength*) defining, except for *Sun*, the power in watt.

In the *Lamp* tab 3 main panels are present: *Preview* (showing the illumination source preview), *Lamp* (defining the dimensions of the light source with respect to the cast shadow) and *Nodes* (summarizing the node chain, exactly like it were a normal material).

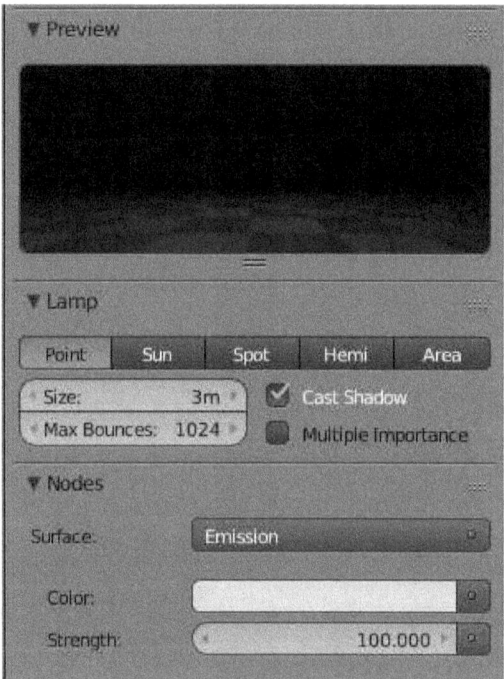

fig. 401 the *Lamp* tab panels

While the **Nodes** panel summarizes the node chain representing the luminous flux, the nature of the light source can be determined in the **Lamp** panel.

More specifically, depending on the line type, the parameters contained in *Lamp* may slightly vary.

Size defines the light source dimensions, yielding more defined shadows (low values) or blurred shadows (high values).

Max Bounces defines the cast shadow resolution based on the samples (by *default* 1024).

Cast Shadow, if checked, casts the shadows on other objects and surfaces.

Multiple Importance reduces the noise produced by the shadows by increasing at the same time the computation speed.

The *Spot* and *Area Lamp* types have some additional parameters other than the ones previously shown.

The first one (*Spot*) adds one more panel, *Spot Shape* containing some parameters defining the shape and behavior of the light cone.

Size defines the cone angle, in degrees.

Blend defines the blurring between the area lighted by the light cone and the shadowed area. For higher values a smoother effect is achieved, gradual.

Show Cone shows the light cone.

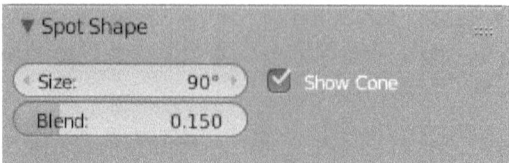

fig. 402 the *Spot Shape* panel relevant to the *Lamp Spot*

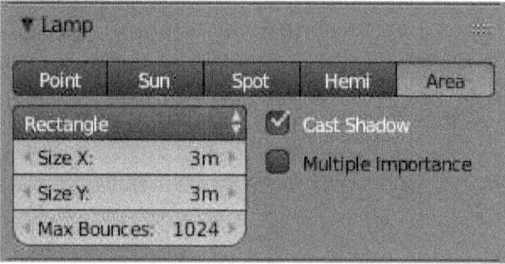

fig. 403 the *Lamp* panel of *Area* type

The second one (*Area*) adds two counters for defining the *x* and *y* dimensions of the emitting panel.

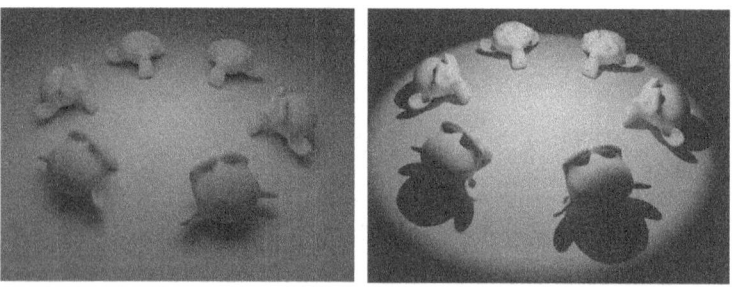

fig. 404 scene illumination (with *Spot*). On the left the *Size* is set to 5 meters and produces soft shadows; on the right the *Size* is set to 0 and produces sharp shadows

3.4.2. Tab World (environment)

A scene, as already seen previously, can be partially or totally influenced by the *environment*, i.e. by the illumination of the surrounding environment.

This environment, which is actually also the background of a scene, can be represented by a plane containing an image in turn associated as a color of an *Emission*, or as an image set as *Environment Texture*, or as a procedural background, for example *Sky Texture*.

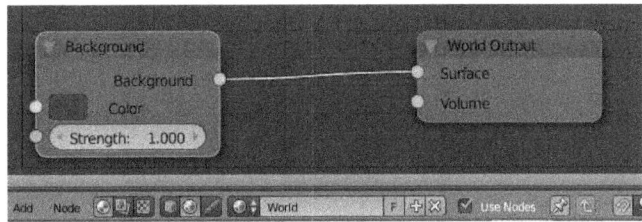

fig. 405 node configuration relevant to the *World* environment

Except for the first case, which is simply a plane placed inside a scene, and thus represented by the nodes in the *Material* environment of the *Node Editor*, the others refer to the *World* environment and the relevant *textures* constitute the color of the *Background* node, corresponding to a tradeoff between *Diffuse* and *Emission* in the *Material* environment.

In the **Surface** panel can be found the nodes determining that environment. They are composed of, as already said, a *Background* node, defining the background color. Setting this color to absolute black, the *environment* will not influence at all the scene illumination, leaving it to only the *Lamp* lights.

It is possible to connect an *Image* node to *Background*, as procedural *textures* to achieve psychedelic effects, *Sky Texture* achieving a sky, *Environment Texture* on which to upload a

355

texture environment, usually of spherical type, or *HDRI* which are elaborations of panoramic images at 360° on the *xy* plane or on the *xy*, *xz* and *yz* plane (spherical image). These images has a *.hdr* extension.

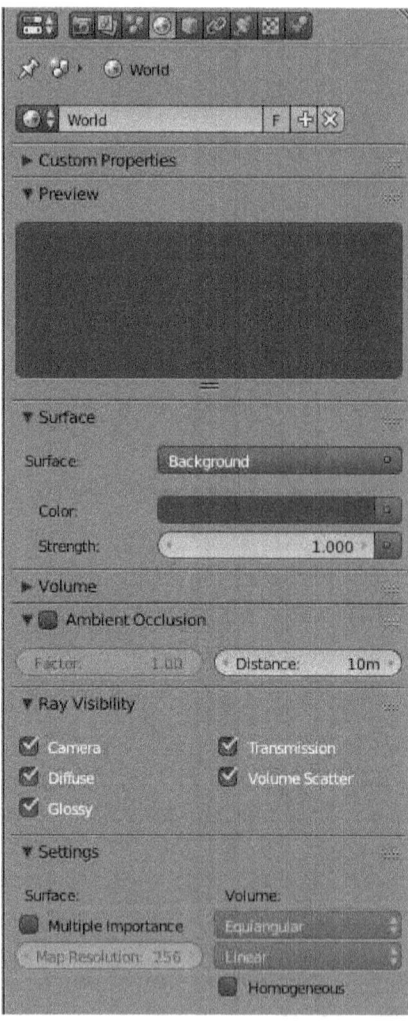

fig. 406 the *World* tab in *Cycles*

fig. 407 hdr image

As already said, the *Strength* parameter of the *Background* node determines the luminous intensity, which the *texture* will produce in the scene, lighting the objects.

This kind of illumination method is very realistic and often does not need even of additional lights or of the sun.

It is recommended to find *.hdr images of good quality.

In order to define the dimensions of the background image, as well as its position and rotation, it is necessary to insert the *Mapping* and *texture Coordinate* nodes, the latter connected to the former by means of the *Generated* output socket.

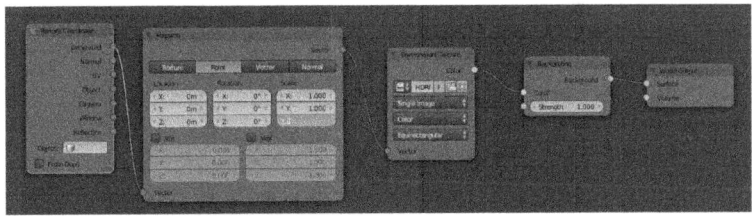

fig. 408 node configuration (in *World* environment) defining the scene global illumination by using a texture*.hdr whose dimensions, rotation and position are defined by the *Mapping* node

fig. 409 panoramic views of the 3Dscene lighted by the *texture* *.*hdr*

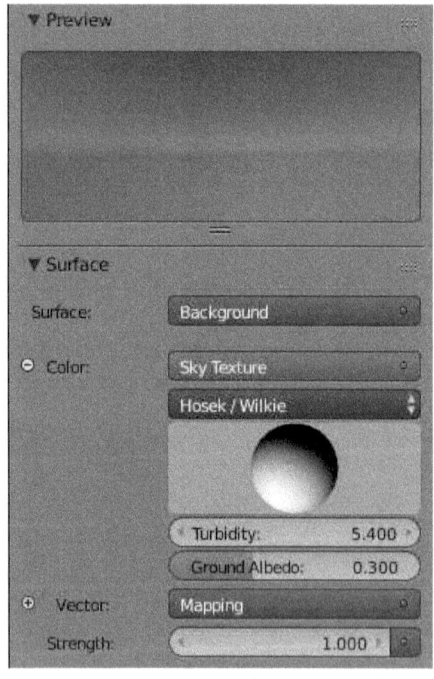

fig. 410 the *Surface* panel of *World* with a *Sky texture* associated to the *Background* node

358

On the other hand, by applying to the *Background* node a *Sky Texture*, such as for *Blender Render*, it is possible to represent and light the background using this special *texture*, whose node configuration is analogous to the previous one.

Like for the version for *Render Blender*, it is possible to regulate the sun direction and height, by acting on the sphere, the atmosphere clearness (*Turbidity*) and the sunrise effect (*Ground Albedo*).

fig. 411 *Sky Texture* generates a sky and a ground in the 3D scene

In the same way it is possible to insert other *texture* types (like a *Noise Texture*, for example, or a normal *Image texture*) achieving the most varied effects.

fig. 412 Noise Texture generates a dreamlike and psychedelic world of the 3D scene

359

By setting as *environment* a non-emitting black color, you can light the scene, or a part of it, using a light-emitting plane or object.

This element associated to a simple *Emission* material, is usually adopted for illuminating and increase the contrast in some key points of the scene.

fig. 413 this luminous plane (working analogously to an *Area Lamp*) if useful to lighten shaded zones, create reflections, even auxiliary, concentrate the detail and the attention on a part of the scene

Remember to prevent the camera to visualize the luminous plane, if framed, canceling the flag *Camera* from the *Ray Visibility* of the *Object* tab, as it will be illustrated in detail in a short.

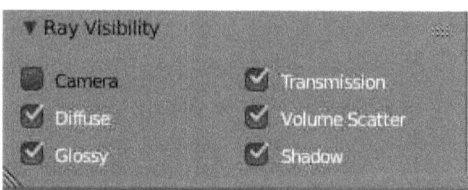

fig. 414 the *Ray Visibility* panel

Obviously an emitting plane containing an image can light a scene and act, at the same time, as background.

fig. 415 an *Image as Plane* assigned to an *Emission* node generates a light emitting background

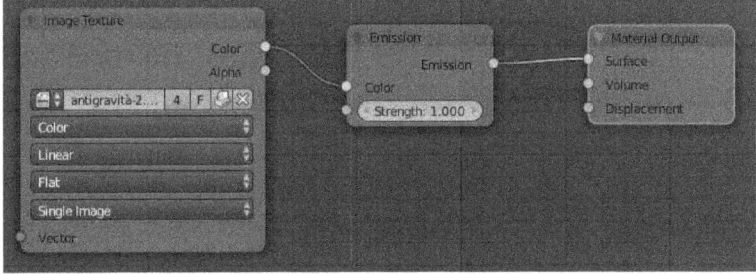

fig. 416 node configuration in *Material* environment of a light emitting image

The **Ambient Occlusion** panel must be enabled if you want to have a diffuse and not shaded light, as granted by this function, identical to the one previously described.

Same for the **Settings** panel.

The **Ray Visibility** panel assigns specific properties of *environment* visualization, exactly as it occurs for the homonym panel relevant to the objects.

By checking the available options, the *environment* will influence, respectively, the *Camera*, the base color (*Diffuse*), the reflection (*Glossy*), the transparency (*Transmission*) and the *Volume Scatter* of the objects in the scene.

3.4.3. Light Setup Scene

For making simpler a material creation, a photographic virtual set has been created in which, in a space with rounded edges, three luminous panels have been placed, one on the left emitting a cold light, one on the right emitting a hot light and one on the top emitting a neutral light.

These three luminous sources produce a diffuse and well balanced light with hinted shadows.

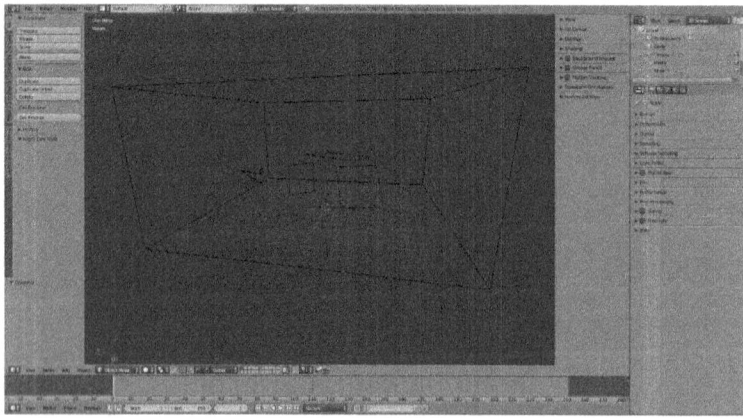

fig. 417 3D view of the *Light Setup Scene*

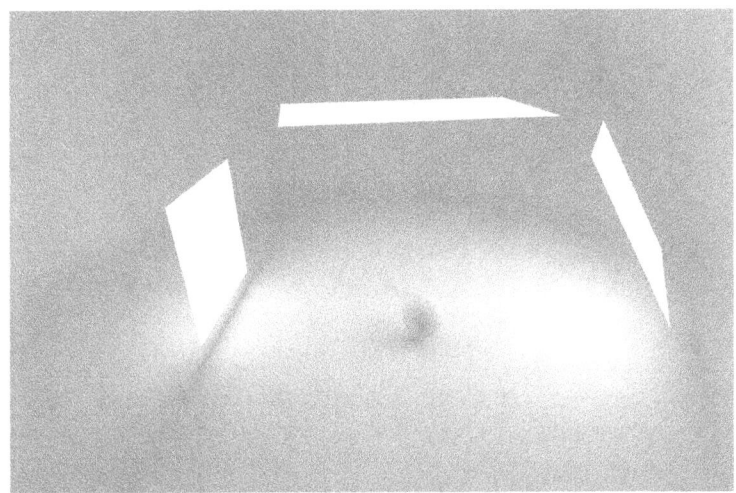

A camera and an empty object are present in the scene, useful for the focus adjustment.

The background and the three lights have been prevented to select and modify the *Wireframe* view 3D ambient, such as not to influence the modeling.

You can download the *Light Setup Scene.blend* file from the files attached to the present volume.

This ambient is also very useful for representing objects, especially those of design in a neutral background.

3.4.4. Bake

Bake is a term you will often find in Blender.

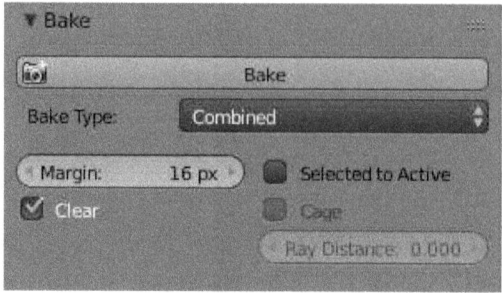

fig. 419 *Bake* panel inside the *tab Render* tab

Bake freezes (or cook) the scene or the object in a precise moment, preserving the event, the color, the effect, the light, the shadow, or the physical simulation impressed in that frame, or with that specific illumination conditions.

In fact the command is used in several cases we will analyze in the foregoing, one by one.

Referred to the illumination and the shadings, in particular on a mesh, *Bake* fixes the illumination, the shadows, the colors and all the components of the material assigned to the object in a new mesh.

The procedure, though slow and tricky, is very useful in the animations and most of all in videogames.

Fixing in a new texture all the components and effects belonging to the illuminations, makes the static scene much more light and makes the animation definitely more flowing, just because the rendering computations have been previously done, during the realization and programming phase, thus avoiding that, in real time, the cpu and the graphic board reserve all the resources for a computation preventing the image and videogame flowing.

Think, for example, to the complex videogames, in which tens of players appear playing together in a lighted ambient.

364

Continuously computing the lighting and the shading for all the objects present in the scene, would make the flowing impossible.

This system is anyway very useful and functional, provided the illumination source be considered fixed and not variable.

fig. 420 the illumination, the shadows and the reflections are fixed in the *textures* relevant to all the objects in this well known *videogame*, thus avoiding the arduous rendering process in real time

 EXERCISE n. 16: ILLUMINATED TEXTURE BAKE

Let us make an example to better understand the operation of this tool.

Insert a cube in a *Light Setup Scene*, a light of *Spot* type and a small sphere placed between the light source and the cube, such that it can cast a shadow.

Assign the colors to the cube and the sphere.

The cube is a high reflecting green material (*Fac* balancing between *Diffuse* and *Glossy* equal to 0.9 and *Roughness* equal to 0.2; whereas the sphere is colored with a red *Diffuse*.

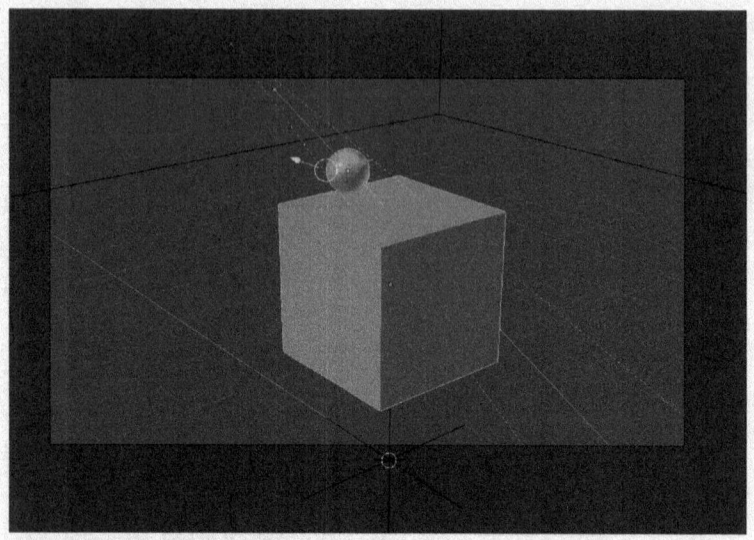

fig. 421 the scene relevant to this exercise

Finally, set the strength to 60 watt and a magenta color for the Spot light.

The outcome you should visualize is similar to the following one.

Note the red reflection and the sphere shadow on the cube and the violet light stroke.

Execute the cube *unwrapping* in *Edit Mode*, then click *New* in the *UV/Image Editor* for creating a new material. Define the dimensions, the color and possibly the name from the menu that will appear and confirm.

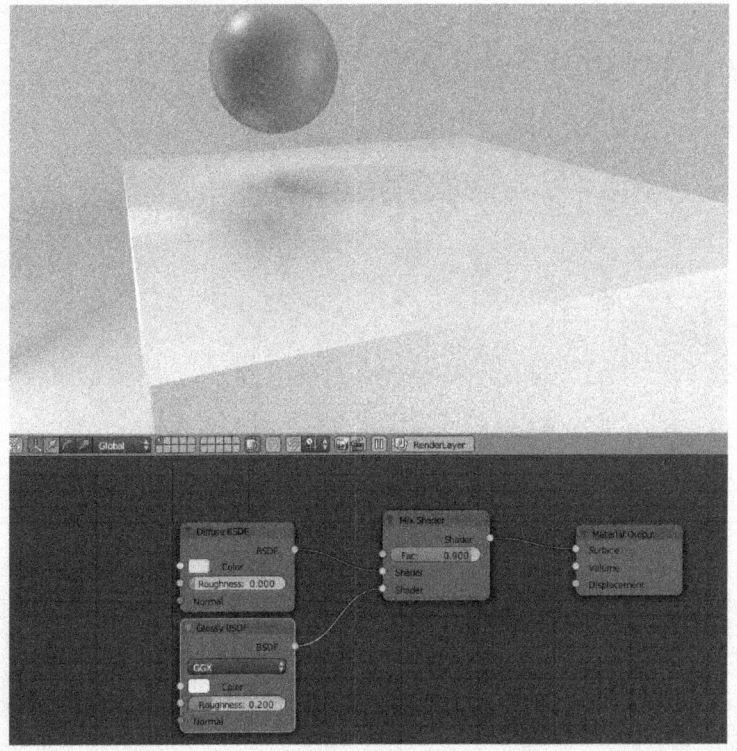

fig. 422 the rendered scene

Now save the new texture using the *Image* menu of the *header* of the *UV/Image Editor* (or directly press F3, choosing from the *Browser* the file destination.

The choice of the file destination path is of the outmost importance for the correct operation of *Bake.*

367

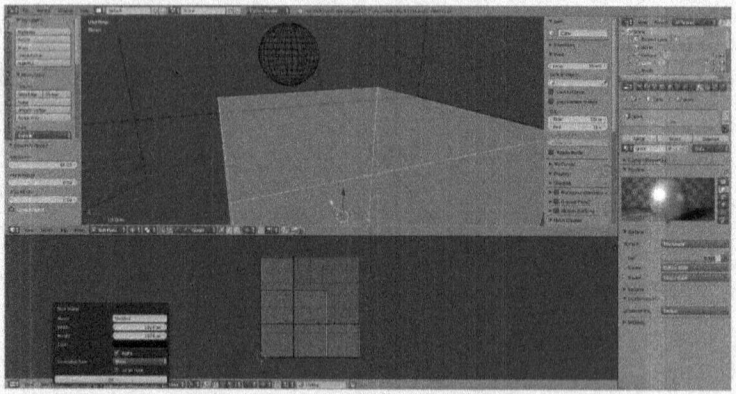

fig. 423 creation of the new empty *texture*

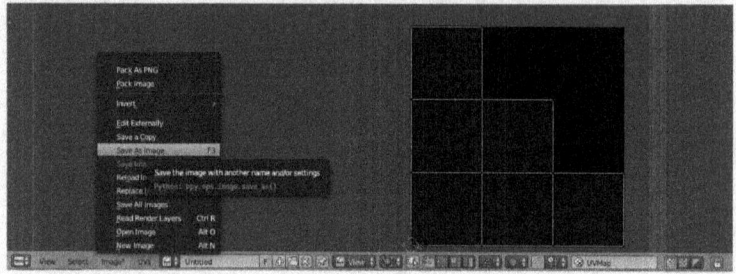

fig. 424 *texture* saving

The *texture* (that will be than replaced by the *baking* tool, should really exist in a saved file and should be then recalled and assigned to the material in place of the original node configuration. After having saved the *file*, open again the *Node Editor*, with the cube material visible (cube selected).

Replace the original nodes with a simple *Diffuse* composition on *Material Output*. Insert an *Image Texture* node on which the just saved file should be uploaded, without connecting it to the *Diffuse*.

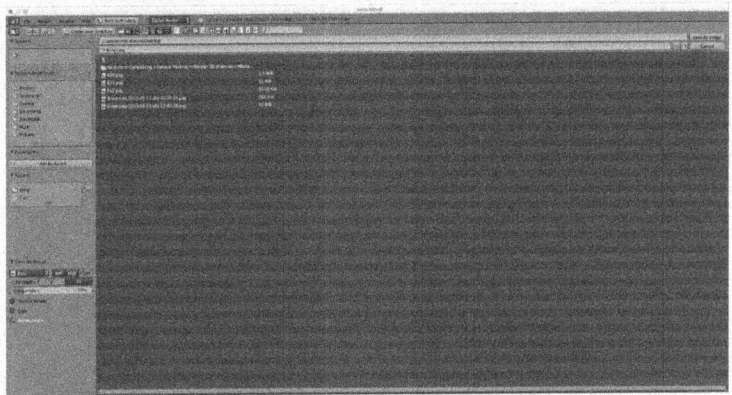

fig. 425 choice of the file destination path

fig. 426 node replacement

Launch then the *baking* pressing the *Bake* command in the homonym panel in the *Render* tab in the *Properties* editor, paying attention that the *Image Texture* node on which the created texture has been uploaded had been selected and active.

fig. 427 *Bake* execution

fig. 428 *baking* process progress

At the end of the process (the progress bar will be visualized in the *header* of the *Info* editor), which could take several minutes depending on your hardware system, the empty *texture* will be replaced by the scene image permanently fixed into an image file.

The new *texture* will be determined by the base green color, with the reflection and the shadow relevant to the red sphere, the violet ellipse produced by the cone light, the global illumination reflections and possible shadows.

In case of a more complex material (*texture*, *Bump*), all these components would have been anyway fixed on the texture baked by the *baking*.

Now you can check if the saved file contains the new color information and reload it in the material, connecting the *Image Texture* node with the *Diffuse* and deleting the nodes not used anymore.

You can delete the *Spot* light and the red sphere and launch the *rendering* again.

The process will be much more fast and the cube mapping will show the reflections, the shadows and the light strokes relevant to the just removed objects.

In much complex scenes, where the illumination and the object position be fixed, spending some time for running the baking on each mesh could solve heavy and long rendering problems.

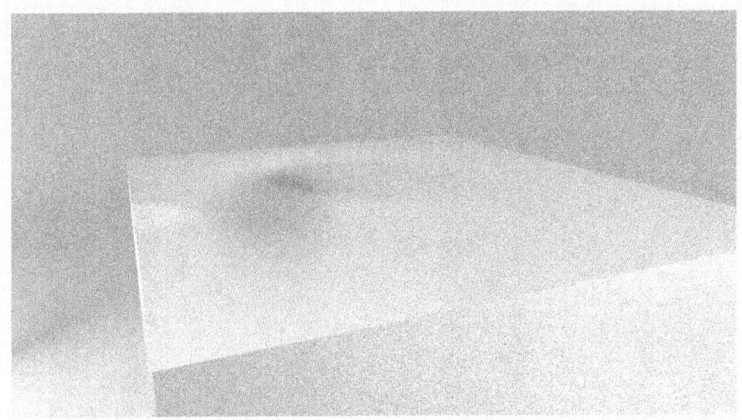

fig. 429 the scene rendering with the *texture* produced by the *Bake* applied to the cube. Note that the Spot light and the sphere have been removed, but the reflections and the shadows have been permanently fixed on the cube texture

NOTE: in the creation of the 3D models for videogames, in addition to the backing process for texturing the meshes thus avoiding future *raytracing* computations in real time by the graphic board of the user support, during the videogame execution, it is recommended to set a low polygonal definition of the meshes themselves. Few polygons make the scene light and this will improve, together with the elimination of the real time raytracing, the game flowing.

3.4.5. Caustics

As defined in *Wikipedia*, the **caustics** are geometric entities composed of the singular concentration of curves. These curves approximately model the behavior of luminous rays, when meeting certain surfaces such as lenses, curved mirrors or areas of a material with different densities, generating as a consequence a different response to the illumination.

fig. 430 light effects and reflections determined by the caustics produced by a diamond illumination

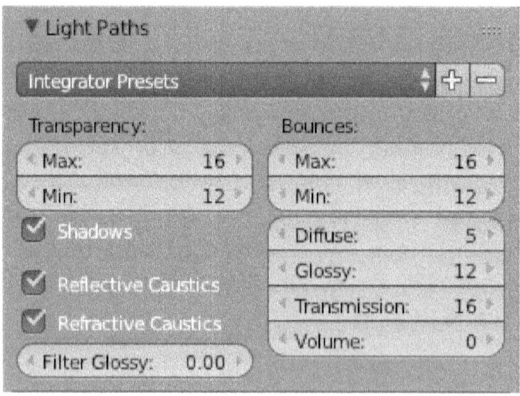

fig. 431 the flags on the options activating the caustic visualization

Some examples of caustics are the lighting effects at the bottom of swimming pools, under the bridges over rivers, or inside certain transparent of translucent materials, like the glass or the diamonds.

These very peculiar reflections can be faithfully reproduced by Cycles, with detriment of the computing speed.

It is then recommended to remove the flags *Reflective Caustics* and *Refractive Caustics*, in the *Light Path* panel of the *Render* tab, if not strictly necessary.

 EXERCISE n. 17: CREATING A DIAMOND

First of all activate from the *Addons* the option *Extras* among the *meshes*.

Among these auxiliary objects, already defined, we find *Diamonds*.

Insert, with SHIFT + A, a diamond in the *Light Setup Scene*.

A simple *Glass* material has been already assigned to it, but it is not enough. The diamond, in fact, due to its purity, is able to split the light into its red, green and blue components (*RGB*) and diffuse them separately.

You must then add 3 additional *shader Glass* nodes in the *Node Editor* relevant to the diamond material, changing their white base color with a pure red, green and blue color at 255.

These 3 new *shaders* will be added together with two *Add Shader* nodes, and the output socket of the second *Add* should be mixed (*Mix Shader*) with the original white *Glass* node.

Use the *Sharp* algorithm for the four *Glass* nodes and be sure that the *Fac* balancing of the *Mix Shader* be set such that the white be the dominating color. A value equal to 0.25 should be sufficient.

Once the diamond has been suitably placed into the scene and framed, launch the *rendering*.

The colors will be separately diffused and the reflections (caustics) will be visualized on the scene background.

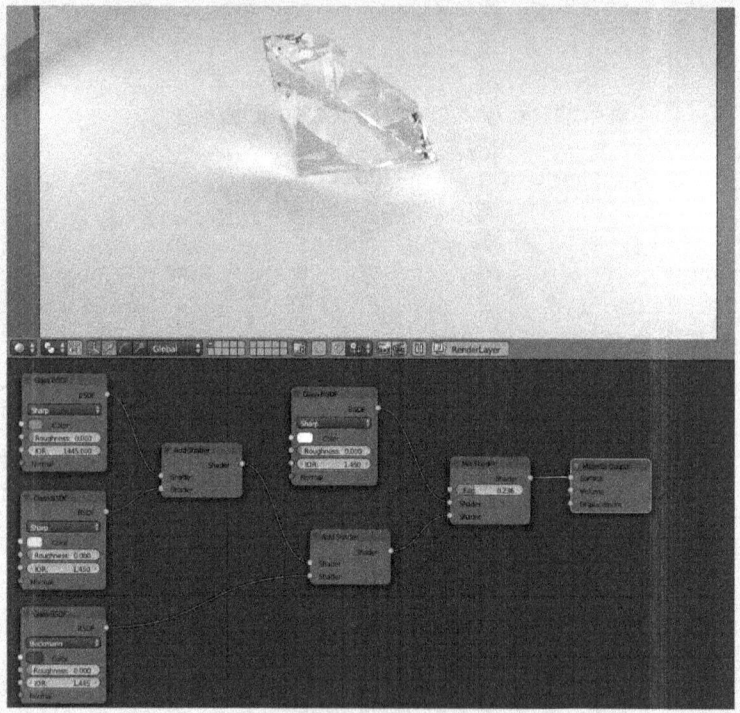

fig. 432 node configuration reproducing the diamond material and the rendering with the caustics

3.5. Applying the materials to the 3D curves

In this final part of the chapter devoted to *Cycles* and to the materials, we will show how to assign a material to a 3D curve, without transforming the latter into a mesh and then unwrapping it.

 EXERCISE n. 18: ASSIGN A MATERIAL TO A 3D CURVE

For assigning a material to any object, it is necessary that the object has a solidity, a thickness and a surface on which to map the material.

Insert into the *Light Setup Scene* a *Bézier Curve* and place it such as to achieve a frame you like.

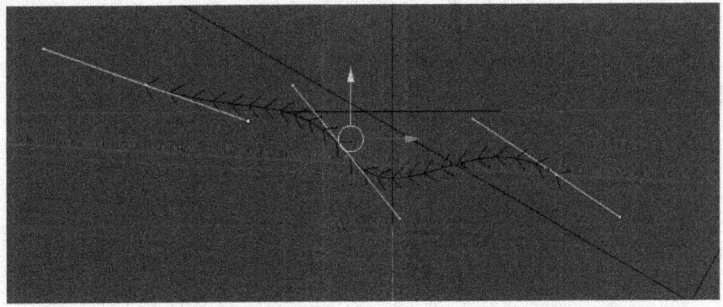

fig. 433 inserting a *Curve* into the *Light Setup Scene*

Now we can give a thickness to the curve entering the *tab Data* relevant to the curve.

375

In this *tab* be sure that in the **Shape** panel the curve be defined as 3D and that the *Fill* menu be set on *Full* to make the curve thicker in any direction.

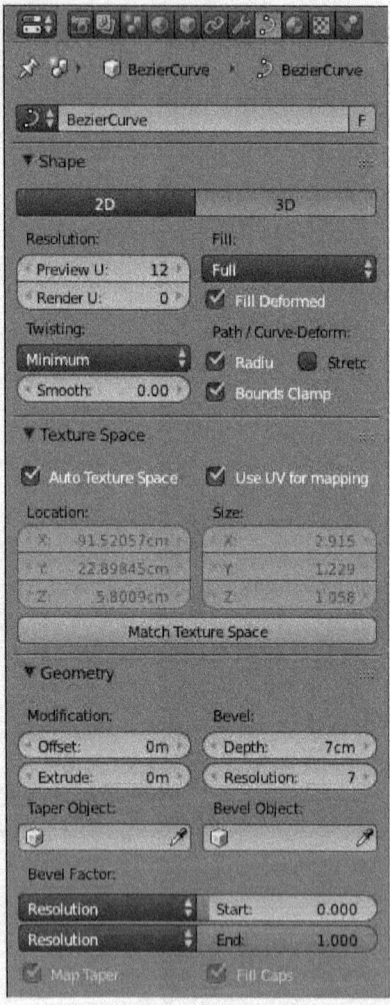

fig. 434 the *Curve Data* tab

In the **Texture Space** panel check *Use UV for Mapping* to allow the texture to be mapped on this kind of object. This operation is equivalent to the *unwrapping*.

Finally, give a thickness to the curve.

In the **Geometry** panel set a value higher than 0 in the *Bevel*. This will give a thickness to the curve, whereas *Resolution* will smooth the surface.

The curve will appear in this way.

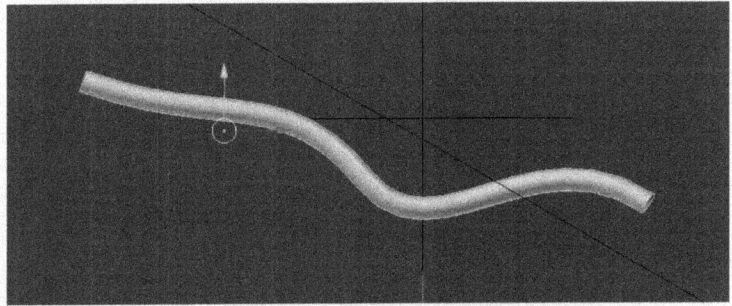

fig. 435 the *Bézier* curve with the thickness

Add now a material and open the *Node Editor*.

Assign a *Noise Texture* to the *Diffuse*. The 3D curve surface will appear colored.

Obviously it is possible to suitably map the *texture* inserting the usual *Texture Coordinate* and *Mapping* nodes at the *texture* beginning.

By connecting the *Fac* output socket of the *Noise Texture* with the *Displacement socket* of the *Material Output* node, the *texture* will correctly perform a *Bump* on the curve.

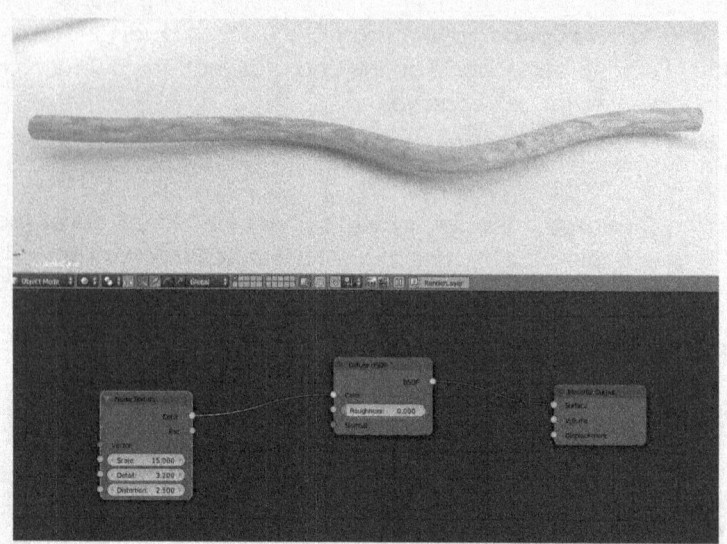

fig. 436 the *Noise texture* on the curve

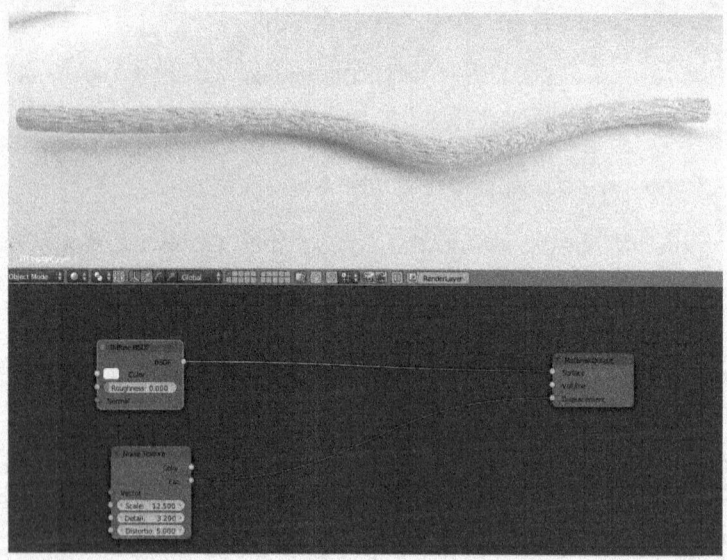

fig. 437 the *Noise texture* acts as a *Bump* on the curve

378

You can now try to create a more complex node configuration, by mixing two brown tones, balanced by the *Noise texture* for simulating the wood veins.

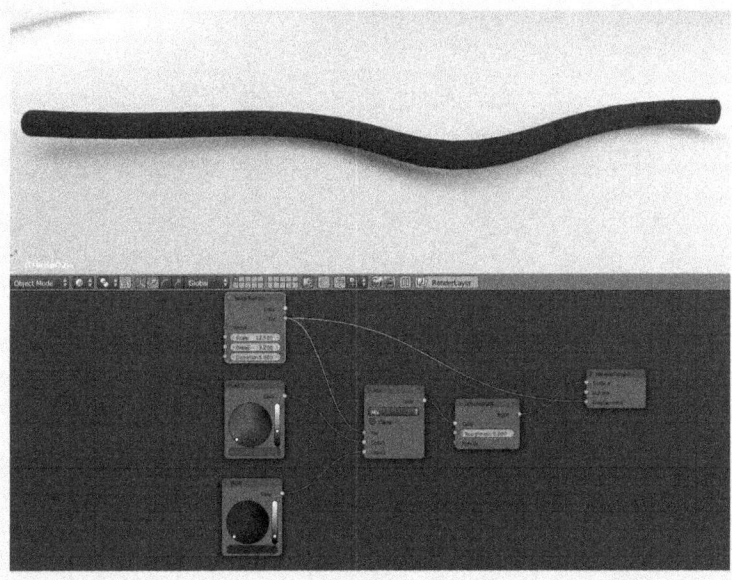

fig. 438 simulation of the wood veins on a curve

4
TEXTURE PAINT MODE

4.1. Painting on a mesh

Up to now we learned how the materials applied to an object can be comprised of a series of events, effects and shaders.

We also saw how the *textures*, meant as base colors (*Diffuse*) of a material, can be uploaded by an external file or obtained through Blender procedural computations.

Finally we saw how, with the use of nodes, the *textures* can be deformed, colored again and corrected.

In this chapter we will learn how to create a *texture* by directly drawing it in Blender, using the mouse or better a graphic paddle.

Several paddles are available on the market, of all types and costs.

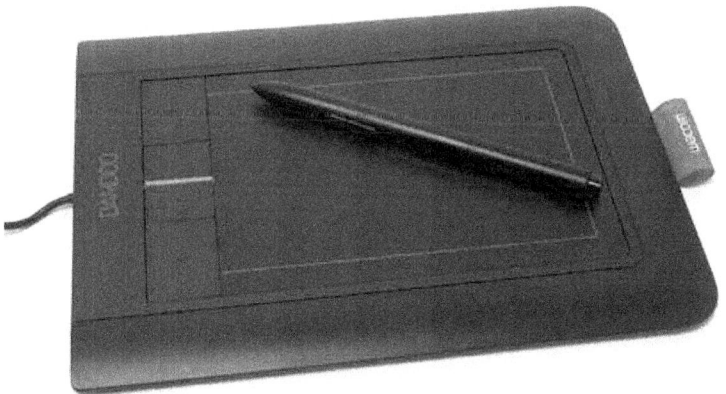

fig. 439 graphic paddle *Wacom Bamboo*

383

Essentially, other than the medium used to draw, there exist two methods for painting, directly creating the *texture* in Blender:

1) painting a 2D image in the *UV/Image* Editor, directly on the selected *texture* or creating a new one (New), using its *UV* mapping for transferring the colors on the mesh faces;

2) drawing the *texture* directly on the *mesh*, in the 3D view, and let Blender using the *UV* mapping presently selected.

Obviously it is also possible to use any photo editing program out of Blender like Gimp, for example, which is still an *open* source code, for creating the image.

The environment and the tool Blender uses to paint a *texture* is called *Texture Painting*.

Before being able to draw on a *texture* of a *mesh* it is necessary to perform the mesh unwrapping.

Then we must create a new *texture* (as we previously learned in the section where we explained the *baking*, or upload an existing one on which to operate.

As already said, it is possible to directly draw on the *mesh* or draw a *texture* in the *UV/Image Editor*, in 2D.

In the first case, in the 3D view, it is only needed to go in **Texture Paint Mode** by selecting *Mode* in the 3D view header.

fig. 440 *Texture Paint Mode* in the 3D view window

In the second case it is needed, once uploaded or created the texture to be painted, to activate the Paint *Mode* among the options present in the *UV/Image Editor* header.

384

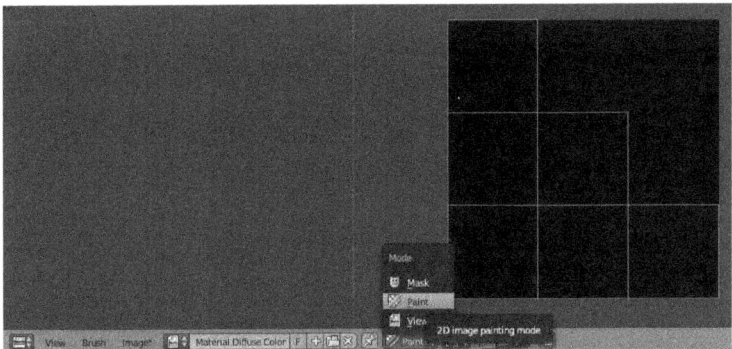

fig. 441 *Paint Mode* in the *UV/Image Editor*

Once activated the *Texture Paint Mode* (or *Paint* in the *UV/Image Editor*), the mouse pointer becomes a small circle, indicating the brush thickness. In this mode the mesh cannot be transformed or modified.

The *Tools Shelf* of the 3D view and of the *UV/Image Editor* contain *tabs* and dedicated panels, which we will analyze in a short.

4.1.1. Menu of the 3d view and of the *UV/Image Editor*

As always happens, also in *Texture Paint Mode* Blender adapts its menus.

The commands that can be found in the 3D view and in the *UV/Image Editor* are essentially the same as in the *Object Mode*.

Only to menus are added, personalized for the modality: *Brush* and *Image*.

The menu **View** does not add any new information with respect to the same menu in *Object Mode*.

385

fig. 442 the *Brush* menu

The drop-down menu **Brush**, common to the 3D view and to the *UV/Image Editor*, contains some options activating some settings.

- the sub menu *Image Paint Tool* activates or deactivates the tools relevant to the image;

fig. 443 the sub menu *Image Paint Tool*

- the sub menu *Enabled Modes* activates or deactivates the effect on the other mesh modalities;

386

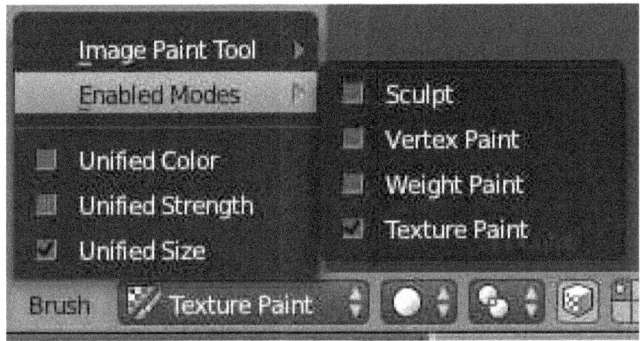

fig. 444 the sub menu *Enabled Modes*

- the check on *Unified Color* makes the color uniform in the painting;

- the check on *Unified Strength* makes uniform the brush strength;

- the check on *Unified Size*, finally, makes uniform the brush size.

The **Image** menu, placed in the *UV/Image Editor* header, contains the commands for the management of the uploaded or created image.

- *Pack as PNG* inserts the *texture* as a*gile* *.png* added to the *file* *.blend;

- *Pack Image* inserts the *texture* as a image *file* added to the *file* *.blend;

- *Invert* opens a sub drop-down menu where it is possible to define the inversion of the texture colors, of the primary colors comprising the texture or of the *alpha* channel;

- *Edit Externally* enables to edit the texture by means of a program out of Blender;

- *Save a Copy* save a texture copy;

- *Save As Image* (key F3) saves the current *texture* in another image file and places it based on the path defined by the *Browser*;

- *Save Image* (ALT + S) saves the current image updating the saved file;

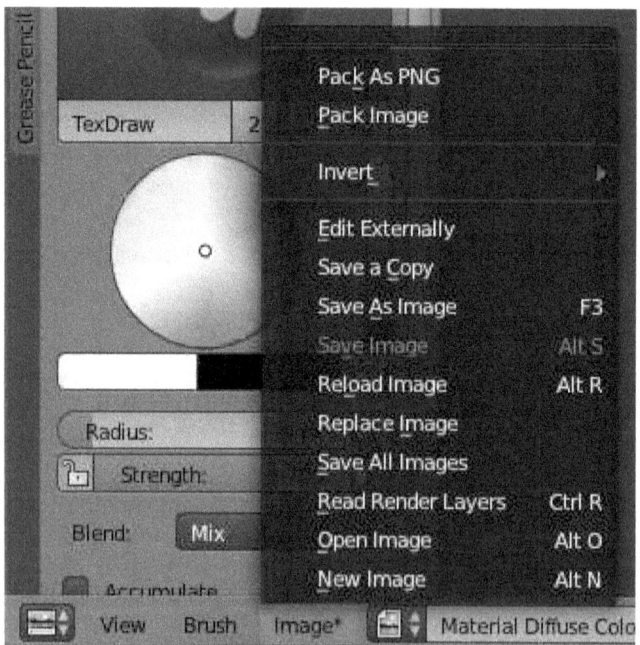

fig. 445 the *Image* menu

- *Reload Image* (ALT + R) reload the image if the latter has been modified or externally substituted;

388

- *Replace Image* replaces the image with another one chosen from the *Browser*;

- *Save All Images* saves all the images created in a *file* on the disk; *Read Render Layers* (CTRL + R) reads all the *Render Layers* present in the scene, if necessary;

- *Open Image* (ALT + O) upload an image from an external file;

- *New Image* (ALT + N), as already seen in the paragraph relevant to the *backing*, creates a new *texture* starting from a background color and from the dimensions.

By creating a new image a window will open in which define name, dimensions, depth in *bit* and *alpha* channel of the new empty image.

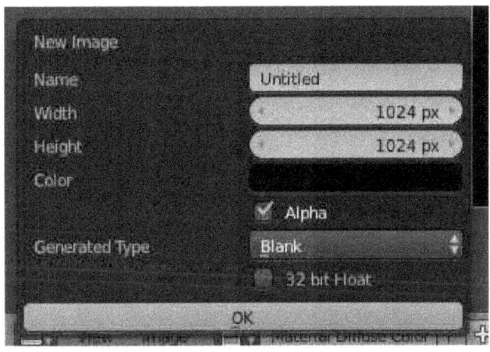

fig. 446 the *New Image* panel

4.1.2. The *Tools Shelf* in ambient *Texture Paint*

The *Tools Shelf* can be activated with the key T and contains some *tab* and some brushes closely related to the *texture painting*.

389

A) *TAB TOOLS*

fig. 447 the *Tools Shelf* panels in *Texture Paint* environment

Inside the *tab* **Tools** the panels closely related to the drawing and painting function cab be found.

The **Brush** panel contains the painting tools.

Once uploaded or created a texture, this panel activates the brush (or pen) option choices.

Clicking in the area on the top it is possible to choose the brush type among the available ones in the list.

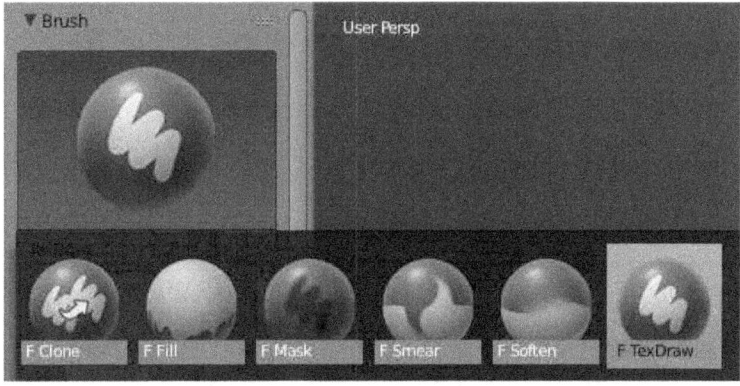

fig. 448 the *Brush* choice

On the bottom it is possible to name the *brush*, duplicate or cancel it.

The palette enables to define the *brush* color, the thickness (*Radius*), and the strength impressed in the drawing (*Strength*).

The menu *Blending Mode* enables to define the way the virtual "*paint*" is applied to the underlying surface.

The main methods are:

- Mix: the brush color is mixed with the existing colors;

391

- *Add*: the brush color is added to the existing color, yielding as a result the sum of the two colors;

- *Subtract*: the brush color is subtracted from the existing one;

- *Multiply*: the base *RGB* value is multiplied by the brush color;

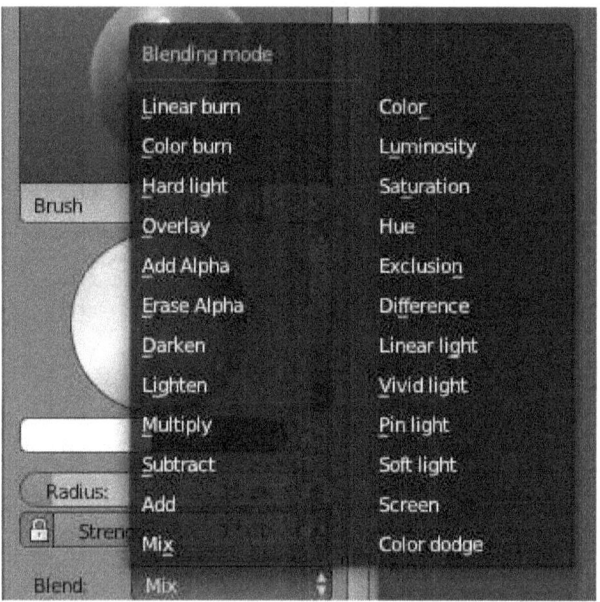

fig. 449 *Blending Mode*

- *Lighten*: the base color *RGB* value is increased of the brush color;

- Darken: attenuates the colors;

- *Erase Alpha*: makes the image transparent to the brush passage, enabling to see through the background colors and the possible textures at the lower level;

- *Add Alpha*: make the image more opaque to the brush passage.

The checkbox *nAccumulate* enables to superimpose the colors one next to the other.

The flag on *Alpha*, if disabled, blocks and keep the transparencies during the painting.

The flag on *Use Gradient* activates a *Color Ramp* defining a technique soft painting, defined in the *Mode* menu.

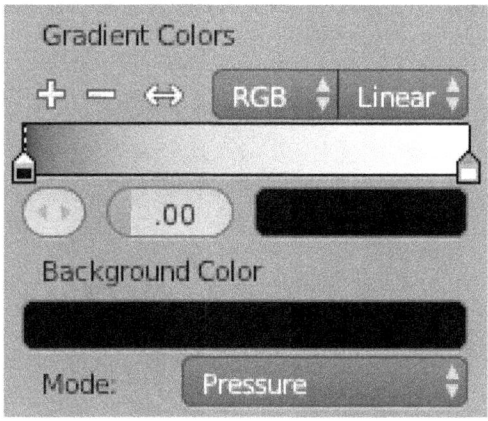

fig. 450 *Gradient Colors*

The **Texture** panel enables to use a *texture* uploaded by the dedicated *Browser* to be used as brush.

That *texture*, in the brush, can be regularly mapped onto the *brush* in such a way as it can be rotated (*Angle*), translated (*Offset*) or scaled (*Size*).

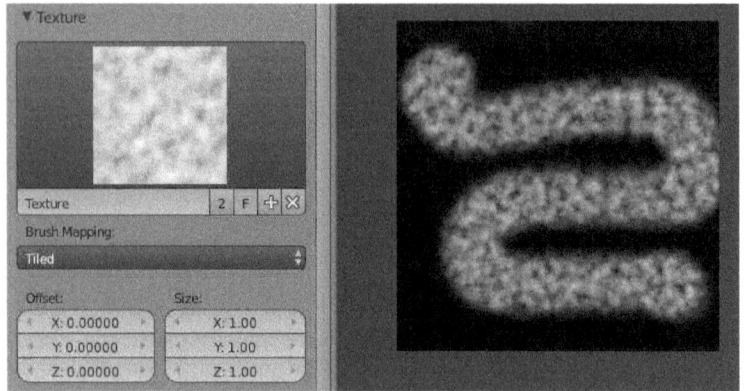

fig. 451 a *texture* used as *brush*

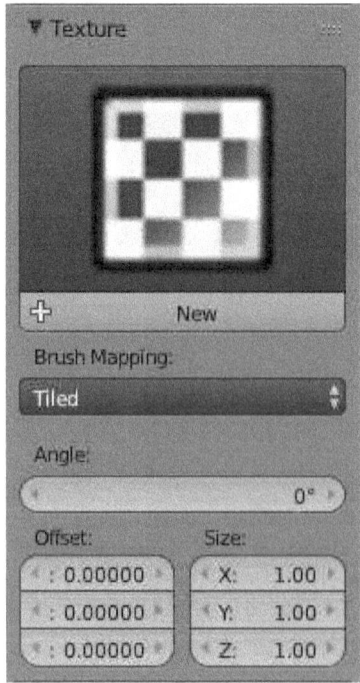

fig. 452 the *Texture* panel

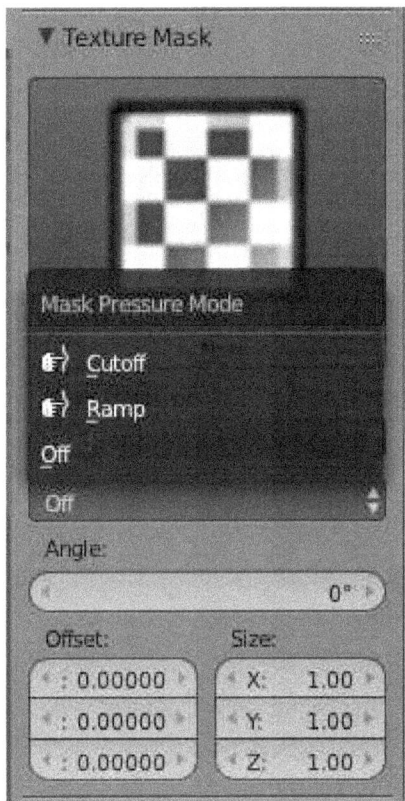

fig. 453 the *Texture Mask* panel

The *Brush mapping* menu sets the method for applying the texture to the brush.

- *View Plane*: in 2D painting, the *texture* moves together with the brush;

- *Tiles*: the *texture* is compensated by the brush position;

- *3D*: same modality as *Tiles*;

- *Stencil*: the *texture* is applied only to the boundary of the *stencil*;

- *Random*: applies the *texture* randomly.

Some of these modalities add some parameters relevant to *angle*:

- *User*: enables to directly insert the angle value;

- *Rate*: *Angle* follows the direction of the brush line. Not available with 3Dtextures;

- *Random*: *Angle* is randomized.

The **Texture Mask** panel offers the same settings of the previous one, but its scope is to make a texture uploaded from the browser to behave as a mask.

A menu is added, determining the Mode of the mask action depending on the brush pressure (*Off*, *Cutoff*, *Ramp*).

The **Stroke** panel defines the parameters relevant to the line.

The *Stroke Method* menu enables to choose the way the effect is applied. It is possible to choose between:

- *Airbrush*, producing a continuous movement of the brush, while the LMB is kept pressed, generated by the setting *Rate*. If disabled, the brush can modify only the color when it changes its position;

- *Space*, creating a dotted line, where the dot spacing is determined by the setting *Spacing*;

- *Dots*, applying the "*painting*" for an mouse movement;

- *Jitter*, modifying the brush position during the painting;

396

- *Smooth Stroke*, generating a line with a certain delay with respect to the mouse movement, following an easy path. When it is active, are also activated:

- *Ray*, setting the minimum distance from the last dot before the continuous line;
- *Factor*, setting the amount of smoothing;
- *Input* Samples, defining the average number of samples acting on the line smoothing;
- Wrap, wrapping the paint toward the top of the image, like the brush could exit out from the other painting side. It is very useful for creating uniform *textures*.

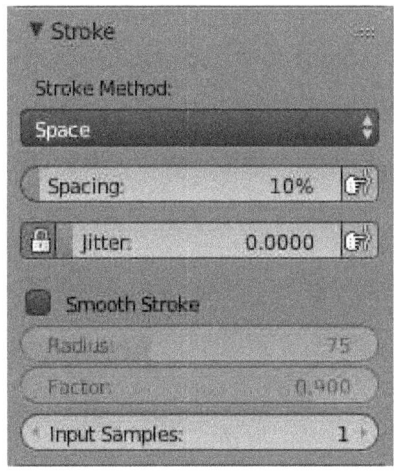

fig. 454 the *Stroke* panel

The **Curve** panel enables to control the decaying of the paint produced by the brush. The curve shape change will make the brush softer of harder.

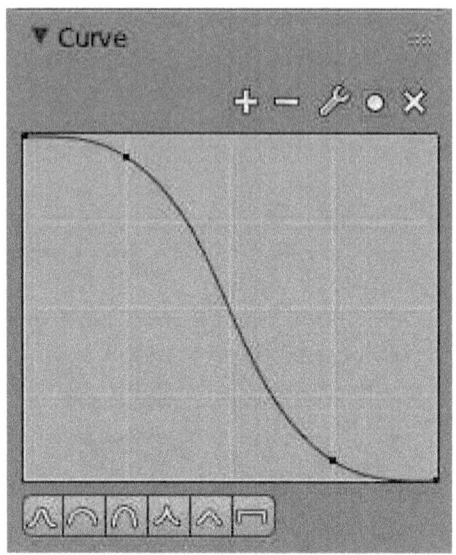

fig. 455 the *Curve* panel

The **External** panel uses the image of external use.

- *Quick Edit*, for example, makes a *screenshot* of the current view in an external image viewer.

- Apply project the edited image on the object.

- The two counters determine the dimensions in *pixel* of the external image.

- *Apply Camera image* projects the camera rendered image on the object.

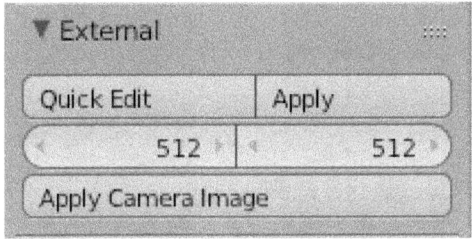

fig. 456 the *External* panel

The **Symmetry** panel enables to define possible symmetry axes, with respect to the selected object, such as the painted lines will be symmetrically duplicated on the mesh.

This function is useful when a texture specular with respect to the mesh is created, to avoid to repeat twice the drawings.

It is possible to set x, y and/or z as symmetry axes.

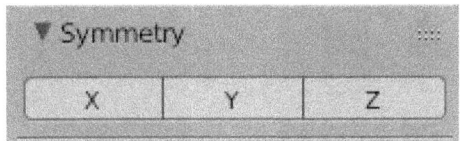

fig. 457 the *Symmetry* panel

B) *TAB SLOTS*

In this tab all the painted textures are contained, placed in suitable slots.

The slots can be visualized in the **Slots** panel. They can be renamed with a double click and the Mode of mesh projection of the paint is set in the *Painting Mode* menu, in which it is

399

possible to choose if the textures should be found in the material (*Material*) or the selected image should be set as texture (*Image*).

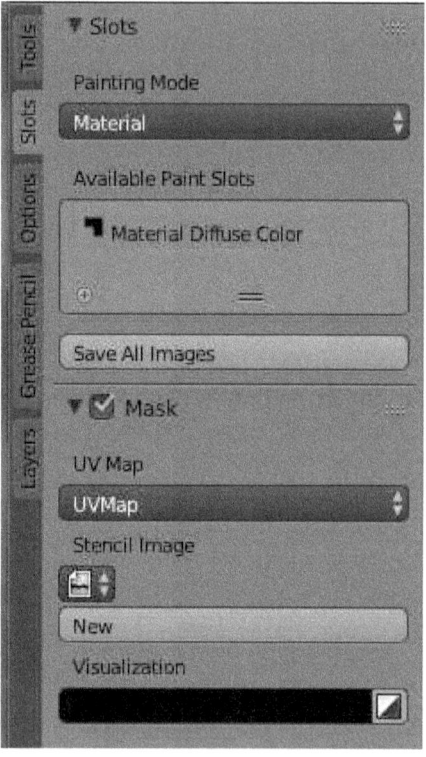

fig. 458 the *Slots* tabs

The command *Save All Images* enables to save on disk all the painted images.

The **Mask** panel, if activated, enables to choose the *Stencil Image* among the ones used in the memory, or to create a new one (*New*).

400

C) *TAB OPTIONS*

fig. 459 the *Options* tab

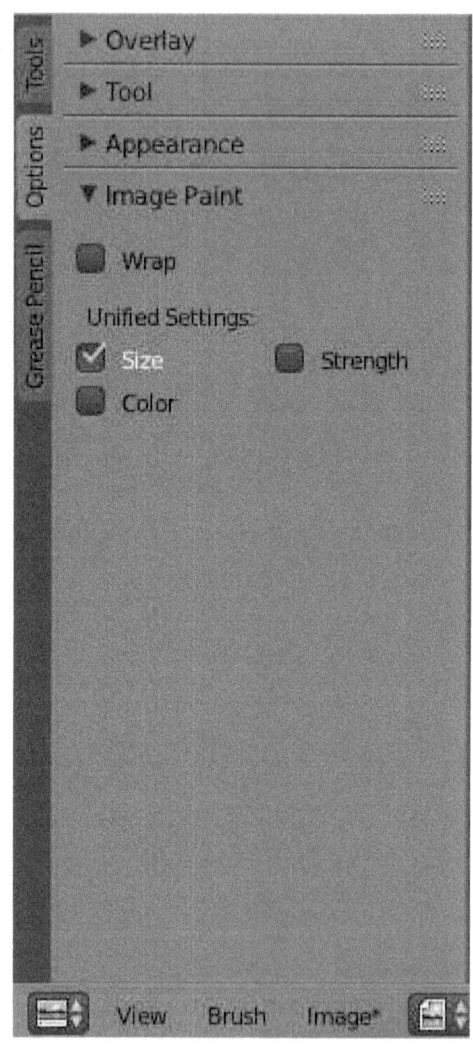

fig. 460 the Image Paint panel (only in the Options tab of the UV/Image Editor)

In the **Overlay** panel it is possible to personalize and balance the curve visualization and the brush line consistency, depending on the percentage values relevant to *Curve, Texture* and *Mask Texture*.

In the **Appearance** panel it is possible to personalize the brush edge color (*Show Brush*), and to specify a personalized icon.

In the **Project Paint** panel some secondary options are defined, relevant to the line projection methodology as a function of the mesh geometry and to the line grain (*Dither*).

The **Image Paint** panel, active only in the *UV/Image Editor*, contains information similar to those contained in the previous panel.

 EXERCISE N. 19: COLOR A TEXTURE DIRECTLY ON THE MESH

After having described all the commands, the options and the tools relevant to the *Texture Painting*, we can develop an exercise useful to practice what we learned.

We will create a cup for coffee which we will paint handmade.

First of all restore the cup *mesh* in the previous exercise.

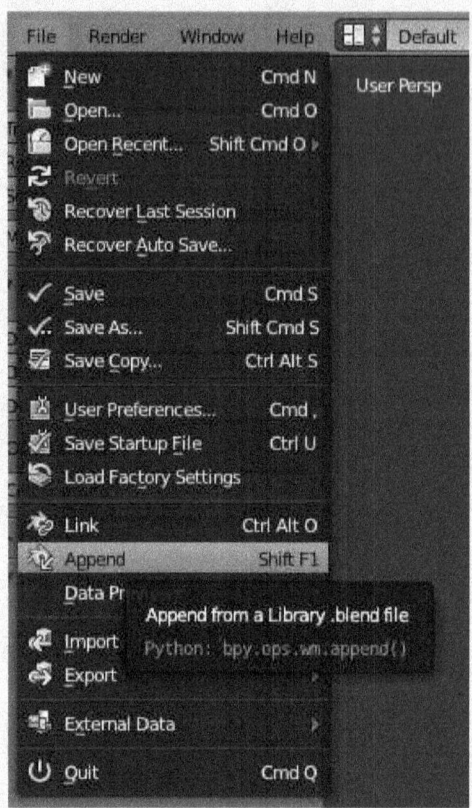

fig. 461 the *File – Append* menu

4.3.1. *Append*

For inserting it in the current project, let's introduce a simple and new command: *Append*.

This command enables to insert an object and all its materials contained in an external file into a current scene.

In the *File* menu of the *header* of the *Info* window, choose the option *Append* (or digit SHIFT + F1).

A *Browser* will open, in which to choose what should be copied into the scene. For our case choose *Object* and then the *mesh* relevant to the cup. Confirm the choice. The cup will be now placed into the scene.

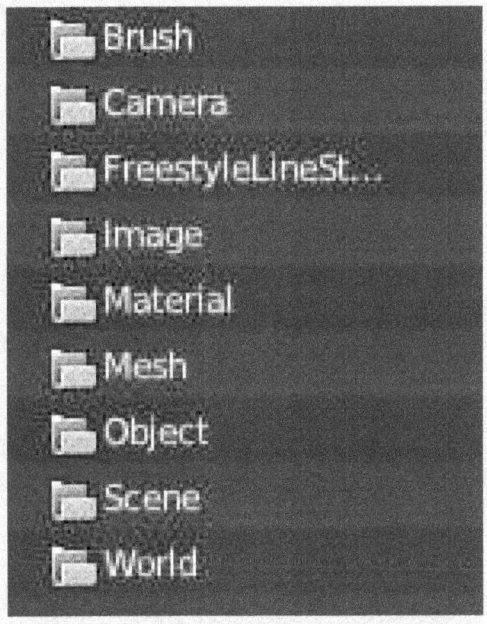

fig. 462 choice of the object to be attached

Now insert a plane and rescale it, then a *Lamp* of *Spot* type for illuminating the cup.

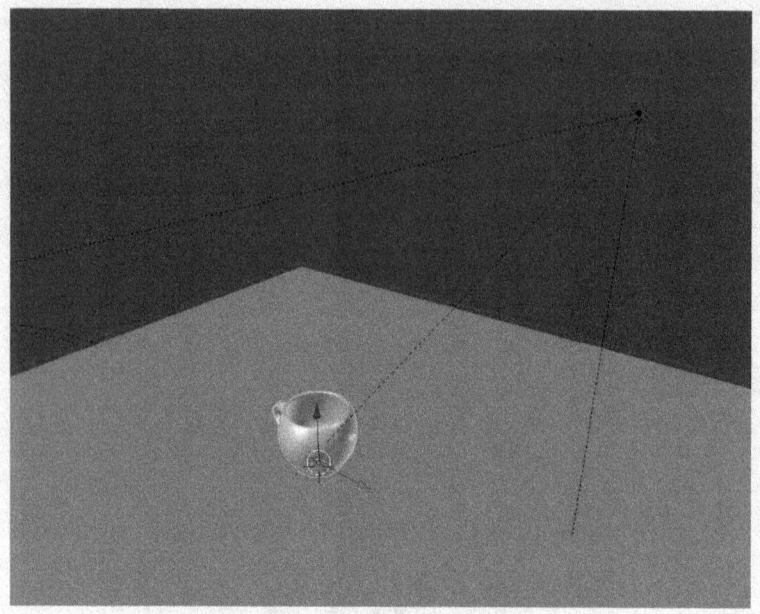

fig. 463 the scene

Select the cup, enter in *Edit Mode*, select all the vertices with A and execute the *unwrapping* by typing U.

Organize the Blender windows such as to have the 3D view, the *Node Editor* and the *UV/Image Editor* on which the unwrapped mesh will be visualized and placed on a plane.

Add now an empty *texture* in the *UV/Image Editor*, clicking on *New* and setting the name, for example "*cup decorations*", the white color and the resolution: 3000 x 3000 *pixels* to get a neat and defined line. Confirm with OK.

fig. 464 the overall project visualized

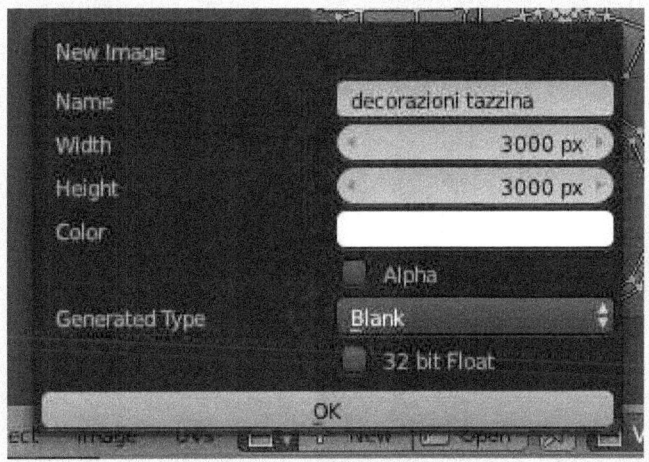

fig. 465 addition of a new empty texture

Insert an Image Texture node in the Node Editor to be connected to the *Diffuse*. In this node, upload the just created *texture*, choosing from the drop-down menu generated by the icon next to the *Open* button.

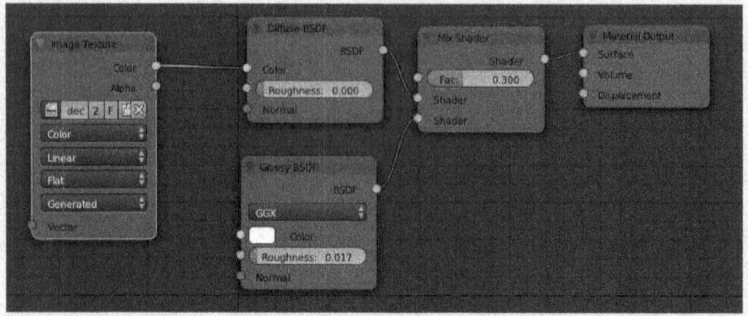

fig. 466 addition of the *Image Texture* node on which upload the just created *texture*

Add an *Emission* panel from the top.

Then select the cup and enter in *Texture Paint*.

fig. 467 *texture Paint Mode*

Select the *Brush* and set the brush radius at 5 *pixels* and the strength at 0.5 to get a not neat paint, similar to a watercolor. Select the gray color and start to paint on the *mesh*.

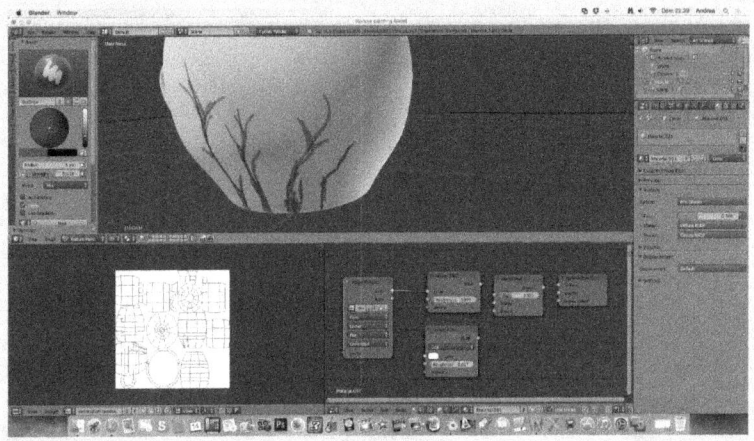

fig. 468 painting on the *mesh*

Note: take into account that the brush dimensions remain constant, thus the line will depend on the proximity with the mesh and the zoom.

In case of overlapping and overlapped landscapes, if *Mix* or *Add* is set, the color will be multiplied or added with the background, appearing darker.

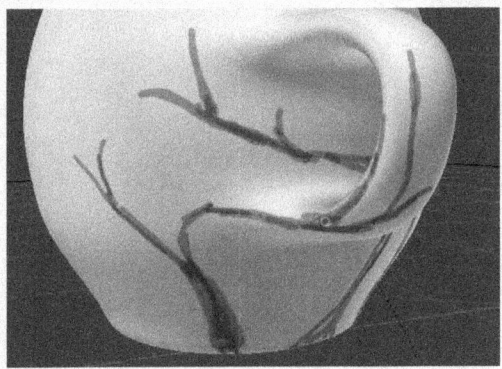

fig. 469 by rotating the *mesh* we can paint in any part of the surface

Note how the *texture* in the *UV/Image Editor* is updated in real time with what is drawn in the 3D scene.

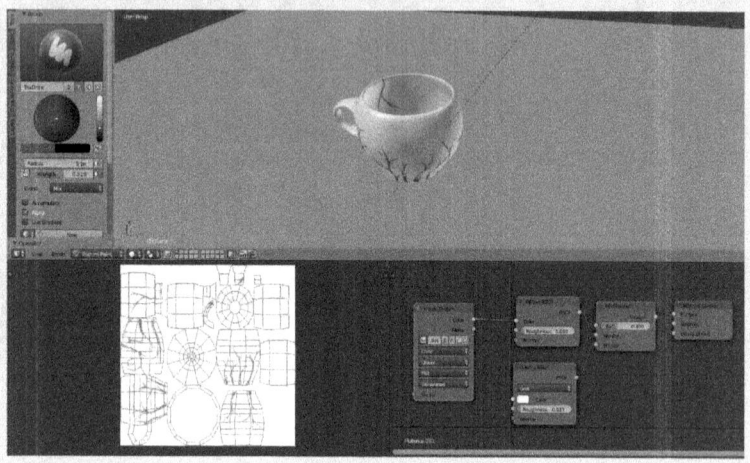

fig. 470 at the end of the operation the *texture* will result updated

At the end of the job, w can set the frame and launch the *rendering*. Remember to save the texture with F3.

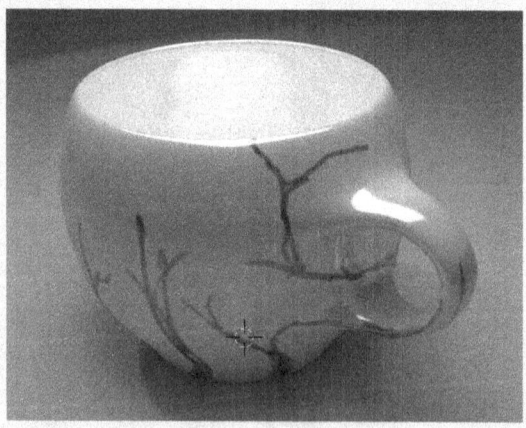

fig. 471 *rendering* of the cup painted handmade

410

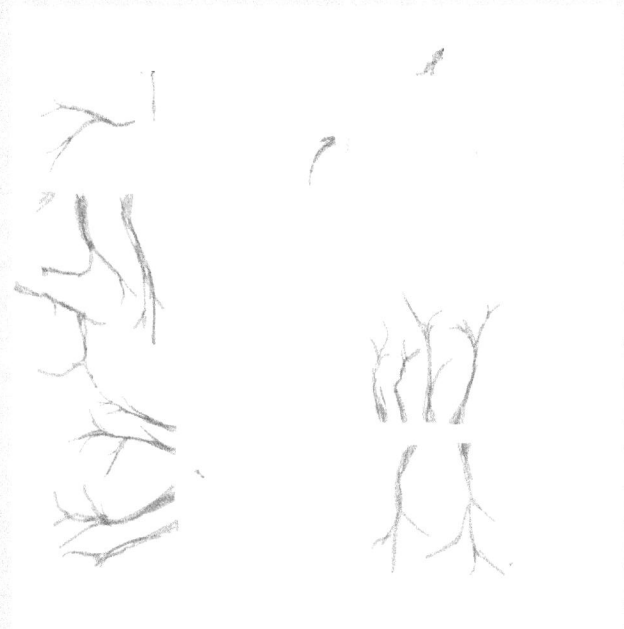

fig. 472 the saved *texture*

5

THE FRAMING

5.1. The Camera

After finishing the modeling, mapping scene lighting processes, the last task to be accomplished before the rendering if the framing.

The tool used for the framing is the camera. The latter can be still (photo camera) or for movement (video camera).

First of all it is useful to remember that Blender is able to insert several cameras inside the same scene, even if only the active one is devoted to the framing.

The local framing axes, defined for convention as x directed horizontally, y vertically and z directed normally to itself, whose positive direction is defined by the vector pointing fat from the observer.

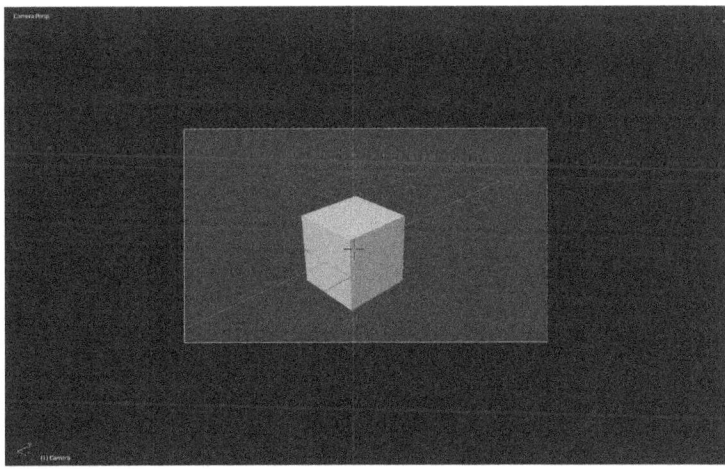

fig. 473 active camera framing of the scene (x, y)

Remember that the *shortcut* to move from the 3D view to the active camera framing of the scene is 0 NUM, or in the *View* menu of the 3D view, the option *Cameras - Active Camera*.

Another method for visualizing which one is the active camera is to observe the icon placed at the right hand side of the camera in the *Outliner*. Differently from the non-active cameras, the active one is circled in light gray.

fig. 474 the active camera represented in the *Outliner*

Inside a scene with several cameras, the active one is not necessarily the one selected and colored in light orange.

In the 3D view, in the Select menu inside the *header*, the option *Select Camera* immediately shows which one is the active camera.

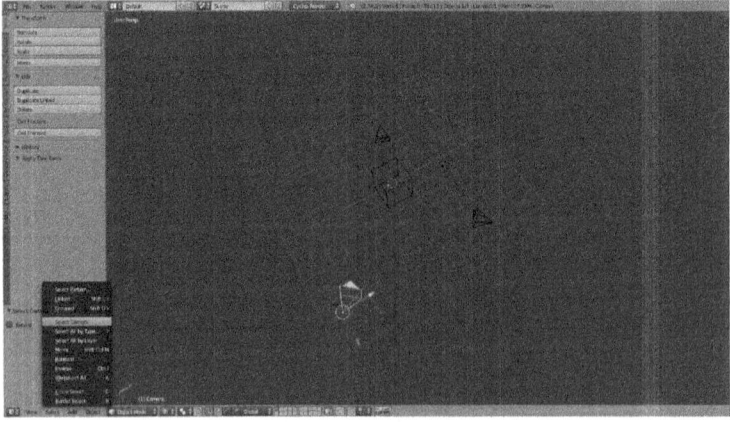

fig. 474 active camera selection

On the other hand, for making active a selected camera, it is only needed to enter the *View* menu and select the choice *Set Active Object As Camera* from the submenu *Cameras*, or to digit the *shortcut* CTRL + 0 NUM.

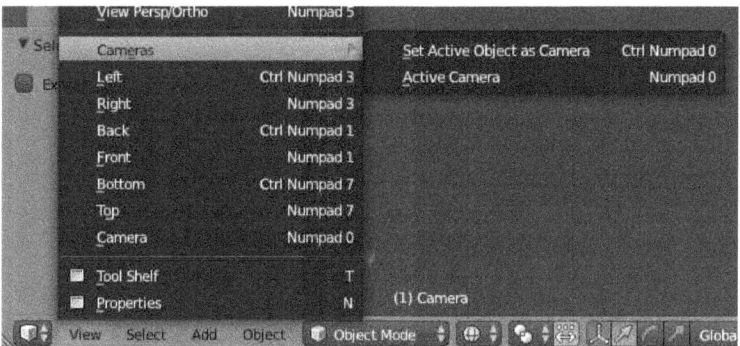

fig. 474 setting as active the selected camera

Thus the framing refers always to the active camera and not to the selected camera.

Nevertheless it is always not recommended to insert into a scene several cameras, unless in case of very simple scenes.

This because the same lighting in the scene is not necessarily suitable for all the framings.

For example a framing of a detail could not properly reproduce it and represent it in shadow, or too flat, or out of focus or too few reflecting, if the same lighting of the overall scene is adopted.

Often the use of auxiliary *ad hoc* lightings, like emitting panels, objects invisible to the camera near the detail, fully change the outcome.

So each framing has usually its own lighting configuration and the latter cannot be suitable to all the other framings.

What to do then?

A solution is to use the layers.

By inserting in separate *layers* camera and lights devoted to each framing could be a fast method when the scene is simple. Blender does not offer too many *layers* and wasting them for the framings in not particularly indicated.

The conceptually most correct method is to use the **Scenes**.

5.1.1. The *Scenes*

In the scenes all the elements belonging to a project are collected, which must be represented by a specific framing. Objects or part of objects not framed can be even eliminated, such s to make lighter the scene itself, the *file* and the *rendering* process.

In the *header* of the *Info Editor*, the *Scene* menu is just used to manage the project scenes.

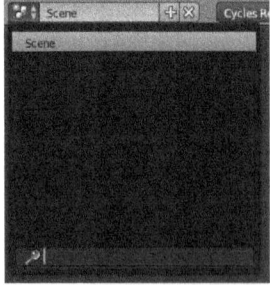

fig. 477 the *Scene* menu of the *Info Editor*

These can be selected from the drop-down menu by clicking on the icon, created (by clicking the key +) or canceled (by clicking the key X).

When a new scene is created (key +), a dedicated menu appears (*New Scene*) from which it is possible to choose the creation parameters.

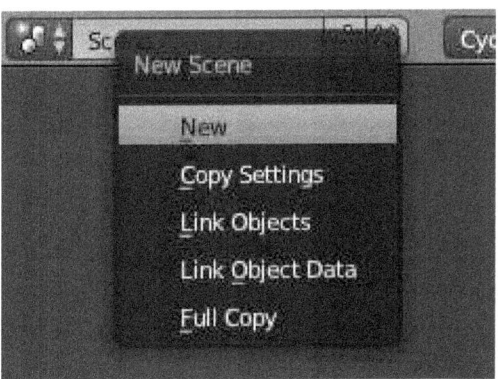

fig. 478 the *New Scene* menu

The options are:

- *New* (creates a new empty scene);

- *Copy Settings* (creates a new scene by importing only the current scene settings);

- *Link Objects* (creates a new scene in which the inserted objects are directly connected with the current scene ones and are subjected to their influence for any modification or transformation);

- *Link Object Data* (creates a new scene in which the inserted objects are the same, with the same characteristics, of the ones present in the current scene, but not related or connected to the them);

419

- *Full Copy* (creates an exact copy of the current scene).

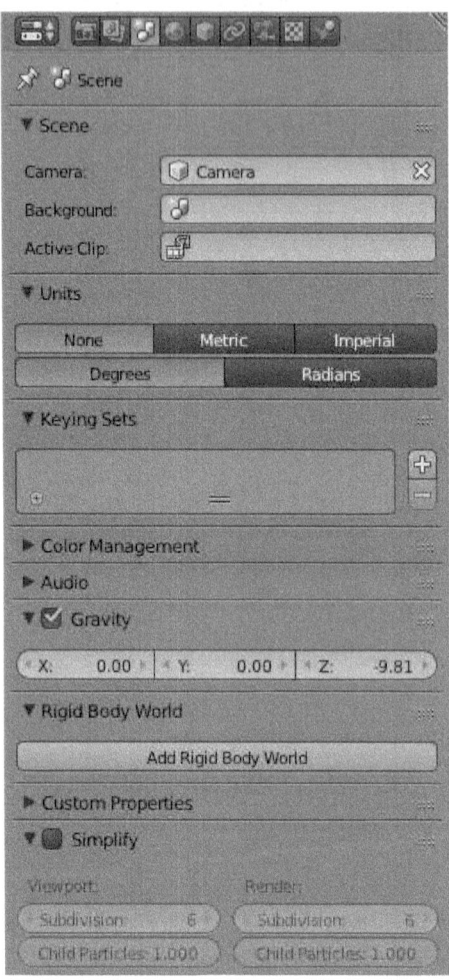

fig. 479 the *Scene* tab of the *Properties Editor*

The choice must obviously be done based on the present needs.

In the new scene the active camera can be replaced, a possibly auxiliary illumination can be added, the global light can be regulated and the objects out of the framing can be removed.

It is recommended to preserve a reference global scene in which all the main objects of the scene are present.

Remember that the scene settings are summarized in the *Scene* tab of the *Properties Editor*, already analyzed in volume 1.

5.1.2. The *View* panel of the 3D view *Property Bar*

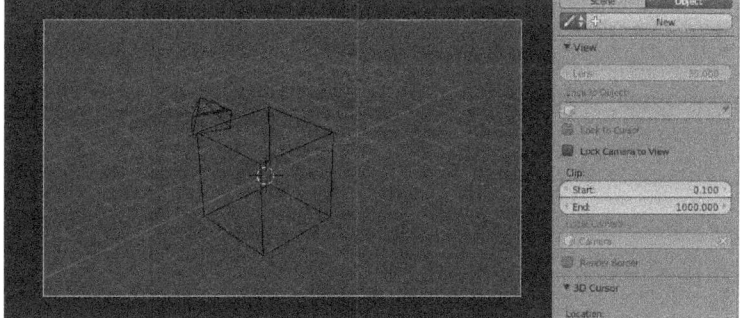

fig. 480 the *View* panel

Remember that it is possible to execute in the **View** panel some functions referred to the current view, even in the specific case of the framing.

In particular remember that *Lens* defines the view lens, but not the camera lens, *Clip* defines the visualization limits, *Lock Camera to View* enables to navigate inside the framing and *Render Border* enables to define an area, selected with a box, inside which the pre rendering will be visible (SHIFT +Z).

421

5.2. Data tab

The **Data** tab of the *Properties Editor* summarizes all the information and parameters relevant to the camera.

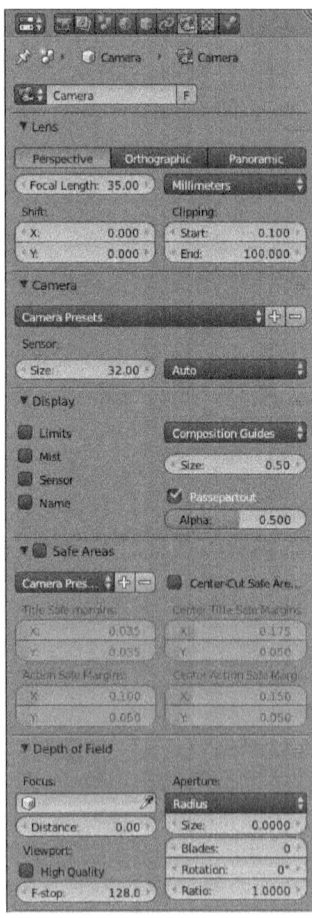

fig. 481 the *Data* tab

Let us repeat what already explained in chapter 3 of the first volume.

In *tab*, from the top to the bottom we find several panels.

The *Camera* icon enables the choice of the current camera;

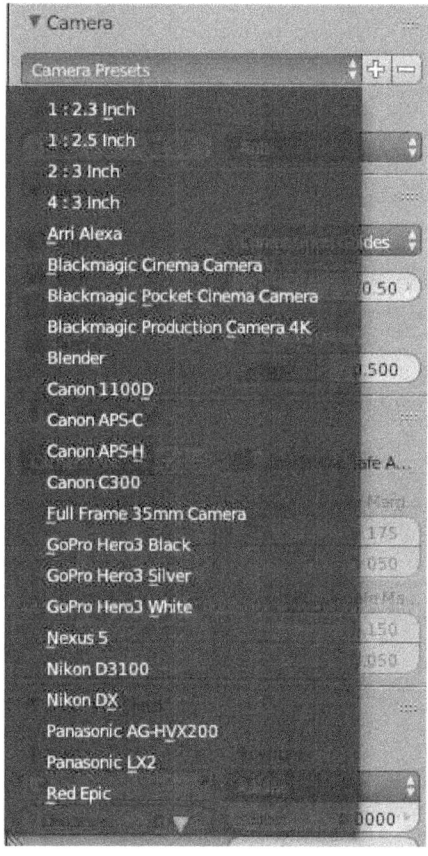

fig. 482 *Camera Presets*

The **Lens** panel contains the parameters and the information relevant to the lens type, choosing among the main visualizations:

- *Perspective;*

- *Orthographic;*

- *Panoramic* (with a choice between *Fisheye* and *Equirectangular*).

- *Focal Length*, expressed in millimeters defines the camera focal length;

- *Shift* enables to translate horizontally (*x*) or vertically (*y*) a frame without image deformation and without displacement of the vanishing points;

- *Clipping* has the same function of the same command in the 3D view;

The **Camera** panel sets the camera physical characteristics:

- the *Camera Preset* menu enables to choose a predefined camera in the settings based on models in use on the market;

- *Sensor* defines the dimensions in millimeters of the camera sensor;

Display defines what to be visualized and rendered:

- *Limits; Mist* (if activated); *Sensor* (the sensor data), *Name* (the camera name);

- *Composition Guide* is a drop-down menu enabling to visualize (but not to render) some guidelines, very useful in photography for a correct framing;

- The line dimensions;

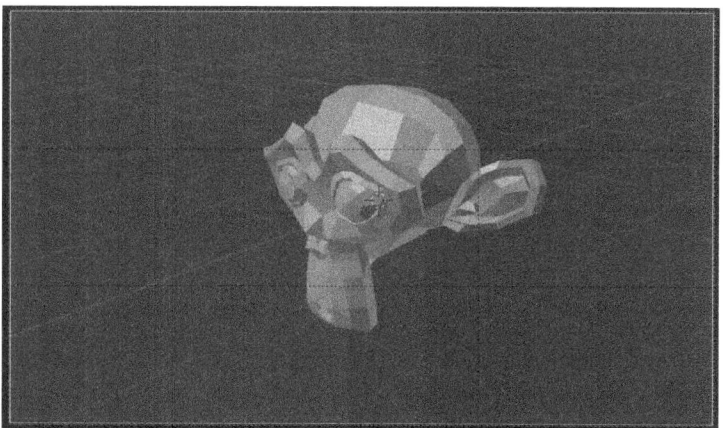

fig. 483 the guidelines (in the image: the average third method)

- *Passpartout* and its *Alpha* value in percentage, make darker the external part of the framing making it more visible.

The **Depth of Field** panel contains all the data relevant to the camera focalization and the objective aperture:

- *Focus* enables to insert an object as focalization target, chosen between the scene object list in the drop-down menu (for example an *Empty* object);

- *Distance*, the focalization distance;

- *Aperture Type*, expressed either with the radial distance(in meters)or in *F-Stop* value (e.g. 5,6);

425

- The aperture value;

- *Blades* indicates the objective blade number;

- *Rotation* indicates the rotation degree number of the blades;

- *Ratio*, indicates the distortion simulating the blade anamorphic effect (with relevant parameter ranging from 1 to 2);

The **Safe Area** panel defines the secure shot area, beyond which the image or the video will be visualized in any case, even if the support format were different. For example: 14:9 instead of 16:9.

The discussion concerning the camera and the shot could be much more developed, but we believe that this is not the best place to present a full dissertation of it, and of the photography and illumination techniques.

Thus we will not discuss in this book topics regarding shot techniques, fields and all the concepts regarding this huge argument.

The interested reader is invited to consider specific photography texts.

6

PARENT RELATIONS
AND CONSTRAINTS

6.1. To parent objects

Working in an orderly way is, as we always said, the best starting point.

We have seen how to model in a neat way, how to group objects having the same nature or in some way related each other in a layer, how to rename them such as to be readily recognized, how to use *layers* and *Scenes*.

Let us analyze now a new topic, very useful and involved in several applications: the parent relation between objects.

This technique enables, for example, to bind one or more objects to another one, or connect the object components to an external element behaving as a parent.

In the animation, as it will be clear in the foregoing books, binding the objects will be essential for a simple and functional management.

Analogously, in the *rigging*, the *mesh* bone could be bound to an external object, or to a lattice, in order to manage the deformations.

The parent is also used in binding a specific path to one or more objects.

Blender supports the parent relation between objects, *bones*, *Curve Deform*, *Path Constraint*, *Lattice Deform*, vertices.

Before starting to discuss in detail the parent relations, let us analyze the *Constraints* tab, contained in the *Properties Editor*, enclosing all the constraint typologies, which can regulate the object behavior.

429

6.2. Tab Constraints

The *tab* **Constraints**, inside the *Properties Editor*, collects all the tools binding, or tying, the objects one to each other, according to certain rules and specific functions.

Even if the *constraints* may result very useful in the static scenes, for example favoring the object placement, rotation and scaling, they have been designed mainly for the animation, since they enable to limit and control the object degrees of freedom, either in absolute sense (i.e. in the global space), and relatively to other objects.

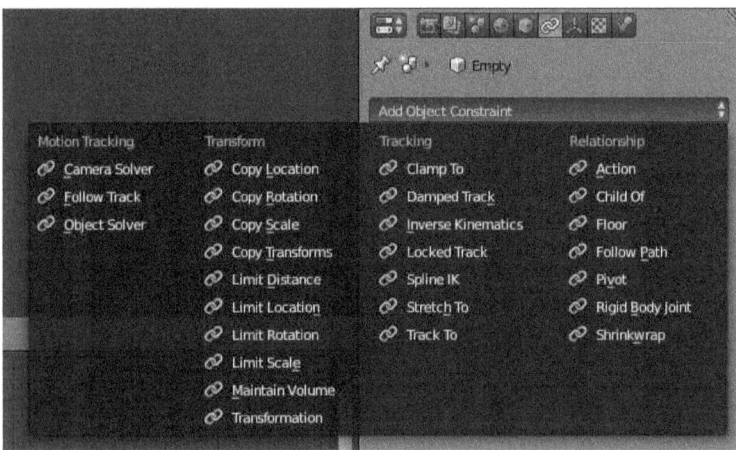

fig. 484 *Constraints* tab

By selecting an object in the scene, it is possible to associate to it a connection by clicking on the *Add Object Constraints* menu.

A window subdivided in 4 sections will open, classifying the constraints by categories: *Motion Tracking* (relevant to the

430

namesake tracing system), *Transform* (associating to the object a transformation bind and dimensional data of another object), *Tracking* (containing the tracing options of an object with respect to another one); *Relationship* (binding an object to the behavior of another one or of physics related action).

In this chapter we will only see the functions contained in the *Transform* and *Relationship* sections.

6.2.1. Transform

These constraints directly control or limit the transformation properties of the selected object bound to another one, in an absolute way or relevant to the target object properties.

Copy Location forces the object to bind its position to the position of another object.

fig. 485 the *Copy Location* panel

- *Target* defines the object whose position will be the reference for the selected one.

- *X, Y* and *Z* bind the position only with respect to the selected axes.

- *Invert* enables to invert the coordinates relevant to the selected axes.

- *Offset*, if activated, enables to add the distance between the selected object and the *target* to the final position.

- The two menus *Space* enable to specify if the position of the *target* object should be relevant to the local coordinate system (*Local*) or global of the scene (*World*).

- *Influence* determines how much the constraint should act on the selected object. By assigning the value 0, the constraint will not have any effect on the selected object. Setting instead 1 the selected object will be overlapped to the *target*.

Copy Rotation forces the object to bind its scaling to the one of another object. The functioning is analogous to that of *Copy Location*.

Copy Scale forces the object to bind its position to that of another object. The functioning is analogous to that of *Copy Location* and *Copy Rotation*.

Copy Transforms binds any transformation on the *target* object to the selected object.

Limit Distance forces a constant distance between the bound selected object and the target object. When this constraint is applied, a dashed blue line appears between the two objects, indicating the presence of the constraint.

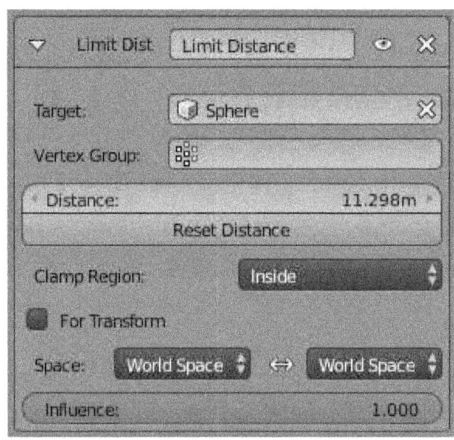

fig. 486 the *Limit Distance* panel

- *Target* defines the object on which to bind the selected one.

- *Vertex Group* enables to define the constraint with respect to only some vertices of the target.

- *Distance* defines the maximum distance between the two objects.

- *Reset Distance* reset the transformations between the two objects and restore the original distance.

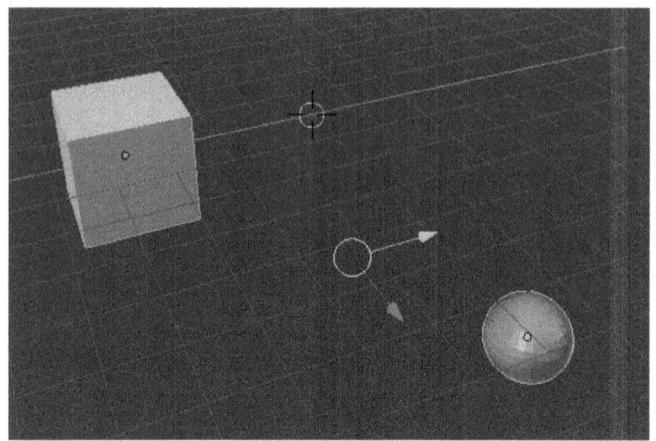

fig. 487 two constrained objects

- *Clamp Region* sets as distance one of the options *Inside* (object constrained inside the virtual sphere containing the target object), *Outside* (object constrained outside the virtual sphere containing the target object), or *On Surface* (object constrained on the virtual sphere surface containing the target object).

- The flag on *For Transform* indicates that also the transformations of the target affect the constraint.

- *Space* and *Influence* have the same function of the previous constraints.

Limit Location acts such as not constrained objects could be owed on the scene along the X, Y and Z direction. This constraint limits the amount of displacement permitted along each axis, through lower and upper limits. The limits referred to an object are computed from its center, and the limits of a bone, as we will see in the foregoing, from its root.

434

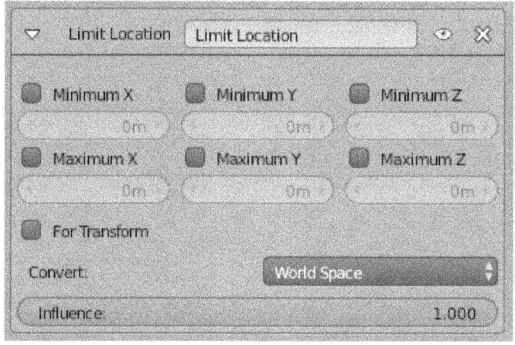

fig. 488 the *Limit Location* panel

Minimum and *Maximum* referred to the three axes *X*, *Y* and *Z* define the limits on the position. The other parameters are analogous to those relevant to the previously described constraints.

Limit Rotation and ***Limit Scale*** are two constraints acting analogously to the previous one and define, respectively, the minimum and maximum transformation limits of the object with respect to the rotation and the scale.

These limits are very useful for the bones and limit some movements. Think for example to a limb rotation, which cannot exceed some limit.

Maintain Volume limits a mesh or a bone volume to have a certain ratio with its original volume.

This ratio depends on the axes *X*, *Y* and *Z*, whereas the counter *Volume* defines the volume object at rest.

Convert and *Influence* parameterize the constraint coordinates and influence, similarly to other constraints.

Transformation is a constraint type more complex and versatile with respect to the other constraints relevant to the transformation. It enables to associate a transformation property type of the target (for example the position, the rotation or the scale), to the same or to another transformation property type of the selected object, in a certain value range (possibly different for each target and property of the selected object). Moreover it is possible to act between the axes, and use the values of the field not as limits, but indeed as "*markers*" for defining a mapping between input (*target*) and output(object) values.

For example, it is possible to use the target position along the X axis to control the object rotation along the Z axis.

- *Target* and *Vertex Group* set the constraint target object and the possible group of vertices.

- *Extrapolate*, when checked, forces the next *Mix* and *Max* as markers for a mapping proportional between the input and output values.

- The *Source* switches define the target input settings. The three *Loc*, *Rot* and *Scale* mutually exclude themselves and enable the property type to be used.

- The counters *Min* and *Max* contain the numeric fields defining the lower and upper limits for the input values, independently for each axis. Note that if a *Min* value is larger than its maximum correspondent value, the constraint will act like it had the same value of the maximum one.

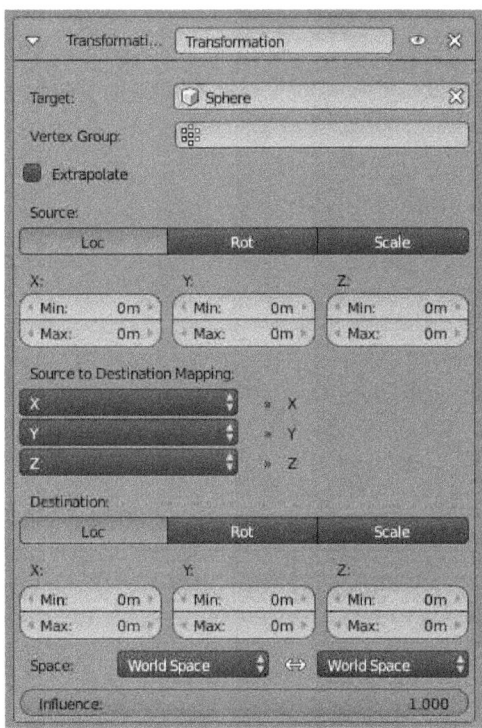

fig. 490 the *Transformation* panel

- The three drop-down menus *Source To Destination Mapping* set the connections between the input and output coordinates *X*, *Y* and *Z*.

437

- The *Destination* switch contains the output settings relevant to the object. Like for *Source*, the three *Loc*, *Rot* and *Scale* mutually exclude themselves and enable to select the property type for the control.

- As for the inputs, the numerical fields *Min* and *Max* control the lower and upper limits of the output value, independently for each mapped axis.

- *Space* and *Influence* define the coordinates and influence of the constraint on the object.

6.2.2. Relationship

The second group of constraints we are going to analyze in this chapter defines the relationships between two or more objects.

Action enables to control a movement action, associated to a frame interval, with the transformations of another object.

- *Target* defines the object undergoing the transformations and *Vertex Group* the vertices of this object.

- *From Target* determines the transformation type (displacement, rotation or rescaling along or around one of the axes) and the global (*World Space*) or local (*Local Space*) coordinate system.

- *To Action* selects the type of associated action. A flag on *Object Action*, if activated, working only for the bone, will force the bone to use the object part related to the action. This enables to apply an object action to a bone.

- *Target Range* defines the upper and lower limits of the target action.

- *Action Range* defines the starting (*Start*) and ending (*End*) action frames.

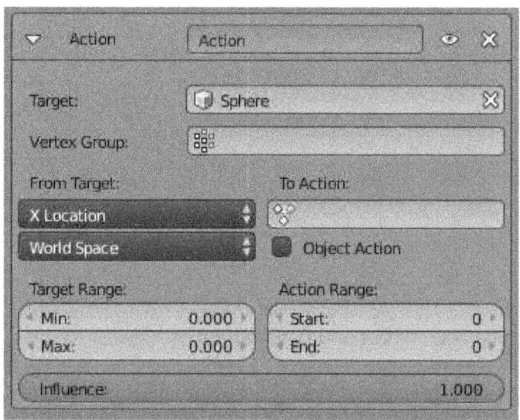

fig. 491 the *Action* panel

Child To forces a parent relationship (see in the foregoing) between a selected object (named *child*) and a target object (named parent) or a target specific *Vertex Group*.

It is possible that an object is a child of different parents, so that undergoes the influence of one or more of these targets, as well as to make sure that most objects are children of a single parent.

By assigning the *Child Of* constraint, the object will be positioned, less than the limits imposed in the coordinates, with the origin coinciding with the same of the target and will respond faithfully to all the transformations undergone by the latter.

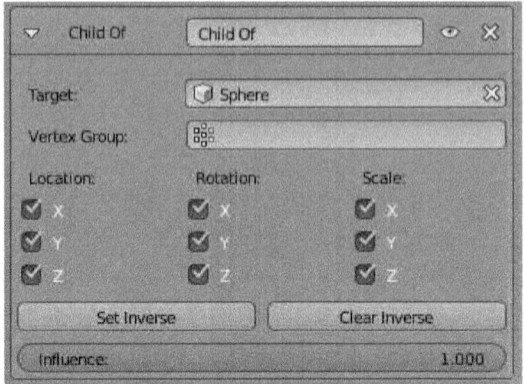

fig. 492 the *Child Of* panel

- Checking *X*, *Y* and *Z* of the *Location*, *Rotation* and *Scale* constraints, the object will bind to specific coordinates and target transformations.

- For predefined setting, the target and the son object origins will coincide. In other words, the son is transformed when also the parent is transformed. However, if the constraint aim were to preserve the son original features before becoming parent, it will be enough to click the Inverse button.

- *Clear Inverse* cancels the previous action.

- *Influence* defines the influence of the parent on the son.

Floor enables to present the selected object to cross a plane. This plane can have any orientation.

The constraint acts only on fully flat planes and cannot be used, for example, for disconnected floors or walls.

fig. 493 the *Floor* panel

The constraint limit is enforced based on the origin of the selected object. This means that it will be the origin to be actually constrained not to cross the target plane. It is possible to apply the constraint to a vertex group of the plane set as *Vertex Group*.

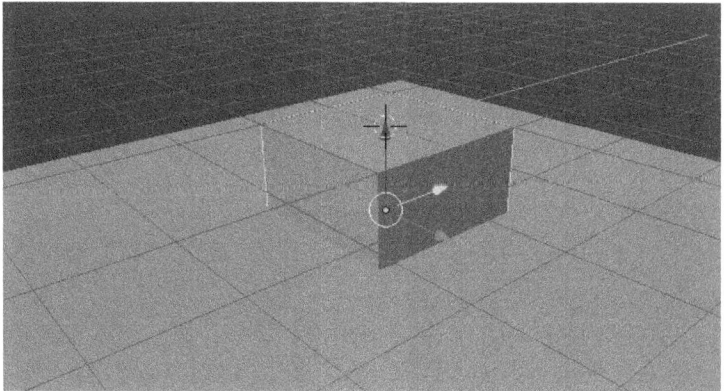

fig. 494 the cube origin cannot cross the target plane

- *Sticky*, if checked, prevent the object to be moved once it touches the plane, for example preventing it from sliding on the surface.

441

- *Use Rotation* forces the constraint to be aligned with the target rotation or slope.

- *Offset* enforces a distance between the object and the floor.

- *Min/Max* are buttons defining the direction along which the target will not be crossed. For example, if the plane is a horizontal floor, the *Z* direction should be selected.

- The *Local* or *World* coordinates and *Influence* are defined by the two last panel parameters.

Follow Path is a very useful tool enabling to bind an object to a certain path, usually a *Bézier* curve or a *Path*.

It is very used in animated cameras, as we will set in the volume dedicated to this topic.

To clarify it, we will anticipate the concepts with a brief exercise.

 EXERCISE N. 20: THE CAMERA FOLLOWING A PATH

In this exercise, we will create an animated camera following a certain path defined by a *Bézier* curve.

Insert in the scene a curve. Enter then in *Edit Mode* an select the first vertex of the curve. With SHIFT + S tell to Blender that the *3D Cursor* must be placed in correspondence of the point (*Cursor to Selected*).

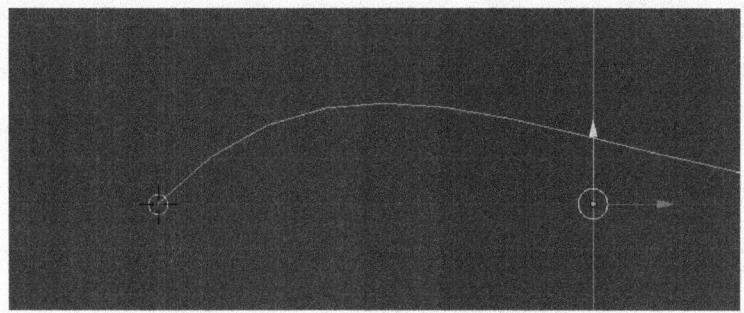

fig. 495 *Cursor to Selected*

In *Object Mode* insert a new camera which will be placed in correspondence of the*3D Cursor*.

Rotate it such as it appears perpendicular to the curve tangent in that point.

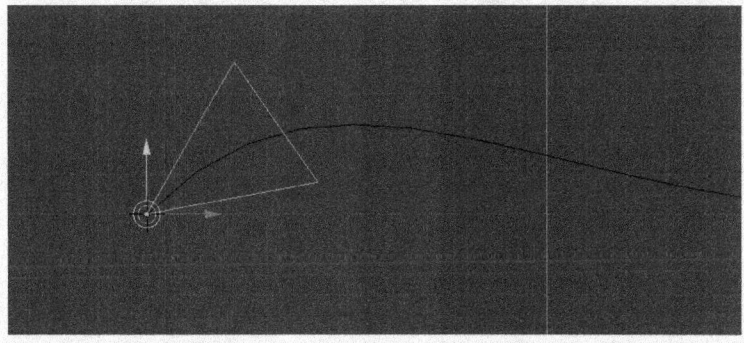

fig. 496 inserting the camera

With the camera selected add the constraint *Follow Path* and assign as target the curve, clicking the button *Animate Path*.

Launch the animation with ALT + A. The camera will start moving following the path drawn by the curve.

443

fig. 497 the *Follow Path* panel

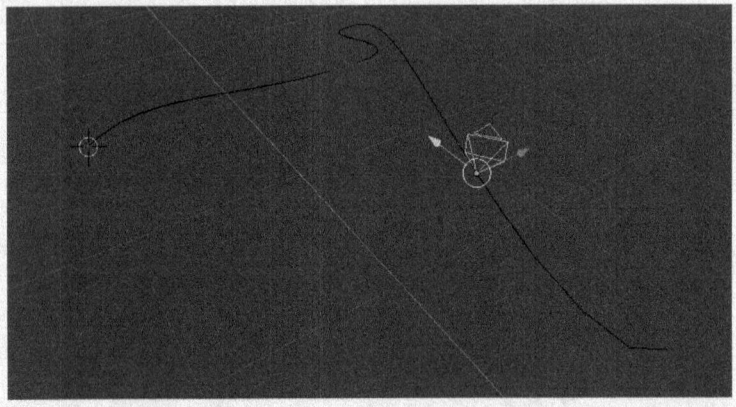

fig. 498 the camera follows the curve path

Note that the camera always frames along the same direction. This is normal, in the present case, since as second target, named *Track To*, has not been assigned. It can be found among the *constraints* of the *Tracking* group and enables to set the frame on an external object.

Anyway this feature will be discussed in the foregoing.

444

- Nevertheless, checking *Follow Curve* it is possible to fix the frame on the *target*, i.e. the curve origin. The camera, in this case, will rotate framing constantly the origin, following the path.

- *Curve Radius* enables the object (the camera in our case) to scale according to the curve curvature radius.

- *Offset* enables to move the object position along a path depending on the animation starting frame.

- *Forward* defines the object orientation with respect to the curve, by aligning it along the path advancement direction, i.e. along the curve tangent in that point.

- *Up* defines the object axis aligned with the world *z* axis. The latter, in case of the camera, is set on *Z*, since normal to the framing.

Pivot enables the object to rotate around a target object.

- *Target* sets the target object.

- *Pivot Offset* (*X*, *Y* and *Z*) defines the object distance from the target.

- *Pivot When* defines the rotation range of the rotation around the pivot.

- *Influence* defines the constraint influence on the object.

fig. 499 the *Pivot* panel

Rigid Body Joint refers to the rigid body dynamics which will be discussed in the next volume.

Shrinkwrap is a constraint corresponding to the namesake modifier. It moves the object origin and, as a consequence, its position toward the *target* surface. This requires that the *target* must necessarily have a surface.

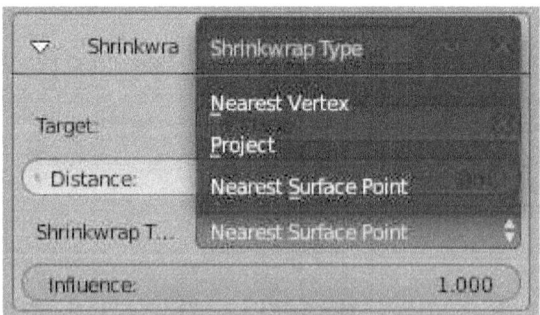

fig. 500 the *Shrinkwrap* panel

446

- *Target* indicates the target.

- *Distance* sets the object offset from the *target*.

- The *Shrinkwrap Type* menu enables to select the method to be used for computing the point on the target surface on which projecting the object center. Three options are available:

  a) *Nearest Surface Point* (the target surface point will be the nearest to the original object position);

  b) *Project* (the target surface point is determined by projecting the object center along an axis, defined by *X*, *Y* and *Z*);

  c) *Nearest Vertex* (very similar to the first option, except that possible replacements due to the object projection are limited to the target vertices).

- *Influence* defines the constraint influence.

 EXERCISE N. 21: TO PARENT AND GROUP SOME OBJECTS TO AN EXTERNAL OBJECT: TABLE AND CHAIRS

It is often useful to have the possibility of managing several objects through the transformation of a single external object, usually an *Empty*.

For example, a table, the chairs, the tablecloth, dishes and cutlery, a vase and the carpet, may be easily parent to an *Empty*, usually, placed for convenience at the group center and on the ground.

Thus insert into the scene the table and the four chairs. Add an *Empty* in the mass center and place it on the ground.

To group by *shortcut* the object to the *Empty*, it's enough to select all of them and the *Empty* at last, then digit CTRL + P.

It is possible to choose from the menu between *Object*, binding simply the object to the *Empty*, and *Object (Keep Transform)* that will assign to all the objects the transformations applied to the *Empty*.

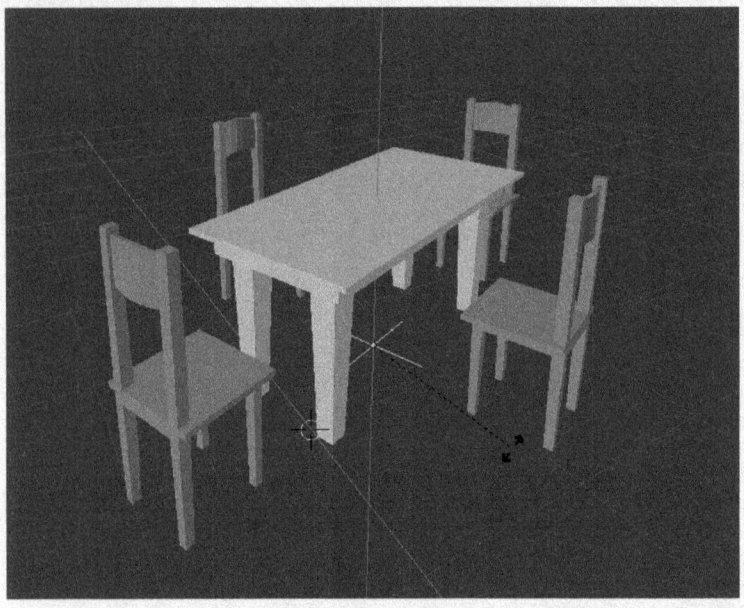

fig. 501 table and chairs are parented to the Empty

A black dashed line will connect the group to the *Empty*.

Try to move, rotate and scale the *Empty*. The associated object group will follow the transformation.

Among the attachments of this volume, you can access to the file under consideration (*table and chairs – parent.blend*).

7
INFORMATION AND
SETTINGS ON THE
OBJECTS

7.1. Tab Object

The **Tab Object** contains all the information and settings relevant to the objects present on the scene.

This *tab* has been already partially analyzed in the first volume, talking about the windows and the transformers.

In this chapter we will then see which panels exist and which information they manage.

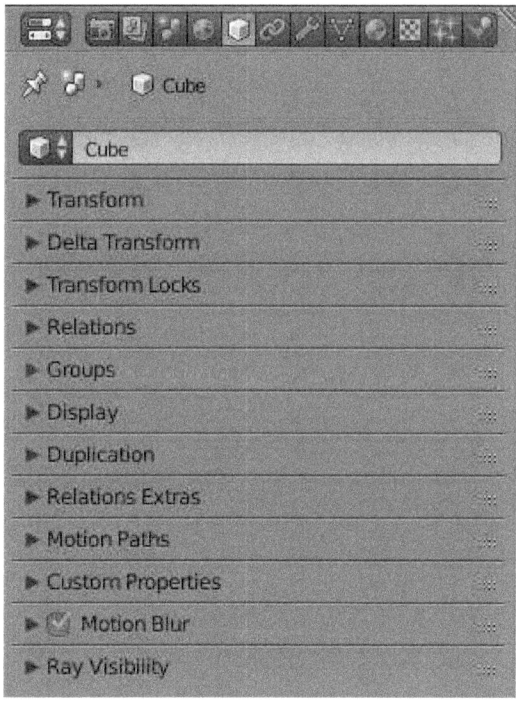

fig. 502 the *Objects* tab

451

The *Transform* panel, as already seen, defines the object information relative to the location (*Location*), the rotation (*Rotation*) and the scale (*Scale*).

The *Delta Transform* panel contains the information relevant to an object already subjected to a transformation, indicating the differences (*delta*) between the present distances, rotations and scaling and the original ones.

Activating the panel locks *Transform Locks*, the transformation of the selected objects are prevented.

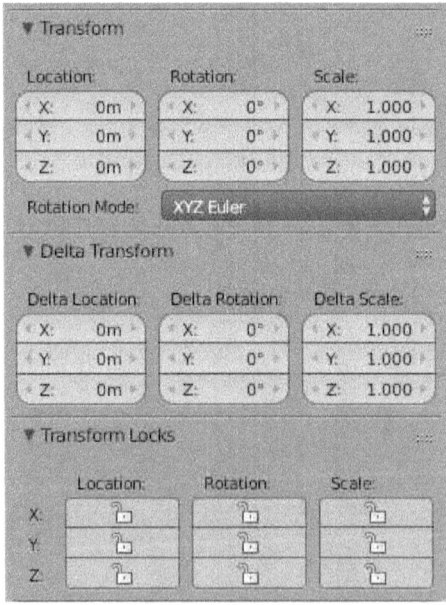

fig. 503 the *Transform* panels, *Delta Transform* and *Transform Locks*

The **Relations** panel visualizes and sets the relationships and parents of the selected object and in particular: in which *Layer* is inserted, to what object is parented (*Parent*) and the possible *Pass Index*, a numeric value needed to assign an object (in this case), but also a material to a certain *Render Layer*, useful for the *Compositing*.

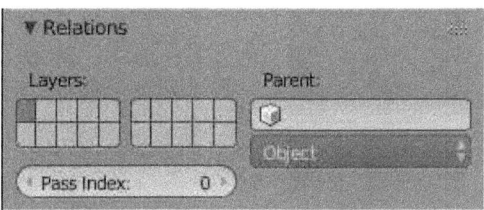

fig. 504 the *Relations* panel

The **Groups** panel enabled to collect into a group (created by simply clicking the *Add To Group* button) a series of selected objects.

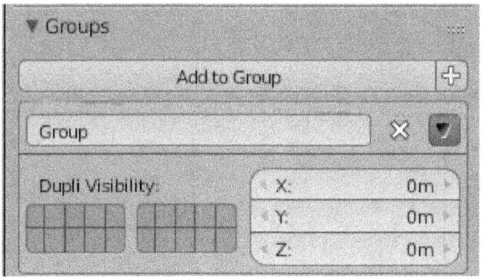

fig. 505 the *Groups* panel

These grouped objects behave analogously to the parent relationship with respect to an external object (see the previous chapter).

Once assigned the group name it is possible to visualize the objects contained in it, divided per layers (*Duply Visibility*), but most of all it is possible to define if the objects must be considered a unique element, by selecting *Select Grouped* from the black arrow menu, or if their behavior must remain independent from the other objects in the group, by selecting *Unlink Group*, or, finally, if to set an *offset* from the cursor (*Set Offset From Cursor*).

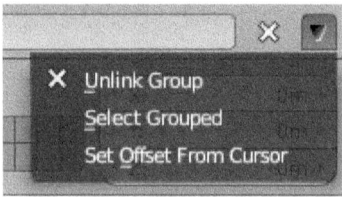

fig. 506 connection of the object of the group

The contour of the grouped objects will appear in green.

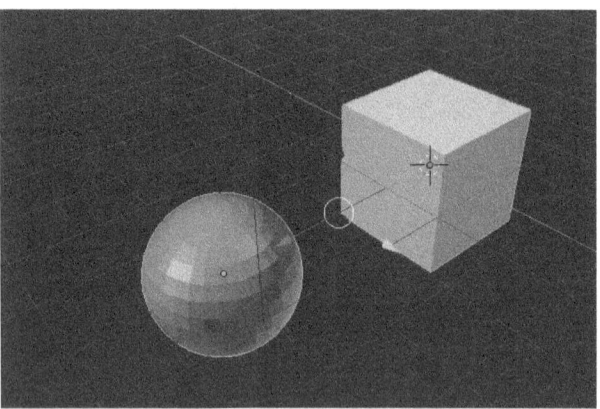

fig. 507 grouped objects

The **Display** panel collects all the settings relevant to the visualization of an object in the scene.

By checking the various options it is possible to visualize in the 3D view, in correspondence of the selected object: the name (*Name*), the axis (*Axis*),the wire (*Wire*) for the *meshes*, all the edges (*Draw all Edges*), the maximum bound (*Bound*) defined in the drop-down menu as *Box, Cone, Cylinder, Capsule* or *Sphere*, the *texture space*, X-Ray visualization (*X-Ray*) for seeing the selected object in all cases as it were in foreground, and a material transparency if present (*Transparency*).

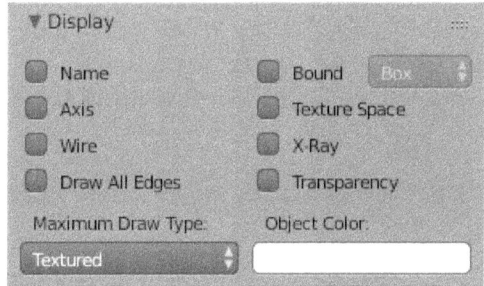

fig. 508 the *Display* panel

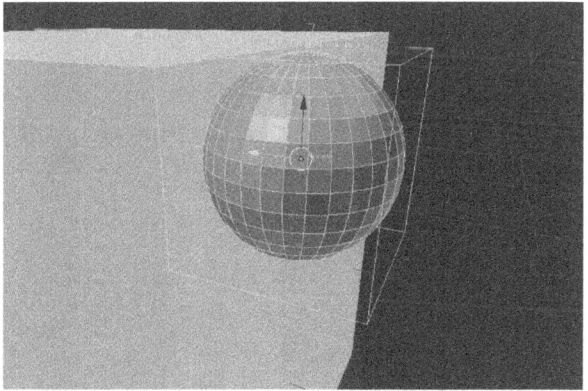

fig. 509 in this sphere all the visualization options have been checked

455

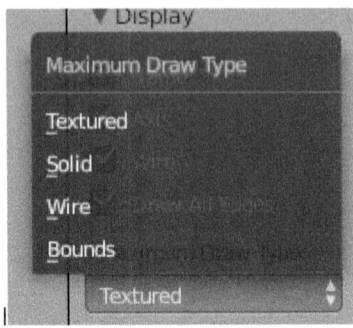

fig. 510 the *Maximum Draw Type* menu

n the *Maximum Draw Type* menu the selected object visualization is forced as *Textured*, *Solid*, *Wireframe* or *Bounds*, in correspondence of any scene visualization setting set in the 3D view header.

Finally the palette *Object Color* assigns a fictitious color to the object in the 3D scene.

The **Duplication** panel defines the object duplication methods.

The **Relations Extras** panel defines some other relationships regarding the parents and the *tracking*, which we will analyze in the foregoing.

The **Motion Paths** panel contains some parameters and information relevant to the animations and *frames*, which we will discuss in the relevant treatise.

456

The **Motion Blur** panel shows the information relevant to the *motion blur*, producing a sort of contrail in the object movement, overlapping each frame with the previous one.

The **Ray Visibility** panel is very useful to assign or unselecting projection effect of the luminous rays with respect to some elements.

By default, all the flags are active. But, if unselected, the following effects will be achieved:

- *Camera* (the object will be prevented to be rendered and visualized);

- *Diffuse* (the object color will not be shown);

- *Glossy* (the reflections will not be shown);

- *Transmission* (transmissions on transparent objects will not occur);

- *Volume Scatter* (the internal volumetric illumination, typical of this shader, will be prevented);

- *Shadow* (shadows will not be projected from this object).

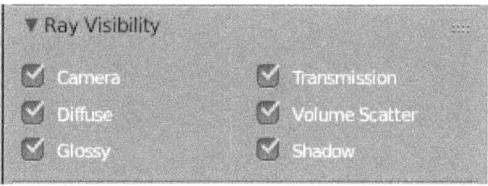

fig. 508 the *Ray Visibility* panel

A classical example if the deactivation of the flag *Camera* from a plane where the shader Emission is set, such as to make the

457

luminous source active on the objects in the scene, but to make also the luminous panel invisible to the active camera.

It is obvious that the *Object* panel disables some panels or some items of the *Object* tab, adapting itself to the typology of objects present in the scene.

For example, the *Motion Blur* panel will not be present for a curve, like *Ray Visibility* will not appear for an *Empty* object, since the latter is already not influencing the scene.

8

CONCLUDING REMARKS

8.1. Conclusions and acknowledgements

I want to thank all who have contributed to the development of this second volume of **Blender – the Ultimate Guide**, my family, my collaborators, my friends who have supported and advised me, like, among all, Francesco Andresciani (who developed the cup decoration used in exercise n. 19 on *Texture Paint*), the 3D *artist* Alan Zirpoli with whom I developed the kitchen models represented in this volume and the cover, Oliver Villar Diz, Massimiliano Zeuli, Giovanni Caruso for the translation in English of this books, obviously all the *Blender Community* and the *Blender Foundation*, all the people following me and the web site www.blenderhighschool.it, and all my editors.

I want to dedicate to all of them the success of this book.

Thanks.

Andrea

8.2. Support bibliography

For the writing of this volume all the following digital and print sources have been consulted:

- Francesco Siddi - Grafica 3D con Blender - Apogeo 2015

- Oliver Villar Diz - Learning Blender - Addison Wesley 2015

- Andrea Coppola / Francesco Andresciani - Blender - Area 51 Publishing 2013-2015

- Francesco Andresciani - Blender: le basi per tutti - Area 51 Publishing 2014

- Gabriele Falco - Blender 2.7 Grafica e Animazione 3D - 2014

- Gordon Fisher - Blender 3D Basics - PACKT Publishing 2014

- John M. Blain - Blender Graphics Computer Modeling & Animation - CRC Press 2012

- Ben Simons - Blender Master Class - 2012

- Andrea Coppola - Blender Videocorso (modulo base e intermedio) - Area 51 Publishing - 2014-2015

- Andrew Price - The Architecture Academy - 2014

Moreover the following web sites have been consulted:

www. blender.org (Cloud)

www.blenderguru.com

www. blendtuts.com

www.francescomilanese.com

www.blenderclick.it

www.blender.it

cgcookie.com/blender

www.blenderhighschool.it

8.3. About the Author

Andrea Coppola, born on 1971, is a polyhedric professional: **architect**, *designer*, **3D** *artist* and **builder** (and many years ago also a musician, arranger and producer).

He lives both in **Roma** (where he works as an interior designer, designer and trainer) and in **Kenya** (where he has designed and constructed five house residences in Watamu: (for information see www.lamiacasainkenya.com). In Kenya he is also founding partner of the construction company Hendon Properties Ltd.

Holder and founder of the architectural firm **in Roma L.A.A.R.** (www.laboratoriodiarchitettura.info), he worked and presently works as interior designer and designer (having designed, in particular, the two kitchen models "Nairobi" and "Skin" for Reval Cucine s.r.l. and the chair "Cra Cra" for Art Leather).

He also worked as security responsible in building sites and as university assistant for the architecture faculty of the University of Rome "La Sapienza", teaching some master classes.

Passionate about computer graphics and in particular about Blender, regularly teaches courses, through the web site www.blenderhighschool.it, one of the main referenceы in Italy for Blender and official partner of Blender Italia (www.blender.it). Through this web site, connected with www.blenderclick.it (managed together with Francesco Andresciani), the Author tries to give his personal contribution to Blender development, thanks to his versatility, offering tutorials, tricks, books and products for free or not, in addition to modeling and rendering services.

As consultant he has developed catalogs for kitchen firms (together with Alan Zirpoli) and for the Mars Society of Bergamo, an interactive project using the real maps of the red planet provided be the NASA (together with Francesco Andresciani).

Besides this guide, he has published 8 e-books on Blender, 1 book on PBR Theory, 1 on the 3D print, 87 video courses, 1 Thematic Academy on Blender; 3 e-books on Autocad; 2 e-books on Arduino 1 course about sound design and 1 *thriller* ("L'Altra Specie"), all edited by Area 51 Editore of Bologna (www.area51editore.com) and Lulu (www.lulu.com).

He's one of the 6 Italian BLENDER FOUNDATION CERTIFIED TRAINERS.

Blender Foundation
CERTIFIED TRAINER

Contacts:
blenderhighschool@gmail.com
www.blenderhighschool.it

For any question, please, use the Author's free Helpline: .
http://www.blenderhighschool.it/helpline.html

465

www.ingramcontent.com/pod-product-compliance
Lightning Source LLC
Chambersburg PA
CBHW071409180526
45170CB00001B/22